Stop Walking On Eggshells For Parents

How To Help Your Child (Of Any Age) With Borderline Personality Disorder Without Losing Yourself

Randi Kreger
Christine Adamec, MBA
Daniel S. Lobel, PhD

16pt

Copyright Page from the Original Book

Publisher's Note

Care has been taken to confirm the accuracy of the information presented and to describe generally accepted practices. However, the authors, editors, and publisher are not responsible for errors or omissions or for any consequences from application of the information in this book and make no warranty, express or implied, with respect to the contents of the publication.

Distributed in Canada by Raincoast Books

NEW HARBINGER PUBLICATIONS is a registered trademark of New Harbinger Publications, Inc.

New Harbinger Publications is an employee-owned company.

Copyright © 2022 by Randi Kreger, Christine Adamec, and Daniel Lobel
New Harbinger Publications, Inc.
5674 Shattuck Avenue
Oakland, CA 94609
www.newharbinger.com

All Rights Reserved

Acquired by Catharine Meyers

Cover design by Amy Shoup

Library of Congress Cataloging-in-Publication Data

Names: Kreger, Randi, author. | Adamec, Christine A., 1949- author. | Lobel, Daniel S., author.

Title: Stop walking on eggshells for parents : how to help your child (of any age) with borderline personality disorder without losing yourself / Randi Kreger, Christine Adamec, and Daniel S. Lobel.

Description: Oakland, CA : New Harbinger Publications, 2022. | Includes bibliographical references.

Subjects: LCSH: Child rearing--Popular works. | Borderline personality disorder in children--Popular works. | Self-care, Health.

Classification: LCC HQ769 .K6844 2022 | DDC 649/.1--dc23/eng/20211109

LC record available at https://lccn.loc.gov/2021046291

TABLE OF CONTENTS

Foreword	v
Preface	xi
CHAPTER 1: An Introduction to Borderline Personality Disorder (BPD)	1
CHAPTER 2: How BPD Affects Your Child	28
CHAPTER 3: Psychiatric Problems That Commonly Co-Occur with BPD	47
CHAPTER 4: Types of Treatment and Finding Treatment	69
CHAPTER 5: Improving Your Mental Health	100
CHAPTER 6: How BPD Impacts the Whole Family	130
CHAPTER 7: Life-Changing Communication Techniques	156
CHAPTER 8: BPD-Savvy Parenting Techniques Part 1	196
CHAPTER 9: BPD-Savvy Parenting Techniques Part 2	222
CHAPTER 10: Parenting a Preteen with BPD	250
CHAPTER 11: Parenting an Adolescent with BPD	275
CHAPTER 12: Parenting an Adult Child with BPD	296
CHAPTER 13: Parenting a Child Who Self-Harms or Is Suicidal	323
CHAPTER 14: Parenting a Child with Extreme Behaviors	347
Epilogue	367
Acknowledgments	369
APPENDIX A: Top Ten Tips for Dads	373
APPENDIX B: Clinician to Clinician: The Underdiagnosis of BPD in Children	385
APPENDIX C: Resources	389
References	400
more books to help you stop walking on eggshells	416
Back Cover Material	418

TABLE OF CONTENTS

Foreword v
Preface ix
CHAPTER 1: An Introduction to Borderline Personality Disorder (BPD) 1
CHAPTER 2: How BPD Affects Your Child 28
CHAPTER 3: Psychiatric Problems That Commonly Co-Occur with BPD 47
CHAPTER 4: Types of Treatment and Finding Treatment 69
CHAPTER 5: Shoring Up Your Mental Health 100
CHAPTER 6: How BPD Impacts the Whole Family 130
CHAPTER 7: Life Changing Communication Techniques 156
CHAPTER 8: BPD-Savvy Parenting Techniques Part 1 196
CHAPTER 9: BPD-Savvy Parenting Techniques Part 2 222
CHAPTER 10: Parenting a Preteen with BPD 250
CHAPTER 11: Parenting an Adolescent with BPD 275
CHAPTER 12: Parenting an Adult Child with BPD 296
CHAPTER 13: Parenting a Child Who Self-Harms or Is Suicidal 323
CHAPTER 14: Parenting a Child with Extreme Behaviors 342
Epilogue 367
Acknowledgements 369
APPENDIX A: Top Ten Tips for Dads 373
APPENDIX B: Clinician to Clinician: The Underdiagnosis of BPD in Children 385
APPENDIX C: Resources 389
References 400
more books to help you stop walking on eggshells 412
Back Cover Material 418

"Children don't come with instruction manuals—particularly borderline personality disorder (BPD) children. This book is a comprehensive guide to *why* your child is so troubled, disrespectful, and prone to rages; *how* you can strategize to improve these and other typical BPD behaviors (and your own health in the process!); and *where* to find the resources to assist you. For bewildered and beleaguered parents at their wits' end, it's the answer to a prayer!"

—**Fran L. Porter, BEd, MA,** 2017 Calgary Philanthropic Award winner, and author of *When the Ship Has No Stabilizers*

"This book is full of useful information for parents and caretakers of children with BPD. It is a great resource for those who need help with the behavior and ever-changing emotions of their child. I highly recommend this book to parents of children at any age to help navigate the uncertain journey with BPD, and help themselves and their child."

—**Donna Toone,** administrator of the Facebook group, Support for Parents of Children with BPD; and mom of a child with BPD

"*Stop Walking on Eggshells for Parents* is a much-needed and welcome guide for families who have a child with borderline behaviors. Using research and interviews with real families, the authors provide comprehensive guidance, information, support, parenting suggestions, treatment options, and extensive examples to help parents respond effectively to the difficult challenges of their emotionally dysregulated children. It fills a great need for practical, understanding support."

—**Margalis Fjelstad, PhD,** author of *Healing from a Narcissistic Relationship,* and coauthor of *Raising Resilient Children with a Borderline or Narcissist Parent*

"*Stop Walking on Eggshells for Parents* takes on the challenging territory of helping parents who have a child living with BPD, and provides actionable suggestions in a framework that is compassionate toward everyone in the family system. Very few books take on the issue of the onset of BPD patterns in childhood and adolescence, and this awareness is essential to helping families with support instead of stigma."

—**Ramani Durvasula, PhD,** clinical psychologist; founder and CEO of LUNA Education, Training and Consulting; and retired professor of psychology at California State University, Los Angeles

I've never met a strong person with an easy past.

—Unknown

I dedicate this book to all the parents struggling with children who have borderline personality disorder (BPD), especially those who allowed us to interview them for the book: the mothers of the Facebook group "Parents of Children with BPD," my own group "Moving Forward," and those who responded to a detailed survey. You are all heroes.

—Randi Kreger

Foreword

When Randi Kreger asked me to write a foreword for this book, I responded without hesitation that I'd be delighted. I had not yet read the manuscript, but I had read her book *Stop Walking on Eggshells* and her two other BPD books while researching *When the Ship Has No Stabilizers,* my memoir about Colleen, my daughter with borderline personality disorder. I knew that, like those books, this one would be a fount of information to help parents of children with this disorder. How my husband and I could have used such information during Colleen's formative years between 1980 and 1996, before she turned eighteen!

Colleen was born in 1978. At that time, there was not the body of knowledge or writing on her condition that exists today. From age two, she showed behavior extremes such as excessive clinginess at times, pushing us forcefully away at other times, and throwing frighteningly intense temper tantrums over seemingly minor issues. Repeatedly we were told, "She'll grow out of it." She didn't. Like any illness that goes untreated, it got worse and worse. She would pound her fists, throw things, and swear at us. When we wouldn't instantly gratify any demand she might make, she would call us names and tell us how much she hated us. Puberty brought smoking, risky sexual activity, hanging out with the drug crowd, ignoring curfews, and becoming addicted to drugs herself.

Yet, despite all this, we were given what I would call "the brushoff" by genuinely caring experts. With the best of intentions, they dismissed us as overly worried parents. Colleen was extremely bright. I'd venture to say she had the highest IQ in our family. The psychologists and psychiatrists who saw her all commented on her intelligence, her facility with language, and her ability to solve almost instantly any puzzle that was put in front of her.

But, as Randi points out, "feelings have no IQ." No amount of reason or logic could quell the extreme emotions that so frequently swamped our daughter. "Take her away," one doctor joked, "and bring me a child with a real problem." Today, after reading this book (and after having read many others written by experts), I'd call that an invalidating response to Colleen's cries for help.

To be fair, though, that is a revisionist statement on my part. Society's awareness of mental health issues at that time was not nearly what it is today. That doctor thought he was speaking the truth. And I, a high school teacher with a master's degree who considered herself fairly knowledgeable in certain areas, can say unequivocally that I had no knowledge whatsoever of borderline personality disorder.

The first time I even heard the term was when Colleen was fifteen and had been sentenced by a court judge to ten sessions with a qualified psychotherapist. She'd been forging our names on checks and withdrawing money from our bank accounts in order to buy drugs. With the sexual and drug history she already had, she, like so many others with BPD, had been categorized as a "bad kid." And, on the recommendation of a support group counselor we were then seeing, we pressed charges. The only positive result that came from that experience was learning the name of her diagnosis—except, maybe, for reinforcing to Colleen our firm belief that such actions should have consequences.

But what blew me away was that until that sentencing, we had spent fifteen years in the dark as to her diagnosis—as had Colleen! Why? We'd been taking her to specialists ever since she was a baby. We'd seen the extremity of her emotional reactions compared to those of her elder sister, Lisa. We'd spotted things that concerned us as early as when she was interacting with other kids in the daycare center she went to when we were at work. And yet none of those specialists had wanted to label our child. As one of them put it, "There's a stigma attached to mental illness. So, we usually don't address problems like that until a person is eighteen."

What? If you suspected your child had a broken leg at age five, would you wait until they were eighteen to treat it?

In many ways, society is only just waking up about issues concerning mental health. New technology has given us functional magnetic resonance imaging (fMRI), which can show the brain in action. What it has shown is that the neurotypical brain functions very differently from the brains of people with BPD. It has also shown that, with training, the brain is capable of *neuroplasticity*, or the changing of its behavior patterns. But for a person with mental health issues, the more those patterns become entrenched with the passage of time, the more difficult it is to change them. The difficulty of changing long-established habits is something most of us know from firsthand experience. So it's critical for us to get our children into treatment as soon as possible.

Let's face it: the stigma that specialist referred to is still alive and well today. Those who haven't walked the walk—as we have—hold all kinds of misconceptions. After my book was released, my husband and I were invited to many speaking engagements and book club events. One book club president, however, said, "Our club is reading your book and finding it amazing, but a few of the members vetoed my suggestion that we invite you and Andy along to a discussion about it. That's because they've heard that BPD is caused by parental abuse."

Another parent told me, "Frankly, I'm astonished a well-respected teacher like you could have had a child who turned out to be as bad as Colleen." Wow! That's like saying, "I'm astonished your daughter has brown eyes when you don't." Unfair though it is, parents are often the first ones to be blamed when something goes wrong with their child. And even when others don't blame us, we blame ourselves and feel guilty. We feel guilty without knowing exactly why, and when we learn about BPD, we feel guilty that we didn't know about it earlier so we could have taken advantage of the specialized parenting tools you're going to learn about in this book.

We, the parents of troubled children, can't change everyone's thinking. But, as the authors of this book indicate, we can try our best to help both ourselves and our children by learning how to interact with them in ways that are not invalidating or demeaning—and how, sometimes, to not interact with them at all. In those cases, it's best to give them, as well as ourselves, some space until everybody has had a chance to calm down.

When my memoir about Colleen was published in 2014, I thought I'd written it for a select few parents like me in the support group we attended. But the overwhelming popularity of the book and the response we received confirmed that the problem is so much bigger than anyone ever realized. We learned there were many other Colleens and many other bewildered and grieving parents at their wits' end. Parents from all over started calling us and telling us their own stories. A woman from New York phoned one morning just to thank us on behalf of her BPD daughter.

The book you are about to read will show you how to thrive, not just survive, and how to be the best parent you can be to your child. It will tell you about cherishing your child, but disengaging: difficult, though essential. It will reassure you that you are by no means alone in your struggles, that you can pat yourself on the back for hanging in there, and that you can forgive yourself for the times when you feel like throwing in the towel. There is a section on dialectical behavior therapy, and other therapies presently used to treat BPD. And there is a section on how to protect your grandchildren. This book will help you realize that BPD isn't your fault and you are far from alone.

We parents of BPD children are all in this together. Education is one of the best proactive tools in our toolbox—and the box you have in your hands is full of all kinds of tools. Read on to find out how to help yourself and help your child. God bless you.

—Fran L. Porter, author of *When the Ship Has No Stabilizers*

Preface

The book you hold in your hands began as a new edition of my 1998 booklet *Hope for Parents: Helping Your Borderline Son or Daughter Without Sacrificing Your Family or Yourself.* I contracted my coauthor Christine Adamec to redo the booklet in 2017 because she had the right writing background and, unlike me, she has kids.

It became evident pretty quickly that the booklet needed to be a book, and it made sense that it be part of the *Stop Walking on Eggshells* series. That meant I needed to throw myself at it full throttle and get to know the subject inside out. I'll be honest: I didn't think that children would interest me that much. But I was drawn into the information very quickly because I realized that parents of kids with BPD were so desperate for help. Four mothers told me they had considered suicide. I quickly realized that the parent-child relationships had more in common with the other relationships I had already been writing about for the past twenty-five years.

Christine had the brilliant idea of adding a psychologist to the team. I had been working on my own for so many years that I hadn't even considered it. But could we find a clinician who specialized in BPD *in children?* As it so happened, my publisher, New Harbinger, had published the book *When Your Daughter Has BPD* by Daniel S.

Lobel. Amazingly, we both had the same outlook about BPD and family support. Daniel acted as our northern star, keeping everything accurate. We all hopped on a Zoom conference together and the rest is history.

As I searched for solutions for a myriad of issues, it quickly became evident that the parents' natural instincts to help their children by any and all means possible wasn't helping the parents *at all*—it was causing them to take actions that were making problems much *worse*—not just for their children, but for themselves.

You and I are sailing in uncharted waters through this book. As you will read in the next section, there are very few published resources on children and BPD. The same was true for adults with BPD when *Stop Walking on Eggshells* came out in 1998. Back then it was almost impossible to find consumer information on *anything* about BPD. So ... *tradition*.

Just like the first edition of *Stop Walking on Eggshells* was not the final say for all of BPD, neither is this book the last word on parenting a child (or adult) with BPD. Rather, this book collects the best practices we know of right now according to surveys of parents, comments from people with BPD, and the medical knowledge of psychiatrists, research studies, and other clinical sources. It is a snapshot in time. We will revise and update this book as we come to know more. And we hope that it inspires more resources for the parents who desperately need it.

Notes on Sources Used in This Book

As we write this book, there are only two other books that we know of with helpful information explicitly for the parents of minors with BPD. One, *When Your Daughter Has BPD: Essential Skills to Help Families Manage Borderline Personality Disorder,* was written by Daniel Lobel, a coauthor of this book. The other one is *Borderline Personality Disorder in Adolescents: What to Do When Your Teen Has BPD* by psychiatrist Blaise Aguirre. Aguirre is the medical director of one of the first inpatient units dedicated to treating adolescents with BPD at McLean Hospital in Belmont, MA. Aguirre gives presentations around the world on the topic of BPD in minors. Because of his vast experience, combined with the fact that there is so little research out there, we will frequently mention his work in this book. His book, originally published in 2007, was updated in 2014. We highly recommend both books if you want to learn more.

—Randi Kreger

CHAPTER I

An Introduction to Borderline Personality Disorder (BPD)

You're tired, worried, overwhelmed, and feel like you're drowning in the ocean. You're asking yourself, *What happened to that sweet child I dressed up as a superhero for Halloween?* Your child is angry, doesn't understand that their actions have consequences, has identity and self-esteem problems, and has unstable friendships and moods. You're always walking on eggshells *and* waiting for the next shoe to drop. Life is an emotional roller coaster, and your child seems to be in charge, taking everyone else for a ride. Life is unmanageable chaos.

For nineteen years, we've been loving and caring for our adopted daughter. We had some initial signs of trouble—severe separation issues, arguing, temper tantrums, and a hard time making friends. Doctors told us she had ADHD. We gave her loving family support and help with her friends, and spent money on every doctor imaginable. In sixth grade she started missing a lot of school, showed signs of depression, and caused constant family turmoil. Her siblings felt put upon because of her episodes and because she was getting all the attention. At this point they diagnosed her as bipolar.

As an adolescent she started smoking pot, barely went to school, and had a revolving door of relationships and part-time jobs. She would either quit or get fired within the first month. As an adult, she is barely functional and wants to move back in with us. But she calls us at 3a.m. and tells us what awful parents we are and how we damaged her—then begs us for money. She was always the sweetest, most lovable, and creative child.

You ask yourself, *Is this my fault?* Your child tells you you're a bad parent, or that they hate you, and it breaks your heart and makes you feel bad. *Is it true?* Every mental health professional you take your child to gives you a different diagnosis. Perhaps they said it's bipolar, ADHD, or oppositional defiant disorder. Perhaps your child also has an eating disorder, is depressed, or has some other disorder. But clearly something else is wrong.

The Basics of BPD

Let's start with some basics—like what borderline personality disorder is. Each person who has BPD has their own unique personality, but—just as people who suffer from bipolar, eating disorders, and schizophrenia have traits of those disorders—people with BPD have common traits too. BPD is a mental disorder characterized by dysregulated (unmanaged or uncontrolled) and extreme thoughts, feelings, and actions.

While people generally base their feelings on the facts in front of them, people with BPD base the *facts* on their *feelings*. For example, your child may be furious at you for making them go to school, even though it's mandatory and you're not capable of homeschooling them. Or they may be nearly suicidal about the loss of a relationship that was over before it even started. Logic will not help them in these instances. They think in black and white. Others are either all good or all bad, to be put on a pedestal or angrily tossed off of it. And their strong feelings cause them to exhibit extreme "pain-management behaviors"—actions taken to decrease pain that can be harmful to themselves or others.

Let's look at BPD as the World Health Organization (WHO) formally describes it in the *International Classification of Diseases*, eleventh edition, as well as some general observations from our twenty-five years of working with families and loved ones of people with BPD (2019; *ICD-11*). Here are some of the traits that people with BPD exhibit in relation to thoughts, feelings, and actions.

Thoughts: Impaired perception and reasoning

- Splitting (extremes of idealization and devaluation)—this one isn't in the *ICD-11*, but it's one of the most common traits reported by people who love someone with BPD
- Having an unstable sense of self
- Instances of stress-related paranoia or dissociation (feeling very "out of it" and briefly feeling detached from reality)

Feelings: Poorly regulated, highly changeable emotions

- Intense, unstable moods and strong reactions to changes
- Irritability or anxiety usually lasting for a few hours or days
- Chronic feelings of emptiness, despair, and unhappiness
- Inappropriate, intense anger or difficulty controlling anger

Actions: Impulsive behaviors

- Impulsivity, especially when very upset or angry, leading to unstable relationships and potentially self-damaging behavior
- Frequent displays of temper, such as throwing things, pushing people, or recurrent physical fights
- Frantically tries to avoid abandonment, whether real or imagined
- Multiple acts of self-harm

These traits lead to unstable relationships, leading to a tragic self-fulfilling prophecy: people with BPD desperately need people, but the ways in which they act to maintain these relationships turn people away from them. A person doesn't need to exhibit *every* trait to have BPD, and some problems will be worse than others. Let's look at these traits in more detail.

Thoughts: Impaired Perception and Reasoning

Your child with BPD may think you're wonderful in the morning and detestable in the afternoon, depending on whether you're giving them what they want. They see people as all good or all bad, which is called "splitting." When your child feels one way, they can't recall feeling any other way in the past, and they can't imagine changing their opinion in the future. Many kids think this way, of course, which is why it's called a primitive defense mechanism. Most of us grow out of it at an early age. But kids and adults with BPD don't. Here's an example of splitting with a preteen:

Deja: Shanice didn't invite me to her birthday party, and she invited everyone else.

Mom: Maybe you just didn't get the invitation yet.

Deja: They hate me. They all hate me. I have no friends.

Mom: I hear that you're feeling bad over this. You sound disappointed and sad. I might feel that way too, if I didn't get an invite. Don't forget, though, that you went to three birthday parties last month.

Deja: I am such a loser.

Here's an example of splitting with an adolescent:
Mom: Are you and Bobbi still going out?

Azad: I wouldn't be caught dead with that loser.

Mom: Azad, you told me she was the best girlfriend you ever had.

Azad: That was before I knew she was tutoring Colin Mack in math. That slut!

Kids with BPD often have an insecure sense of self. This can be particularly challenging for adolescents, as adolescence is a time when children begin to define themselves. According to Blaise Aguirre, medical director of an inpatient unit for adolescents with BPD, kids with BPD tend to describe themselves as a composite of characteristics of their close friends or peer groups more than a singular person (2014). He says that as they change peer groups, their self-identity adapts to the new groups. Their values, morals, and identity are fluid and change often, which isn't generally the case for children. Here are some examples of what this fluidity looks like, first for a preteen and then an adolescent:

Hedra: Mom, can you buy me some more black leggings and sweatshirts?

Mom: You have plenty of exercise clothing.

Hedra: I am Goth now. I need black clothes.

Mom: Most of your clothing is pink. I thought that was your favorite color?

Hedra: That's for losers. All of my friends dress Goth.

Paranoid thoughts are another form of impaired perception and reasoning in kids with BPD, as is dissociation. Let's consider paranoia first. Your child may imagine that not only are *you* acting against them, but that other people are plotting against them too. In fact, they may think the whole world is concentrating all its resources to make their life a living hell.

Dissociation is a feeling of not being real or present. What does that mean? Think of your state of mind when you're doing something you've done so many times that the action no longer needs any of your brainpower, like driving to work. During these acts your brain is functioning automatically, and you may not remember much about how you got to work. Dissociation is like that, but it's triggered by extreme stress. Generally, dissociation is unwanted because the person is unaware of how they're feeling and reacting to what's going on around them. Its opposite is mindfulness, a healthy practice covered in chapter 5.

Tatiana was regularly bullied on the bus by some boys who lived down the road. She pleaded with her mother to take her to school, but her mother worked and had no choice but to send her on the bus. When Tatiana's mother asked her how the bus ride went each day, Tatiana always said, "I can't remember." Mom thought everything was fine until she found that Tatiana had wet herself one day during the ride home. She asked her daughter what happened, and Tatiana wasn't even aware that she had wet herself.

Feelings: Poorly Regulated, Highly Changeable Emotions

Many kids with borderline personality disorder have an intense fear of being rejected or abandoned, and the smallest thing can trigger this fear. So, when a family member or friend shows anger or annoyance with your child, they may engage in frantic attempts to regain the love (or at least the continued interest) of the other person. They may make promises to change, show remorse, and do everything they can think of to thwart the perceived coming abandonment.

If your child thinks people are angry at them or are rejecting them, they may internalize and magnify that perceived anger or rejection, seeing themselves as worthless or bad people. This can occur even when others are *not* annoyed with them or are only mildly annoyed. BPD always puts your child on the defensive. This is a big reason why you walk on eggshells. (Since logic doesn't work well with kids with BPD, in chapter 7 we'll discuss how to best respond to them using a communication technique called validation.)

Or perhaps your child gets angry and attacks. Their thinking is, *You're not going to reject me, I'm going to reject you first!* This happens frequently in adult BPD relationships as well. Relationships that are going well can make the person with BPD feel tense and uncertain because they anticipate their friends will find out how unworthy they are and will inevitably leave them. So, they break up the friendship. They would rather reject than be rejected.

The important thing to know is that, no matter what you do—including giving your child unconditional love and everything they ask for—you cannot make this trait go away. That black hole of emptiness cannot be filled by you or anyone else; only treatment works. One father said that trying to meet his kid's needs as they related to perceived abandonment was like trying to fill the Grand Canyon using a water pistol, except the Grand Canyon has a bottom. People with BPD try to fill this hole with all the behaviors in the BPD definition. They sour on relationships because they think this new person will fill the hole, and when they don't, they get disappointed, bitter, upset, suicidal, or angry, which leads to another BPD trait: unstable relationships. Here are preteen and adolescent examples of this trait in action.

> *Zendaya spends as much time as she can with her mother in the morning before school. She anticipates her mother leaving to go to work and dreads the moment. As it gets closer to the time when her mother leaves, her anxiety increases and she asks her mother to stay home with her. When her mother says no, she starts to get a stomachache. Sometimes she throws up or has diarrhea, and other times she goes to school very sad.*

> *Andy is used to seeing his boyfriend, Francois, every day in school. When Francois tells Andy that he is going to Europe with his family for two weeks, Andy panics. Andy tells him that he cannot live without him and threatens to kill himself if he goes.*

When a child has BPD, their emotions may be all over the place. One minute, your child is happy; the next minute, their arms are crossed and they have an angry look on their face. A half hour later they're lying on their bed, depressed. This constant roller coaster of emotions is difficult for everyone—including your child, who is not changing their moods deliberately. Sometimes their moods result from something that is actually happening in life; at other times they are the result of imagined conflict or situations.

Some children with BPD have strong emotional reactions when another child in the family receives special attention, as with a birthday party or an award at school. Here are two examples of this trait in action, first with a preteen and then an adolescent.

> *Lorna went to her friend Harriet's house for the weekend and met her dog Ruffy. She loved dogs and was excited to play with Ruffy, as she didn't have a dog at home. Ruffy was only interested in Harriet. He ignored Lorna and rubbed against Harriet and begged for her attention while rejecting Lorna's efforts to pet him. When Lorna got home she told her*

mother that Harriet's dog was mean and that she never wants to go to her house again.

Astrid was excited to go on vacation with her family to Hawaii because she loved the ocean. In the airport she met a young man about her age who was also going to Hawaii with his family. They agreed to hang out once they got to their hotels. Astrid kept her phone with her at all times waiting for the young man to call. By dinnertime she was frantic that he hadn't called. She refused to go to dinner with her family because she was "too upset to eat." She stayed in the room to wait for the call. By the time her family got back from dinner, Astrid reported that her vacation was ruined and she wanted to go home. Her family couldn't snap her out of it. She stayed in her room the whole trip and refused to go out.

Raising a child with BPD can be so frustrating because you may feel like all the love you pour into your child washes away like rain off a sidewalk. Some parents say that their child ignores all the signs of love they give and picks up on the one critical thing they said above all else. They are highly sensitive to any "clues" that confirm how "bad" they are, and positive feedback can roll off their back because they don't feel worthy enough to accept it. Here are two examples of this trait of feeling empty in a preteen and adolescent.

A new girl at school took Aaliyah's seat at lunch. None of the other girls "protected"

Aaliyah's seat for her. When she got home, she asked to be homeschooled. She told her mother she didn't want to go back to the school because "They all hate me." Her mother validated her feelings of intense disappointment and anxiety, and then explained that most likely the other girl had simply gotten to the seat before her, and that it wasn't personal. Nevertheless, Aaliyah refused to go to school the next morning, claiming that she was sick.

Coreen found her daughter cutting her arm in her bedroom with a razor. She asked her daughter why she was doing this, and her daughter explained that it distracted her from feeling lonely and empty.

Rage and extreme anger, common traits for kids with BPD, are tough for most parents to cope with. When your child is screaming the f-bomb at you, telling you that you should die and that you are a "f@#$%&* monster," or making other terrible comments out of proportion to whatever you said or did, it's very hard to be calm. Or maybe a friend has insulted your child (or they *believe* they've been insulted). Trying to convince a raging child that they're wrong about whatever they're mad about won't work because it comes off as invalidating. In chapter 7, we'll teach you how to validate your child, which should be your first response to intense emotions. Here are two examples of out-of-proportion rage in a preteen and adolescent.

Ginger wanted a green jacket like her friend Emily had. Her father took her to the store to buy one, but they didn't have green in her size, only purple and brown. Ginger was so upset that she collapsed on the floor in the store, sobbing uncontrollably.

Alice's phone was dead, but she couldn't find the charger. She looked all over her room several times, getting more and more frantic with each unsuccessful search. She then asked her little brother if he had taken it, and he said no. She accused him of taking it and insisted that he give it back. When he repeated that he didn't know what she was talking about, she began screaming at him at the top of her lungs.

Actions: Impulsive Behaviors

Children with BPD tend to act impulsively when they're experiencing intense emotional pain. Impulsive behaviors include running away from home, misusing prescription drugs, using street drugs, sharing prescription medication, ruining friendships, drinking, being sexually active with strangers, hitchhiking, shoplifting, sexting, putting nude photos of themselves online, spending money recklessly, or speeding in the family car.

Here are some examples of impulsivity, first for a preteen and then an adolescent.

Glen had to attend his mathematics class remotely because of the COVID quarantine. He turned on his computer a few minutes before class and tried to log on several times, but the link he had was defective. He quickly became frustrated. He didn't want to be late. He hit the computer each time his login attempt failed. Eventually, he knocked the computer onto the floor, and it broke.

Camilla went to a party hoping to get the interest of a boy from history class. She spent hours on her hair and outfit. When she got to the party the boy was talking to two other girls. Camilla attempted to get his attention by flirting. He finally did notice and asked her to go for a walk. He wanted to be intimate with her in the woods nearby. She lost her virginity that night, and when he ignored her the next day at school, she regretted it and felt used.

Children with BPD may threaten suicide or hurt themselves, but these two actions are taken for very different reasons. Suicide is about ending all pain, whereas self-harm is used to reduce emotional pain. (More about both in chapter 13.) Following are two examples of self-harm behavior.

Sofia picks at her fingernails when she's nervous. Sometimes her hand gets bloody or infected. When her doctor asked why she does this, she said she doesn't even realize that she's doing it.

Natasha was upset when Boris broke up with her, and she couldn't wait to get home and cut. She touched the cold steel razor to her upper arm, where she thought no one would see it, and started to draw blood. She immediately felt better. After a while, she bandaged her arm and took a nap.

The suicide rate among people with BPD who acknowledge they have BPD and have done some self-introspection is high. That's why this book has an entire chapter (chapter 13) dedicated to suicide and self-harm. Any threat of suicide should always be taken seriously.

Minors Can Have BPD

Many mental health professionals believe that children and teenagers are too young to be diagnosed with BPD. They even believe that the American Psychiatric Association's *Diagnostic and Statistical Manual of Mental Disorders* (DSM-5) states this as a fact. This is not true! In fact, the *DSM-5* states that most BPD traits begin by early adulthood (663). The BPD diagnosis is also greatly stigmatized, so some clinicians don't want to risk making a diagnosis prematurely, which could prejudice other providers against them in the future. For these reasons, perhaps, mental health professionals haven't suggested a diagnosis of BPD for your child, even if they meet all the criteria.

Other authoritative sources support the diagnosis of BPD in adolescents, as indicated below.
- "Recent data indicate that an estimated 18 million Americans will develop borderline personality disorder (BPD) in their lifetimes,

with symptoms commonly emerging during early adolescence and adulthood." Substance Abuse and Mental Health Services Administration, *Report to Congress on Borderline Personality Disorder* (2011, 1).
- "All available data indicate that adolescence is a critical point for early identification and therapeutic treatment of BPD." Andrea Fossati in *Borderline Personality Disorder in Adolescence: Phenomenology and Construct Validity* (2014, 23).

According to Blaise Aguirre, bipolar disorder is the most common diagnosis adolescents have when they arrive at his inpatient BPD unit (2014). While children can have both BPD and bipolar, the latter is often a misdiagnosis. Why? For the reasons outlined above regarding clinician hesitancy with making a BPD diagnosis, and because bipolar is often the first thing that comes to a clinician's mind when they hear "mood swings." But the disorders and their treatment, including medications, are totally different.

If your child has been diagnosed with bipolar, we suggest that you have a thorough discussion with the mental health professionals who diagnosed your child. Ask specific questions. Here are the most important ones to start with:

1. Did you suspect or believe my child has the traits of BPD, but gave them another diagnosis because you believe children can't have the diagnosis?

2. My child experiences frequent changes in mood. How do you tell whether this is bipolar disorder or BPD?
3. Have you had any special training in the diagnosis and treatment of BPD and other personality disorders?
4. How many individuals with BPD have you treated?
5. How many of them were younger than twenty-one years old?
6. What are the different treatment approaches that you use with bipolar disorder and BPD?

Even if you doubt your child's diagnosis or decide that their mental health professional isn't the person you want treating your child, don't just discontinue any prescribed medications, as that could have dangerous side effects. If you strongly believe the criteria for BPD is a much better fit, and the mental health professionals you are working with dismiss this out of hand, consider finding another. (See chapter 4 for more information.)

> Evidence shows that the earlier you treat BPD, the better. Early diagnosis and treatment are pivotal for helping children and adolescents recover (see appendix B).

It is too early for research studies to compare the different outcomes for people with BPD who get treatment early versus those who wait, but the researchers and authors who back this up include the following:

- "Two things are absolutely clear. First, adults with BPD almost always recognize that their symptoms and suffering started in childhood or adolescence. Second, some adolescents have symptoms that are so consistent with BPD that it would be unethical not to make this diagnosis and treat them accordingly." Blaise Aguirre in *Borderline Disorder in Adolescents: What to Do When Your Teen Has BPD* (2014, 21).
- "BPD has been a controversial diagnosis in adolescents, but this is no longer justified. Recent evidence demonstrates that BPD is as reliable and valid among adolescents as it is in adults and that adolescents with BPD can benefit from early intervention ... BPD diagnosis and treatment should be considered part of routine practice in adolescent mental health to improve these individuals' wellbeing and long-term prognosis." Kaess, Brunner, and Chanen in *Pediatrics* (2014, 1).

The bottom line is this: adolescents and even younger children with symptoms of borderline personality disorder *need* to be diagnosed and treated as soon as symptoms present themselves.

As Fran Porter said in the foreword, would you wait to treat a broken leg? Many adolescents self-harm and are suicidal, and if you only treat the behaviors but not the underlying disorder, you're only treating the *symptoms,* not the *cause.* The difference could literally be life and death. Why take the risk for a negative outcome? And there *are* BPD treatments proven to be effective, such as dialectical behavior therapy (DBT), cognitive behavioral therapy (CBT), and others.

Boys with BPD

Men and boys with BPD tend to have a more difficult time getting an accurate diagnosis even though they make up about half the borderline population (Grant et al. 2008). That's because the stereotypical person with BPD featured in websites, conferences, treatment centers, studies, books, blogs, feature articles—and pretty much everything else—is a woman in her teens to thirties. The following attributes are more common in men with BPD than in women (naturally, studies have not been done on children) (Sansone and Sansone 2011):

- Substance abuse
- Unstable relationships
- A combination of BPD and narcissistic personality disorder or antisocial personality disorder
- Impulsivity

- Aggression, even after controlling for differing levels of the traits by gender

These attributes are more common in women with BPD than in men with the disorder:
- History of being in therapy
- Eating disorders
- Anxiety disorders
- PTSD
- Major mood disorders, such as depression or bipolar
- Taking medication for a mental disorder

If your son has BPD, you may need to advocate for him even more than you would if he were your daughter, because many clinicians are not familiar with recent research showing that BPD is as common in males as it is in females. You may also need to help your son with BPD understand the shades of his emotions. If his father or another trusted male role model can tell him it's okay to have all sorts of feelings (other than anger) and name them, it would do a world of good. Right now, his emotions are probably a mystery to him.

Risk Factors for Developing BPD

There is no one cause of BPD, but rather a constellation of risk factors that involve both nature and nurture (Aguirre 2014). The more risk factors a person has, nature or nurture, the more likely it is they'll develop BPD. Regardless of the biological risk, we believe that you can reduce the chance that your child will develop BPD by following the strategies and techniques described in this book.

Biological Factors

In the mid-1800s, a man named Phineas Gage was working with explosives on a Vermont railroad when his head was punctured by a three-foot-seven-inches-long, one-and-one-quarter-inch-diameter iron tamping rod. He survived his injuries and lived another twelve years. However, his personality went through a complete change. Before the accident, he was a smart, energetic, and persistent businessman. A real gentleman. Afterward, he was fitful, irreverent, profane, rude, impatient, and obstinate. His friends said he was "no longer Gage" (Kreger 2008).

At the time of his injury, his behavior change was a mystery to doctors. But in the 1990s, scientists determined that the rod damaged parts of his brain responsible for emotional processing and rational decision making. This extraordinary case was the first clue that specific physical structures of the brain are associated with our personalities. A glitch in the way the brain operates in people with BPD may explain why they get so angry so quickly, why their memories can be unreliable, and why simple events and innocuous statements can trigger extreme rage. The amygdala, a part of our brain that plays an important role in regulating emotions like fear, aggression, and anxiety, seems to have unusually high levels of activity when someone with BPD is under stress, overwhelming the prefrontal cortex, which allows us to temper those feelings with logic.

Not only may differences in brain structure relate to the onset of BPD traits, but so too may imbalanced brain chemistry. Neurotransmitters carry vital information across the brain's synapses (spaces between brain cells, or neurons). You've probably already heard of neurotransmitters—serotonin, for example, is associated with impulsivity and mood; and dopamine, with feelings of being rewarded. Imbalances in neurotransmitter systems seem to underpin the three core dimensions of BPD we discussed earlier: dysregulated thoughts, feelings, and actions (Friedel 2004). These brain differences seem to be inherited.

> There are many ways in which a person's brain chemistry may come from inherited factors, such as a genetic risk for a mental disorder. However, there are also environmental factors that affect a person's ability to cope and manage life.

Environmental Factors

Environmental factors, when combined with a genetic vulnerability, can create BPD in a person. Important environmental risk factors include (Friedel, Cox, and Friedel 2018; Linehan 1993):

- Negative family and peer influences, ineffective or *perceived* ineffective parenting, an unsafe or chaotic home situation, a poor match between the temperaments of parent and child, or the sudden loss of a parent or a parent's attention.
- Being raised in an invalidating environment, which means one in which caregivers tell children their feelings or experiences are wrong and untrue, or who find fault with kids who don't perform "well enough." (These children tend not to trust themselves and look to others for confirmation of how to feel and act. Chapter 8 covers how to create a validating environment.)
- Experiencing sexual, emotional, or physical abuse, especially over a long period of time. While people tend to blame caregivers, the abuse can come from many different sources.

Did I Cause My Child's BPD?

If you've done any research about BPD, you've probably read that child abuse, neglect, or trauma are among its primary causes. Parents are often confused by this information. Many misconstrue a *correlation* between a history of abuse and BPD for cause and effect. (A *correlation* is a mutual relationship or a connection between two or more things.) However, not everyone with BPD was abused or otherwise traumatized in childhood, and even if they were, no one should assume a parent was responsible.

Even if you were an almost perfect parent and received a national award for parenting, you'd still be going through your memories trying to spot where you went "wrong," because you *must* have done something wrong for your child to be this way, right? Ironically, feelings of guilt will urge you to do all the wrong things for your child with BPD, as we'll show you in chapter 8. Rather than trying to find where you're to blame, channel that guilt you might feel into following the recommended strategies in this book.

BPD Is Very Treatable

When your child is suffering from BPD, and you are suffering as well, it might help to know that of the ten diagnosable personality disorders,

BPD is widely considered the most treatable (Dingfelder 2004). It's easy to find people with BPD who have recovered.

The difference between a person who's in recovery and one who's not is the person's willingness to acknowledge their unhappiness with life and to take responsibility for making changes that will make their life worth living. Treatment and emotional support are musts, of course. But many people with BPD who have recovered describe an epiphany of sorts (sometimes it takes hitting rock bottom) when they realized that only they could put themselves on the road to recovery. And the more effort they put into it, the more they will recover. As a parent, you can't change them directly, but you *can* change your behavior to make it more likely that you let this epiphany occur naturally. In this book, we'll show you how.

Top Takeaways from This Chapter

Here are the top takeaways that you should remember from this chapter:
- BPD is a story of dysregulated (unmanaged or uncontrolled) thoughts, emotions, and actions. Kids with BPD base their facts on their feelings, not vice versa. When your child thinks or behaves in a way that is illogical and beyond your understanding, your mantra should be, "For my child, feelings equal facts."

Write it down and tape it up somewhere they can't see it.
- People with BPD cannot generate self-esteem internally. They rely on others to give it to them by trying to control their environment and the people in it. Understanding that your child's behaviors that feel manipulative are really survival strategies to help them get through a world of pain is the first step to understanding your child and knowing how to respond.
- Minors *can* have BPD, and anyone who tells you otherwise is behind the times. It's vitally important that you become informed and get your child the appropriate treatment as soon as possible (see chapter 4).
- Your child's disorder *is not your fault.* The sooner you accept this, the better parent you will be. You won't be acting out of guilt, but out of what is best for your child.

CHAPTER 2

How BPD Affects Your Child

When Colleen's father had to leave for a week, as we were dropping him off at the airport as usual, on the way home in the middle of heavy traffic, Colleen [a fifteen-year-old with BPD] screamed, "Turn the car around right now! Go back to the airport! We have to stop dad's plane! It's going to crash."

Colleen started sobbing and screaming and Fran [Colleen's mother] tried to calm her down. At breakfast the next morning, Fran told her husband Andy, "Colleen said to me, 'Why did you make such a big deal yesterday about Dad on the way home from the airport?'" Fran was flabbergasted because she wasn't the one who had made the big deal the day before. Andy responded, "It's like she speaks a language we don't speak, and she can't learn ours."

—adapted from Fran Porter, *When the Ship Has No Stabilizers*

Right now, the behavior of your child is probably inexplicable. You are on the outside of borderline personality disorder while your child lies inside it. You see the behaviors, but they often don't make sense because the emotions and thoughts they spring from are invisible. In this chapter, we will travel to your child's inner world to see how they experience themselves, the world, and other people.

Most of the BPD traits and characteristics discussed in this chapter are not part of the official clinical definition of BPD, but they are well known to family members, people with BPD, and clinicians who have experience treating people with BPD and their families. Knowing about them can help you better understand your child with BPD.

The Voices of People with BPD

In this section we offer you BPD characteristics as the sufferers of this disorder see them. Most of these examples come from adults, because it was not ethical to interview children (many of whom don't know of their diagnosis). But we can learn what our children are going through by listening to adults with the same personality disorder. If you are reading this book as the parent of an adult child with BPD, you may recognize these traits in your child.

Identity Confusion

Destiny: You can't remember who you are, and how you ever felt differently. Sometimes your emotions are so big you are drowning in them, leaving you feeling fragmented and split, with your inner self becoming less and less accessible in these emotional storms. You don't know who you are, and you can't remember who you've been. When the pain recedes, all you feel is emptiness and a feeling of being dead inside.

We Feel Everything, All the Time

Rosa: When people ask what it's like to have BPD, I tell them to imagine every feeling they have ever had in their lifetime and feeling them all at the same time—and then having people tell you that every one of those emotions is wrong. It's like you're constantly begging for help or understanding, but no one else speaks your language.

Sam: Having BPD is chaos, like being a small kid inside an adult's body with people having expectations of you that you just can't seem to meet. Hating yourself, not feeling good enough. Being seen as crazy, manipulative, and evil, when you're just a mess inside and don't mean any harm to anyone.

About My Mood Swings

Adam: *Nothing I feel is average. Either I'm figuratively drunk, sobbing in a sticky, dark corner of the bar, or the life of the party, making all the jokes and toasts. When I'm in between, I don't feel much of anything—and I'm craving something that gives me the urge to create drama so I can feel something. My mood can change on a dime based on what I read in the news, something I am worried about, or how I feel about life. Internal things. Or it can be external things, like how others are treating me, reacting to me, or talking (or not talking) to me. My mood fluctuates like the stock market. I know intellectually there is no need to react that strongly. But I can't help it.*

Stan: *If I make even the smallest mistake, I am sure everyone is going to leave me. No one will love me. I try to combat this thinking by constantly reminding myself: "I am chosen. I am cared for. I am loved." Sometimes it takes saying it about a thousand times, but it works.*

How I Feel About Myself

Mimi: *Imagine a world in which you are positively sure that you are a complete and utter failure, and everyone thinks you're an idiot, aren't worth listening to, and can't be* trusted. When you get a chance to show them differently, it turns out wrong no matter what you do. So, you wrap yourself in self-loathing.

Jamal: *I feel like a monster—disgusting, guilty, and confused. I ruin people's lives, so I push them away and hide from them. At the same time, I want them to come to me and reassure me, "No, you're not a monster," as I push them away screaming, "Run for your life! Go away!" But then again, I want to say, "Hug me, maybe? But ... not too much, because I don't deserve it."*

I Hate You—Please Don't Leave Me

Donald: *Every day, I get pure flashes of honest hatred for the people whom I love most. I know that I am splitting them [seeing people in black and white] and that it's not "real," but still it hurts my heart to feel it. Half the battle is knowing that my brain needs to be fixed and that my emotions are not reality. Just because you feel something is true does not make it true. That was hard for me to learn.*

Sophie: *Everyone is lying to my face. No one really cares about me. That's what my brain keeps telling me all the time. The only thing I can do to combat those thoughts is ask my friends and family repeatedly if they're lying to me or if they really do care about me. I ask them so many times I make* both of us exhausted and sick. I feel terrible that I do that to us both, but I don't know how to stop asking.

You Can't Imagine My Worst Pain

Jody: It's like I'm constantly screaming for help and understanding, and nobody hears me.

Imani: Having BPD feels like you're being stabbed in the heart on a regular basis. You hate yourself. Sometimes you hate everyone else. You don't know what to do. You may feel like an alien looking in whether you're with strangers, friends, or family. Everyone is badmouthing you, and you have to admit they're right because you are terrible. Teenagers can seem pretty borderline, and borderline people can seem pretty much like teenagers.

Bai Ling: Heartache makes the world go around and I hate it. I just don't want to exist anymore. I don't want the possibility of someone hurting me anymore. I want to stop existing because life is too painful. It's too exhausting to live this life. I push the people away I love the most, and I can't seem to stop myself or even realize what I have done until it is too late.

Why We Do What We Do

Ellen: We can act so shit-ass crazy because of the pain. I'm not going to deny that or make excuses. But I'm going to be honest when I say we do damage because we are incredibly sick and experiencing pain beyond what most people can imagine.

Denzel: I know you don't understand me. I don't understand me either. My most common thought is, Why did I just do that?

Rodney: Imagine being set on fire over and over again, unable to do anything about it. That is where the impulsivity comes from. We will do anything—cutting, drinking, smoking, doing drugs, spending large sums of money, having risky sex, quitting our jobs, and attempting suicide—to stop the scarlet flames from licking our skin. I read it's like we have exposed nerve endings. How do you tell a person on fire to use logic? The crazy thing is that when I'm happy it's just as intense.

Alejandro: When I am frantic with worry that someone I love is going to abandon me, I hurt them because I lack self-control in the face of overwhelming emotion, not because I lack compassion. After I have taken a step back and surveyed the wreckage, I am filled with guilt and self-loathing. Fear of abandonment is desperation mode, and I usually resort to nasty threats. I don't think I would *follow through with them, but considering my impulsivity and loss of control, I can see why they would scare people away.*

About My Anger

Stephanie: *When I'm angry, it takes over like a tidal wave and I lash out and say mean things, curse, and scream. I want to hurt the ones I love in that moment, so they know how I feel. Most people don't realize the root of the anger is hurt—although I have to admit sometimes I am just pissed off. When it's over, I feel ashamed of myself. I can apologize, but the damage has been done.*

Thoughts

Judgments: People with BPD believe that others are judging them all the time. For example, Carol, a preteen, says she's not going to grandpa's anymore because she thinks he prefers her older brother: "He loves Jimmy better. He only pays attention to him."

Object constancy: When we're lonely, most of us can soothe ourselves by remembering the love that others have for us. This can be very comforting if these people are far away—sometimes even if they're no longer living. This ability to hold others close in spite of their physical absence is called *object constancy*. Many people with BPD find it difficult to evoke an image of a loved one to soothe them when they feel upset or anxious (Cardasis, Hochman, and Silk 1997). To someone with BPD, if that person isn't physically present, it's harder for the person with BPD to emotionally feel that they exist. That's why your child may want you and others to be physically present, or to call, text, and email frequently. Depending upon their age, "transitional objects"—tokens of home or you—can help kids with BPD soothe themselves, especially if you're going to be separated (Cardasis, Hochman, and Silk 1997). Think photo albums, teddy bears, and actual letters.

Difficulty concentrating: People with BPD sometimes confuse feelings and facts, see things in black and white, and may experience paranoia and dissociation. When you add great big emotions and emotional sensitivity, it's no surprise they find it hard to pay attention and concentrate for very long. Imagine trying to figure out a complicated math problem while waiting to hear the results of the biopsy of a lump in your breast. When your child is highly emotional, lower your expectations for logical thinking.

Poor decision making: Emotional pain and weak coping skills sometimes lead kids with BPD to make poor decisions, which leads to chaos. They have a difficult time thinking through the ramifications of their actions. For example, a teen may loan their computer to a friend, who then has an accident with it or loses it. If you know about a choice your child needs to make, rather than tell them what you think, help them think it through. Ask questions. "If you don't study for the test tomorrow, what do you think the consequences will be? If you flunk the test, will your grade point average be good enough to attend camp this year?"

Feelings

Feelings equal facts: We talked about this in chapter 1, but it bears repeating. Whereas most people base their feelings on the facts in front of them (most of the time), people with BPD base the *facts* on their *feelings*. To an extent, we all use our emotions to determine what we believe. Advertisers and politicians know this and exploit it. But kids with BPD take this much further. The validation section in chapter 7 will show you how to elicit some of the "facts" on their mind so you can respond more effectively.

Weak empathy: Because kids with BPD are consumed with survival strategies and their nonstop pain, they have a difficult time putting themselves in other people's shoes. To family members, this comes across as having weak or even no empathy. For example, Jason, a preteen, rushed while clearing the table and broke his mother's favorite coffee mug. When his mother got upset, Jason said, "It's just an effing mug!"

This weak empathy, which is especially striking when the person with BPD is upset, leads to family members feeling underappreciated and overworked. Don't be afraid to point out when you need a please and thank you, or when you're sick or need help. Without shaming your child, don't be afraid to explain how you feel and how you wish to be treated. Just because they don't think of helping you doesn't mean they won't.

Sensitivity to criticism: Kids with BPD are very sensitive to criticism because they already think the worst of themselves. For this reason, be positive when you can be. Catch them being good and notice it. For example, when it's their turn to unload the dishwasher and they do it, thank them. Watch out for the good they do instead of the bad. Celebrate the cessation of unhealthy behaviors—for example, showing restraint while frustrated. Rewards can include smiles, praise, positive body language, attention, and points that can be traded in for privileges or treats. You can say, "You acted in a very smart [helpful, sensitive, intuitive] way" when it is authentic to say so.

Shame and self-loathing: Shame is one of the most painful emotions people with BPD feel. The difference between guilt and shame is that guilt has to do with something you've done, whereas shame is about who you *are* (Brown 2012). Your child is always on high alert for any hint of rejection or abandonment because it confirms what they already believe: people will eventually find out that they are worthless. For example, a preteen refuses to go on a field trip, saying, "Nobody likes me and I don't blame them."

Emotional sensitivity: It's not easy for kids with BPD to maintain relationships because of their emotional reactivity, or their over-the-top intensity that's out of proportion to whatever triggered it. This sensitivity is related to how their brains function differently. Their emotions are not only more intense, but they also stick around longer. It's helpful to remind yourself that this is not an attempt to "manipulate" you; rather, it's a way for them to cope.

*   **Conan:** *Our son is supersensitive (Understatement!) to every word, nuance, tone, smell, and sound he sees as rejecting, and he believes he even knows when we are thinking something negative about him. He wants us to do everything for him even if we don't have time, are ill, or it's an entirely unreasonable request. He's failing school despite his high IQ, which we didn't know because he had been lying to us about his grades and time spent studying (he said he was going to the library when he was really doing something else). He has been to multiple therapists and convinced them that we, his parents, are insane and abusive. This feels hopeless.*

Lower level of emotional development: An average two-year-old has tantrums when they're frustrated, objecting to changes in routine, and feeling jealous because they're not the center of attention. They have frequent mood swings, are egocentric, and have a low awareness of other people's needs. People with BPD are still struggling with some of these tasks, which may make you frustrated. Keep in mind they are still learning to overcome some of these two-year-old challenges.

Neediness: Most children enjoy growing older, becoming more independent, and learning to do things for themselves. Children with BPD are the opposite. Parents doing things for them equals love. They view their parents' gentle push into independence as threatening and abandoning, and they may resist forcefully, causing major upsets. When parents try to "help" by preventing them from experiencing the natural consequences of their behavior, or do so because they want to avoid temper tantrums, their children learn that tantrums work and use them repeatedly. As you will see later in this book, this is called "feeding the monster" (BPD). It makes BPD worse. The story below is that of parents who "fed the monster" for thirty-two years with a bad result.

Karunakar: *Our daughter is very needy, and though she is an adult, she still calls us several times a day, often trying to get us to help her or otherwise get involved with her life and drama. She doesn't recognize the consequences of her bad choices. We have tried for thirty-two years to offer her grace and forgiveness, hoping she would change. This hasn't worked, however, so now she will* *experience consequences without a soft place to land. Maybe that will change her life course, but we really have no control over her choices. We are in our late sixties, and the physical and emotional toll has been heavy.*

Low frustration tolerance: This extremely common characteristic can cause a lot of grief. Sticking at something despite its difficulty allows people to think before they act, something people with BPD, with their impulsivity, don't often do. When they want something, it will always be a crisis. When you rush to satisfy those immediate wants, you signal that enduring the frustration is impossible. If you've ever had a cat, you know that if you give in and feed it before dinnertime, it will want dinner even earlier tomorrow. The same behavioral principles work with your child. Their crisis shouldn't be your crisis. Learning to tolerate frustration is vital to everything they will encounter in life.

Actions

Testing others: You may feel as if your child controls the household, but they think you do, because you have the power to reject or abandon them, blame or criticize them, or otherwise do something that makes them feel terrible. This causes incredible tension. In adult relationships, many people with BPD deal with that by breaking up with a partner before their partner breaks up with them. Your child does something similar: since they can't break up with you, they'll challenge your directives or act in extreme ways to see if you'll still stick by what you said you would do.

For example, Esther's mother offered her a cookie. Esther took two. Mom said she was supposed to have only one but let her keep both. The next day, Esther took three. Sergio, an adolescent, knew that the household rule was to keep food out of the bedrooms. One day his mother came in and caught him eating potato chips. When his mother commented on it, he said, "This is a snack, not food."

Lying: It may not be popular to say so, but some kids with BPD lie—a lot. We don't know if they lie more than kids who don't have BPD, but it is an extremely common parental complaint. Sometimes they lie because they truly believe something (feelings equal facts), or they choose to believe what they want to be true rather than what is actually true. They might lie to get attention or gain sympathy, because they want to impress someone to counter self-loathing, or because they want to hide unacceptable information, such as using drugs. More than a few parents learned that their children were spreading horrific made-up stories of child abuse, reason unknown.

For example, Sharon, the mother of a daughter with BPD, ran an online group for parents of kids with BPD for twenty years. She advises, "You need to accept two things: your child will lie, and punishment won't change that fact. Instead, try to stay on top of things the best you can. If you find out they lied, talk with them and try to understand why they felt they had to lie to get through what was happening to them."

Sharon's method, which may or may not work for you, was to reward her daughter by helping her problem solve why she lied and suggest better coping methods. In any case, it is essential that you hold your child accountable for lying by withholding your trust and explaining why you are doing so. So, if your child wants you to trust them to come straight home from a movie, but the last time they went to a friend's house instead, their punishment is that you now don't trust them and thus refuse the privilege of your trust.

To My Loved Ones, from Your Family Member with BPD

I hate the way I am as much as you do. For all the pain that I cause you, I am suffering ten times as much. I struggle daily with the fear that those I love are going to leave me, often desperately attempting to avoid the inevitable abandonment. I know you think my fear is irrational—and maybe it is—but it feels so real to me.

Every day I wake up never knowing what sort of day I will have. Just like you, I wish I could live a happy life, free from the chaos that seems to follow me wherever I go. The chaos I feel is best described as like having a beast that lives inside me. Sometimes the beast is sleeping and it is easy to forget he is there. Even I can begin to fool myself into thinking that maybe the beast has disappeared. I never know when my beast is going to awaken, ready to wreak havoc on myself and everyone I hold dear to me—all I know is that he will awaken. Just like you, I feel as if I am walking on eggshells most of the time—except that you are walking on them as you fear me, and I walk on them as I fear my beast.

When my beast does rear its ugly head, my world is turned upside down and I lose control. I may self-harm, jump into a relationship, fight, drink, or use any of the other coping mechanisms I have taught myself over the years. You see, to you, my behaviors are simply destructive, but to me, they are survival skills that I use when I don't know how to cope anymore.

To the outside world, I behave in a way that is completely unacceptable. I understand why people have this view—except that nobody knows what is going through my head or how I feel, yet these are the driving forces behind my behavior. Yes, I am highly emotional, and no, I do not consider the consequences of my actions, but I know no other way to be right now. This is who I am. This is me.

There is help out there for people like myself with BPD. There is no cure but it can be managed. I need recovery as much as you need me to recover, but it will be much easier for me if I know I have your love and support.

I must also tell you that recovery takes time, and there will be times when you feel as if I am going backward—I am not; it is just part of the journey. I hope there will come a time when together we can look back on the way that I was as a distant memory. I know that we can get through this and come out the other side stronger—all I ask is that you have understanding and patience. I know that my behaviors are damaging, but please know that I am not a bad person; I'm a person struggling with a disorder that I never chose to have, but I am choosing to learn to live with.

—Shehrina Rooney, *The Big Book on Borderline Personality Disorder*

Top Takeaways from This Chapter

Hopefully you have a better sense of the internal strife your child is enduring, and why they're behaving the way they are. Here are the top takeaways from this chapter to keep in mind:

- Your child is dealing with problems like self-loathing, sensitivity to criticism, emotional pain, and difficulty thinking and concentrating. Emotionally, they are operating at the level of a toddler. They often don't understand why they feel the way they do or why they do what they do.
- Your child can improve and get better, and the key is a willingness to take accountability for improving their own life.

CHAPTER 3

Psychiatric Problems That Commonly Co-Occur with BPD

Regina's daughter Madison was diagnosed with depression when she was eleven years old and treated with Prozac. It helped a little, but Madison still struggled in school and at home. She frequently got into tearful arguments with other children and her parents over minor things that didn't bother other kids, like being told to do her homework before she could play outside. Madison never seemed to understand why other kids—or for that matter, her own parents—didn't automatically do whatever she wanted them to do.

One day she said she hated her best friend, Jessica, because she was "too stuck up." She went to Jessica's house, apparently said some very mean things, and stomped home. The next day, Madison changed her mind about Jessica and regretted everything she said. But Jessica said she didn't want to be her friend anymore and asked Madison to stop texting *her or sitting with her at lunch. It was a blow to Madison's self-esteem.*

Madison, who hadn't yet learned that angry words have consequences in relationships, lay in her bed with the door closed for days crying, uninterested in anything, and refusing to eat or go to school. She complained of aches that wouldn't go away, appeared sad and anxious, and slept all day. Regina and her husband called Madison's psychiatrist, who said it was possible that she might be clinically depressed in addition to her previous BPD diagnosis. The doctor wanted Madison's parents to bring her in right away.

Having borderline personality disorder alone is challenging enough, but many, if not most, people with BPD have one or more psychiatric problems at the same time. It could be that one of the conditions or disorders started before the other, or perhaps both conditions developed at the same time. Sometimes one condition or disorder may end, but the other continues or worsens. An additional psychiatric problem adds more symptoms to the mix, making your child's behavior more confusing (and painful), and requires additional treatment. This chapter covers the most common psychiatric problems that co-occur in people with borderline personality disorder. We'll discuss them from the most to least common based on research studies of large groups of individuals (Grant et al. 2008; Friedel,

Cox, and Friedel 2018; Weiner, Perroud, and Weibel 2019; Zanarini et al. 2010):
- Clinical depression (occurs at some point in over 80 percent of people with BPD)
- Anxiety disorders and panic attacks (60 to 90 percent)
- Eating disorders, including anorexia and bulimia (20 to 55 percent)
- Post-traumatic stress disorder (PTSD) and complex PTSD (30 to 50 percent)
- Narcissistic personality disorder (NPD) (30 to 50 percent)
- Bipolar disorder type I (30 percent)
- Substance abuse disorders, including alcohol abuse (65 to 80 percent)
- Attention deficit/hyperactivity disorder (ADHD) (15 to 40 percent)

Unfortunately, a co-occurring psychiatric problem complicates your child's disordered or dysregulated thoughts, emotions, and actions. It makes treatment—and life—more difficult for both of you. For example, the combination of BPD and depression, anxiety, or substance abuse escalates the risk for suicidal behaviors. In this chapter, we'll give you enough information about these problems so you can recognize them in your child. If your child is willing to see a therapist about a co-occurring problem, ask the BPD treatment professional you're already seeing if they're capable of treating both disorders. If not, ask for a referral. Eating disorders and substance abuse, especially, have their own treatment protocols.

Major Depression

Clinical depression is a common mental disorder in the United States, and a large number (over 80 percent) of people with BPD experience it—probably due to the constant struggles with managing this beast of a diagnosis and its many facets. To get the proper treatment, a mental health professional must discern whether your child is experiencing a typical fluctuation of mood associated with BPD or a co-occurring major depressive episode. The following table draws on the work of Robert Friedel, who is on the scientific advisory board of the National Education Alliance for Borderline Personality Disorder, to show you the differences between a major depressive episode and what Friedel refers to as "borderline depression," or your child's emotional response to their BPD symptoms (Friedel 2004, 109).

Borderline Depression vs. A Major Depressive Episode	
Borderline Depression	**Major Depressive Episode**
Feelings of isolation, sadness, and distress that go along with the BPD traits outlined in chapter 1	Continuous low mood or sadness
Sleep, appetite, and fatigue problems that relate to what's happening in the person's life and usually go away when the current stress has ended	Changes in appetite or weight (increases or decreases) Lack of energy
Acute thoughts of suicide and self-harm that relate to what's going on in the person's life at that moment, such as the ending of an important relationship	Suicidal thoughts caused by the depression even after acute stressors disappear
Any troublesome symptom that gets better as the stressful situation improves	Symptoms don't get better on their own

Treatment for depression may involve giving the patient antidepressant medications, increasing the dosage of a current antidepressant, trying a different antidepressant if the current one is not working, or adding a second medication to increase the power of the first antidepressant. Psychotherapy can also be used. As noted before, the co-occurrence of BPD and major depression increases the risk of suicide. Take or encourage your child to see a therapist, but understand that if they are over eighteen, to seek therapy or help is ultimately their decision.

Julia's fifteen-year-old daughter, Emily, diagnosed with both BPD and major depression, would sometimes stay in her room for twenty-four hours, only coming out to go to the bathroom. She wouldn't talk to her mother or anyone else, wouldn't eat or do anything. Julia decided that if the behavior lasted one more day, she was going to call her doctor. Emily's behavior didn't change, so Julia called Emily's psychiatrist, who asked to see Emily again. After the doctor saw her, he switched her to a different antidepressant and increased her therapy sessions with a psychologist to once a week.

Anxiety Disorders and Panic Attacks

Heightened anxiety and panic attack symptoms may occur in people with BPD when they're under stress. The possible triggers (for example, anticipating a therapist's planned vacation, not getting picked for something at school, or getting in trouble for something at home) are unlimited. A person experiencing anxiety often feels distraught, on edge, and upset, like something terrible is about to happen. Sometimes they cannot identify a clear reason for the anxiety. Worry may cause insomnia or other sleep disturbances. Moderate to severe anxiety can lead to physical symptoms, such as headaches, stomach pain, and irritable bowel syndrome. A person diagnosed with generalized anxiety disorder may have trouble concentrating or find their mind suddenly going blank for no apparent reason. The individual may be irritable, out of sorts, and overtired (NIMH 2016a).

A panic attack is like a black hole of anxiety. It has enough gravity to pull in everything surrounding it. Panic attacks frequently cause immobilization and disrupt functioning. When people experience panic attacks, they have a fixed period of intense fear in which they experience some of the following symptoms, which can appear out of nowhere and dissipate slowly or quickly (NIMH 2016b).

- Fear of dying
- Fear of losing control or going crazy
- A pounding heart or increased heart rate
- Feeling dizzy, unsteady, light-headed, or faint
- Sweating, trembling, or shaking
- Shortness of breath or feeling smothered
- Chest pain or the feeling of choking
- Nausea or stomach upset
- Numbness and tingling sensations
- Chills or heat sensations

Be Cautious About Using Benzodiazepines for Anxiety or Panic Attacks

Psychiatrists often treat anxiety disorders and panic attacks with benzodiazepines, such as Xanax, Klonopin, and Valium. *These drugs might not be suitable for some people with BPD because they can be addictive and can be used impulsively, sometimes resulting in an overdose* (Ripoll 2013). Low dose antipsychotic medications can be useful for some people struggling with anger issues, impulsivity, anxiety, and paranoia (Ripoll 2013; Wasylyshen and Williams 2016). Also, medications are not the only answer. Cognitive behavioral therapy (CBT), which helps people reframe their thoughts, changing their emotions and altering their behavior, is another positive and non-medication option proven to help many people with anxiety and BPD (Matusiewicz et al. 2010). In mild cases, therapy can be used without medications.

Eating Disorders

People with BPD are more likely to have an eating disorder than people in the general population (Zanarini et al. 2010). Some experts suggest that certain BPD symptoms, such as impulsivity and urges to self-harm, may lead to problem eating, which may eventually cause an eating disorder. (An eating disorder is also a form of self-harm in that it involves either starving the body or purging it unnaturally.)

Research concerning people with both BPD and an eating disorder has focused on anorexia and bulimia, although they are not the only eating disorders (Zanarini et al. 2010). People with anorexia are unusually fearful of gaining weight, are preoccupied with being thin, and eat very little to achieve that goal. They have a distorted view of how they look: they see themselves as huge and gross, even when looking in the mirror, while everyone else sees a dangerously thin person.

People suffering from bulimia eat huge amounts of food and then compensate by inducing vomiting, overusing laxatives, or excessively exercising. They may engage in these behaviors several times a day.

Your child may have an eating disorder if you notice several of the following signs:

- Your child behaves in an unusual way around food, such as frequently skipping meals and making excuses for it or sitting at the dinner table and refusing to eat, saying they're "not hungry."
- Your child goes to the bathroom during meals, possibly to purge their food, or quickly disappears after a meal for the same reason.
- Your child eats unusually large quantities of food (a binge), which may later be followed by a purge. (When the person does not compensate with a purge or excessive exercise, it is known as binge-eating disorder.)
- Your child has ritualized ways of eating, such as always cutting an apple into sixteen pieces and chewing each bite for thirty seconds.

- Your child obsessively weighs themself.
- Your child gets upset when they cannot control their food and eating situation, such as on a vacation or while eating a meal at grandma's.
- Your child constantly talks about food and weight, especially about how fat they are when they are already too thin. They pinch loose skin and claim it is "fat."
- Your child withdraws from friends and activities.
- Your child exercises compulsively.
- Your child is obsessed with how their body looks, and the number on the scale determines their mood and how they feel about themself that day. Preoccupation with food and weight takes up so much space in their life that they lose interest in the people and things they used to enjoy.
- Your child has secretive eating habits.

Here are some of the physical signs to look for:
- Cessation of menstruation
- Fluctuations in weight
- The growth of fine, downy hair on the face, back, and arms
- Dizziness, especially upon standing, and feeling cold all the time

- The aftereffects of frequent vomiting: dental problems (enamel erosion, cavities, discoloration of teeth, and tooth sensitivities), cuts and calluses across the top of finger joints (from inducing vomiting), and constipation

Post-Traumatic Stress Disorder (PTSD) and Complex PTSD

In his book *Borderline Personality Disorder in Adolescents*, psychiatrist Blaise Aguirre reports that of the patients with BPD who are hospitalized at the adolescent dialectical behavioral therapy center at McLean Hospital, where he serves as director, up to 50 percent also have post-traumatic stress disorder (PTSD) (2014, 126). PTSD is a condition that may be experienced by a person who has suffered from severe traumas, such as a sexual or other physical assault. The symptoms may include the following, according to the National Institute of Mental Health: flashbacks of the traumatic event, bad dreams or nightmares, and easy startling (2019a).

Note that this does not mean that 50 percent of *people* with BPD have PTSD, only that 50 percent of his *inpatients* have PTSD. He also estimates that 33 percent of his patients experienced some childhood trauma, which, as mentioned, often results in PTSD. Sadly, because experts are aware of the connection between trauma and PTSD, sometimes parents have been unfairly blamed for harming their own children. The thinking is, if the child has PTSD, then it must be the parents' fault.

As a result, for many years, parents were blamed for BPD, with the implication being that they abused their children. In fact, many people with BPD were abused, except it was by someone else they knew (not necessarily a parent) or a stranger. For example, Kiera Van Gelder, author of the memoir *The Buddha and the Borderline,* reports that she was abused by a male babysitter—and her parents had no idea about this abuse (2010).

PTSD and BPD can be misdiagnosed because people often exhibit the same symptoms in the emotional regulation, self-image, and interpersonal problem categories. This table should guide you in giving your child's therapist a proper history so they can more accurately diagnose whether your child has co-occurring PTSD (Dierberger and Lewis-Schroeder 2017; Cloitre et al. 2014).

| Differences between PTSD and BPD ||
PTSD	Borderline Personality Disorder
The cause is exposure to actual or threatened abuse, injury, or violence.	Caused by a combination of biological and environmental factors.
The patient tends to avoid interpersonal relationships, and tends to have a deep sense of social alienation.	Interpersonal relationships are unstable, especially due to splitting and the profound fear of abandonment.
A person's perception of their own identity is stable but may be consistently negative.	A person's perception of their own identity may be unstable and the sense of self may fluctuate dramatically.
Frequently involves flashbacks, nightmares, and other symptoms linked directly to traumatic memories.	Not associated with memory flashbacks; negative feelings are not usually attached to a traumatic incident.
Treatment focuses on healing the trauma and reducing the emotional impact of traumatic memories.	Treatment focuses on reducing suicidality and self-harm, regulating emotions, improving interpersonal relations, and developing a more solid sense of self.

Narcissistic Personality Disorder (NPD)

It is also possible to have two personality disorders at the same time—in fact, it's well known that BPD and narcissistic personality disorder (NPD) can occur at the same time (Grant et al. 2008). This is especially true among people with BPD who use people, excessively criticize others, do not think they have problems, will not seek treatment, and blame others for all their problems. It is much less common in those who seek treatment, self-harm, and blame themselves for things they didn't do. NPD is also more common in adult children than minors.

While people with BPD look to others to manage their moods, people with NPD rely on others to prop up their low self-esteem and shore them up so they can deny their deep feelings of shame. Because people with NPD can't generate self-worth for themselves, they require an unlimited "narcissistic supply" from others in the form of admiration, praise, attention, being envied, special treatment, being feared, approval, affirmation, respect, applause, celebrity status, and any other means of being viewed as special (Mayo Clinic 2017).

As they clutch their narcissistic supply, like a nonswimmer clinging to a capsized boat, people with NPD create a bubble for themselves, which maintains their narrative that they've always been strong, powerful, smart, well liked, and a winner. Intolerable feelings are buried so deep that they can't be accessed on a typical day. Only a "narcissistic injury" (for example, an insult on a social media site, a perceived slight, a spouse asking for a divorce, or losing an election) can threaten this little ecosystem. It punctures the narcissist's bubble and triggers feelings of deep vulnerability, shame, and inadequacy. They may respond by attacking the person who "injured" them or trying to get even.

Bipolar Disorders I and II

There are two forms of bipolar disorder: bipolar I and bipolar II. People with bipolar I experience manic episodes that last at least a week or more or are severe enough to require hospital care. During a manic episode, people feel euphoric and elated, or irritable and touchy. They have a decreased need for sleep and may stay awake all night, thoughts racing, trying to figure out things like a cure for cancer or world peace. They strive for such lofty goals during a manic episode because they may feel like they're more talented or important than they really are. They may act jumpy or wired and refuse to eat as they chatter away about a host of different subjects in a stream-of-consciousness soliloquy. They may impulsively do risky and reckless things, such as have unprotected sex, eat and drink too much, or spend or give away too much money (Friedel, Cox, and Friedel 2018).

Eventually, the manic episode gives way to a depressive episode, which typically lasts two weeks or more. Instead of talking one hundred miles per hour, they speak at the pace of a child dragging their feet on the way home from school after receiving a failing grade. When they do talk, they feel like they have nothing to say. In short, they have the same symptoms of a major depressive episode: feeling suicidal, irritable, hopeless, worthless, and unable to do simple things. They lose interest in previously pleasurable activities and have trouble concentrating or making decisions. A person can also rapidly cycle between depressive and manic states. In between episodes, people with bipolar I can have normative emotional states.

People with bipolar II also have depressive episodes, but not the full-blown mania typical of bipolar I. Instead, they have "hypomanias" (small manic episodes), a reduced duration or less extreme case of the mania described above. A person can rapidly cycle between depressive and hypomanic states. Hypomania can also show up as significant insomnia, irritability, agitation, anxiety, and difficulty concentrating. In between depressive and hypomanic episodes, people with bipolar II can also have normative emotional states (NIMH 2018).

BPD and bipolar disorders share common traits:
- Mood changes
- Impulsivity
- Extreme behaviors
- Suicidal thinking
- Possible alcohol and drug abuse
- A history of troubled, unstable relationships

But there are also striking differences, namely the three detailed in the following table (NIMH 2018; NIMH n.d.).

Differences Between BPD and Bipolar Disorders		
	BPD	**Bipolar Disorders**
Length of mood cycles	Very short, hours to days	Weeks to months
Reason for cycle	Dependent upon events in the person's life	Less frequently tied to what's going on in the person's life; more internally driven Significant stressors can ignite a bipolar episode (Fast and Preston 2006)
Types of emotions that cycle	All emotions fluctuate frequently in intensity: jealousy, anxiety, fear, love, anger, frustration, and so forth	Only depression and mania decrease or increase in intensity, in contrast to all emotions for the person with BPD

The good news is that there is a great deal of data on the treatment of bipolar disorder. The illness can be managed successfully with therapy and medication, and relationships with friends and family can be greatly improved (Fast and Preston 2006). However, like BPD, bipolar disorder is usually a lifelong illness and often involves a combination of medications and psychotherapy. At times, hospitalization may be necessary.

If Your Child Is Diagnosed with Bipolar Disorder

In our experience, children with BPD are mistakenly diagnosed with bipolar disorder more than any other illness, and children with bipolar disorder are mistakenly diagnosed with BPD. Mood swings are common with both disorders, so clinicians mistake the two. Sometimes parents aren't comfortable with the bipolar diagnosis because it explains some of their child's symptoms and behaviors, but not all. A proper diagnosis is vital because the treatments are not the same.

Why might a therapist erroneously give a bipolar diagnosis?

• First, some therapists believe a BPD diagnosis will "label" children with a disorder that lacks meaningful treatment options. (They are incorrect in believing there is no treatment for these children.)

• Second, some therapists don't realize that children can be diagnosed with BPD, *and* they don't know that there are effective treatment options.

As a parent, you've been studying your child's behavior for their entire life in thousands of circumstances. If a diagnosis doesn't feel right to you, get a second or third opinion from qualified clinicians. If they dismiss you or insist children can't be treated for BPD, get another opinion.

Substance Abuse Disorders

Substance abuse disorders include taking illegal drugs, abusing alcohol, misusing prescribed drugs, and using any other unhealthy or self-destructive mood-altering substance. No matter the type of drug, the purpose is the same: numbing the intense emotional pain of BPD. Of course, the numbness only lasts until the next dose, and addiction leads to a new set of problems (including a potential overdose) that cause suffering and danger—not just for the person with BPD, but for family members as well.

While your child is abusing substances, it is incredibly difficult for them to make significant progress in therapy, because therapy is a process of learning how to feel those emotions and to manage them in a healthy way, and because studies have found that substance abuse significantly delays BPD recovery (Aguirre 2014). The use of illicit drugs also makes it difficult to properly prescribe psychiatric medications, such as antidepressants, because the prescriber cannot tell which effects are due to the illicit drugs and which are due to the prescribed medication. We will discuss the issue of substance abuse further in chapter 14.

Attention Deficit/Hyperactivity Disorder (ADHD)

Attention deficit/hyperactivity disorder (ADHD) occurs at least five times more frequently in people with BPD than it does in the general population (Friedel, Fox, and Friedel 2018). The following table highlights some of the similar and dissimilar symptoms found with each disorder. We didn't include *every* symptom, just some of the most significant ones. Symptoms differ by age, thus we listed them accordingly: the first symptom occurs in young children; the last, in teenagers (NIMH 2019b; NIMH n.d.).

Symptom Similarities and Differences with BPD and ADHD	
Common Symptoms of ADHD Alone	Symptoms in Both BPD and ADHD
Lots of toe tapping, squirming, and so forth	Doesn't always recognize the needs of others
Little follow-through	Unstable emotions
Problems listening and remembering	School problems
	Friendship/relationship difficulties
Poor organizational skills	Mood swings
Very distractible	Takes a long time to come back to baseline once angry
Tendency for procrastination	

Top Takeaways from This Chapter

We didn't discuss all possible co-occurring disorders and psychiatric problems in this chapter—just the most common ones. We've given you enough information to get a feel for whether or not they apply to your child, which will help you determine if they were diagnosed correctly. A co-occurring psychiatric problem might mean a change in the course of BPD treatment. Of course, rely on a *competent* clinician for an accurate diagnosis and treatment, if you can, because even though you know your child better than anyone else, you're not an expert on whether particular symptoms indicate BPD or something else. If your child does have a co-occurring issue, you have plenty of company. Keep in mind that children with the same diagnoses have recovered, and their parents have managed too.

Here are some key takeaways of this chapter to keep in mind as you read on:
- Co-occurring illnesses are extremely common in people with BPD, with depression being almost universal.
- You need to determine if your child's current treatment provider can handle the co-occurring illness, or if you need another specialist. If your child is abusing drugs or has an eating disorder, you will almost certainly need outside help.

- If your child is abusing drugs, that illness needs to be managed before or at the same time as BPD treatment (Aguirre 2014). People who abuse drugs and alcohol often do it to numb themselves (make their internal pain go away), and the process of therapy involves examining that pain—and there is evidence that addiction impairs BPD treatment and recovery far more than in many other disorders (Aguirre 2014).
- Bipolar disorder is a very common misdiagnosis for children with BPD (Friedel, Cox, and Friedel 2018). Once you are familiar with both disorders, we suggest you follow your gut. If you feel like your child has been misdiagnosed, get second and third opinions. If your child has BPD and has also been diagnosed with bipolar disorder, find someone who specializes in bipolar disorder and get your child the right treatment. Not to diminish the skills and knowledge of professionals, but keep in mind that you know your child best.

CHAPTER 4

Types of Treatment and Finding Treatment

Klaus: *I am a completely different person since therapy and medication. After many suicide attempts, I hit bottom and realized the pain I was in and causing others. My life had to change, or I knew I was going to die. I went through dialectical behavior therapy twice, and now I feel like a different person. I'm able to stop myself before I take an impulsive action. I have a lot fewer angry outbursts. Even when I get flooded with emotions, it's a lot less intense. I'm able to step away from the situation, get a grasp on my feelings, and decide how I'm going to deal with the situation. I will always have BPD; I have just learned to better manage and cope.*

The good news is that treatment works! The bad news is that it generally takes six to twelve months to take effect. But when the person with BPD truly commits to recovery, the right treatment can help reduce the frequency and intensity of their symptoms, and perhaps eliminate some traits altogether. The more effort your child puts in, the more they will get out of treatment, and the fuller their recovery will be.

BPD is like a chronic physical illness for which a person might need to deal with persistent symptoms. For example, for a person in recovery from BPD, the tendency to fear abandonment is still there, but it doesn't necessarily lead to impulsive, reckless behavior. Through treatment, they learn to differentiate the *fear* of being abandoned—say triggered by a partner coming home late because they are enjoying time alone with their friends—from *real* abandonment, such as their partner breaking up with them.

In this chapter, we're going to cover some of the common methods of treatment: medications, therapy, residential treatment centers, and inpatient hospitalization. Armed with this information, you'll be better equipped to make choices—and help your child make choices—about which treatment options may best fit their situation.

Medications Used in BPD Treatment

When medications work, they can help relieve BPD *symptoms* (not BPD directly, which requires psychotherapy) and can help your child focus better on psychotherapy. But meds don't always help, and occasionally they can cause serious side effects. There is little information on medications for children with BPD, because the myth that children can't have BPD has inhibited research in this area. Therefore, we relied in part on medical information provided by Blaise Aguirre (2014), medical director of the inpatient unit at McLean Hospital for adolescents with BPD, in his book *Borderline Personality Disorder in Adolescents* for this section. Let's go over some of the types of medications that have been used with teens and adults who have BPD, and the symptoms they aim to treat:

- *Antipsychotic medications* may reduce anxiety, paranoia, anger, and hostility. They can reduce interpersonal sensitivity (the hair-trigger responses your child has to what people say and do in respect to them), which can improve relationships. These medications also help with thought clarity.
- *Antidepressant medications* can reduce chronic depression and work with antipsychotic medications to reduce impulsive aggression. (*Impulsive aggression* is characterized by an explosive response that greatly exceeds what most people would call "normal" given the situation. It's what happens when the other shoe drops, the eggshells break, and your child has a total meltdown.)
- *Mood stabilizing* and *anti-seizure drugs* may even out moods. They can significantly decrease irritability and anger, the tempestuousness of relationships, and impulsive aggression (191).

For space reasons, we didn't list the names of all the drugs and their potential side effects, which can be quite serious. If your child has been prescribed meds to treat BPD, we cannot emphasize enough how important it is for you to have a long discussion with the prescribing psychiatrist. And it *should* be a psychiatrist, because treating BPD often requires more than medication, and the medications must be given at just the right dosage in order to balance the benefits with side effects. In addition, if working with children and adolescents, doses may need to be adjusted to lower body weights and other metabolic factors associated with a developing body. Also note that pharmacists are often even better at discussing medication side effects than most doctors, but they do not prescribe. Whenever your child gets prescribed a new medication, ask the following questions:

- What is this medication for?
- How is it supposed to be taken?
- How do I know if this medication is working?
- What are the most common side effects? How about the lesser-known ones? What should I do if these occur?
- Has this medication been tested in children?
- Will this drug interact with any of the other medications my child is taking, including over-the-counter meds and supplements?

- Should my child avoid anything while taking this drug?
- How long does this medication take to work?
- Can my child overdose on this medication?
- What should I do if my child misses a dose?
- What are the side effects of discontinuing this drug?
- Are there alternatives to this medication?

A doctor usually prescribes a very low dose at first to make sure there are no harmful side effects, then increases the dose to determine if the medication works, doesn't work, or works but has unacceptable side effects. If your child experiences one of the latter two outcomes, the psychiatrist will generally prescribe another drug, perhaps one in a different class. Unfortunately, this all takes time. Some medications take many weeks to work. *It is vital that you only try one new medication of any type at a time, so you and your doctor know which drug is having which effect and possibly a side effect/s.* If your child is taking any other drugs for a medical concern or for a co-occurring disorder, make sure all doctors are informed. Your child's primary physician should have a complete list.

Keep careful track of the medications your child is taking, noting what they are for and their dosages. Take note of any side effects and how bothersome they are. Be prepared for the prescribing doctor to ask for your observations about changes in your child's behavior, mood, activity level, appetite, or sleep patterns, as well as side effects. Keeping track of these target behaviors will help the doctor determine the best dosage for your child.

Dispensing Your Child's Meds

Take charge of dispensing your adolescent's or tween's medication. Psychiatric medication is powerful, and your child shouldn't oversee their own meds until they reach adulthood—although as they get older (the exact age is your judgment) and perhaps become more trustworthy, and you're sure they won't abuse the drugs, you may want to let them manage their own meds. Follow your gut feeling. Help them become more independent a little at a time, as long as they're safe.

Getting Your Child to Take Their Medications

According to Blaise Aguirre (2014) in his book, *Borderline Personality Disorder in Adolescents,* your child is most likely to take their medications as directed when the both of you agree on four things (184–85):
1. The purpose of the medication
2. Who is responsible for medication administration
3. Their understanding of medication instructions

> 4. The effectiveness of the medication
>
> Open, honest communication about these factors is essential.

Standardized Psychotherapies

We're going to talk about the first and most prevalent standardized therapy designed for BPD: dialectical behavior therapy. (We'll also discuss cognitive behavioral therapy in a different context.) There are others, but they are more difficult to access. A "standardized" therapy is one that was developed specifically for a particular disorder, in this case BPD. Like fast food, a standardized therapy is the same program wherever it is offered.

Dialectical Behavior Therapy

Marsha Linehan, the psychologist who recovered from BPD herself partly through her personal involvement in Buddhism, developed dialectical behavior therapy (DBT). Fundamental DBT concepts include:

- Patients must be motivated and willing to change. If your child doesn't meet this criterion, it may be best to hold off on DBT because it is a lot of work, with therapy twice a week and homework in between. If your child is unwilling to do the work, no therapy can overcome that. DBT is not inexpensive either, depending on your insurance, so you may want to make sure your child wants to change before committing major resources to their treatment.

- *Radical acceptance,* letting go of something you can't control and accepting a situation for what it is instead of constantly wishing things were different, is essential to recovery. We'll talk more about this in chapter 5.

DBT clients attend individual therapy at least twice a week: a session with a personal therapist and a group skills-training session. Besides the skills acquired in the latter type of session, many people find the group sessions supportive and validating. DBT has four key skills modules: core mindfulness, distress tolerance, emotional regulation, and interpersonal relationships (Linehan 2015).

1. Core mindfulness: *Mindfulness* is being present in the now, paying attention to what's going on around you (including your thoughts and feelings) without daydreaming or looking forward or backward. Mindfulness is beneficial for every family member, so we'll talk about it more in the next chapter.
2. Distress tolerance: Being able to sit with painful feelings without making things worse through the pain management behaviors we discussed in chapter 1.

3. Emotional regulation: Managing negative and overwhelming emotions while increasing positive ones. This module has three components: understanding your emotions, reducing emotional vulnerability, and changing emotional responses.
4. Interpersonal relationships: Getting along better with people. The goal here is to decrease interpersonal chaos, reduce the fear of abandonment, and encourage a positive outlook. This module also contains a lot of information about being assertive.

You can find a DBT therapist in your state or region at https://www.behavioraltech.com. If you can't find a DBT provider, look for a therapist who uses DBT principles and skills as part of their practice. Lacking that, the website lists books that go over DBT skills. Some include worksheets that clients use in DBT practice. You can find info on DBT all over the internet, including at http://www.dbtselfhelp.com. There's also a plethora of videos about DBT principles on YouTube.

> **Elsa:** *Sometimes you feel like all the therapy you pay for is going in one ear and out the other, passing a set of defiantly crossed arms on its way through. But then you overhear your child in an online child-development class in high school. The topic is "adverse childhood events and resilience." Your immediate thought*

is, Oh boy, this is going to be so triggering and cause a blow-up later. *But then you hear your extremely shy, withdrawn kid hesitantly begin to share a breathing technique they learned in DBT class. And you realize that on some level, the skills are sinking in.*

Cognitive Behavioral Therapy

Cognitive behavioral therapy (CBT) is a key type of therapy used for many types of psychological problems. It's not a standardized therapy like DBT, but DBT still falls under the general umbrella of CBT. Most often, CBT is not practiced alone but with a variety of other approaches. CBT is based on the theory that the way we think and interpret life's events affects how we feel and ultimately how we act. In other words, we experience an event, interpret it—which leads us to feel a certain way—and then take action based on those emotions.

For example, if kids at school teased or bullied you (event), it might lead you to assume you're worthless or bad. If you're bullied for a reason (too many freckles), you may come to believe that freckles are "bad." As a result, you may act very shy and find it hard to make friends (action). A CBT therapist would explore the thoughts (assumptions) you have (worthlessness, freckles are bad) and gently help you come to the realization that the people who bullied you were not authorities on your worth, nor were they the arbiters of beauty. When you begin to internalize those truths, you feel more self-confident and less shy. The behavior change is that you are better able to meet people and make friends, increasing your happiness.

CBT is much more widely available (it's hard to find a therapist who *doesn't* use it) and is sometimes less expensive than DBT. If you live in a state or region where you can't find a DBT therapist, a CBT therapist may be the best bet for your child.

The Relationship with the Therapist

Research has shown that the quality of the relationship between therapist and client can be more important than the type of therapy used. Some studies have even called it the most important common factor in successful outcomes. An American Psychological Association task force found that the relationship between a client and a therapist can be just as important as the treatment method in determining the client's success (Norcross and Wampold 2011). However, this is not to say that the therapist should be a "friend" to your child. It is critical that the therapist make your child feel respected, validated, and understood while consistently practicing the types of boundaries that we want the child (or adult) to learn.

Searching for an Eclectic Therapist

An "eclectic" therapist is a person who uses a mixture of treatments and adds their own personal style. The vast majority of therapists in your area most likely practice in this way. If you can't find specialized BPD treatment, you will need to closely evaluate the therapists who are available to see if they are appropriate for your child.

I suggest starting with a search at *Psychology Today*, which has a large database that allows for very specific searches. For example, you can search for a therapist who has a special interest in BPD in your state, city, or zip code. Each therapist profile comes with a short biography, the types of treatment the therapist uses, their interests, their experience, a photo, and sometimes the type of insurance they take. If you strike out with this search option, here are a few more:

- **Pediatricians and other physicians.** Briefly describe the most distressing and frequent behaviors of your child to see if your child's pediatrician or physician can recommend a psychiatrist or psychologist.
- **Local university.** A nearby university or college may offer an advanced degree in psychology, and teachers and administrators

there may be able to recommend a therapist in your area.
- **Nearest medical school.** People in the psychiatry department of the nearest medical school may be able to recommend psychiatrists or therapists who treat borderline patients. If you call one of the recommended doctors, be sure to say that the psychiatry department recommended them. You're more likely to get through to the doctor this way. Even if the doctor isn't taking patients, they may be able to give you the names of other psychiatrists who are accepting patients with BPD.
- **Social media.** If you use social media, search for local BPD groups that you can join. You can ask other members for a referral.

Be aware that therapists who don't specialize in treating personality disorders may not be effective at working with BPD, and in some cases they may make it worse. For this reason, we recommend that two providers be engaged in a team approach with your child, including an experienced psychologist, therapist, or social worker, and, if medication may be needed, a psychiatrist.

Once you've found a potential therapist or two, the next step is to chat with them on the phone. (A therapist may be willing to do this, but a psychiatrist will likely require an in-person visit.) Before calling, create a history of previous treatments—including medications formerly prescribed, if you can—and a list of concerns you have for your child, including specific behaviors. It's likely that you'll have to leave a message, and if they don't call back, they're probably not taking new patients. If that's the case, call someone else. Note that some mental health professionals cannot take the time to talk to potential clients on the phone. If the therapist is well regarded but will not talk on the phone with you before intake, consider making an appointment for an in-person visit.

Here are some questions you may want to ask:
- Do you believe people with BPD can get better? (If they don't, pick another therapist.)
- Are you comfortable treating co-occurring disorders?
- What are your views on the use of medications?
- How often will you see my child, and are you available after hours?
- How will you work with me as a parent? (This question is relevant if your child is a minor.)

This is just a sampling of possible questions you can ask. Be sure to spend some time thinking about your child's needs before making a call, so you're well prepared on your quest to find a therapist or doctor who's a good fit.

The Pros and Cons of Telling Your Child About Their BPD Diagnosis

You're going to have to decide for yourself whether or not you should tell your child about their BPD diagnosis. You know your child best, but it's a tough decision to make, so we'll outline arguments for both.

Whether or not you tell your child, we don't recommend making it commonly known among friends, acquaintances, and extended family because there is so much misunderstanding and stigma surrounding the disorder. Fictional characters in books and on TV and film who are portrayed as having BPD are not very realistic.

However, you do need support! If you have a very close relative or friend who will not judge you, will be supportive, and is willing to listen to you talk about the intricacies of the disorder, feel free to make them part of your support team. Look for online support too (see appendix C). If you decide not to tell your child their diagnosis, you can explain how BPD affects them without using the term (see chapter 5).

Pros of Disclosure

- **It can be a relief to the person with BPD:** One of the best reasons for letting a child know about their diagnosis is to avoid them finding out on their own. There are so many resources available now that it's hard to believe your child won't come across information that leads them to the conclusion that they have BPD. Oftentimes people with BPD sense that something is off with them, and because of the plethora of BPD information that's now available, it's not a stretch to imagine someone diagnosing themselves. Also, knowing about their diagnosis can reassure the person that what they have is a known entity, that other people have it, that they can get support from these people, and, most of all, that there is treatment. Sometimes not knowing what is wrong makes things worse—is that flutter in my chest indigestion or a heart attack?

- **It can lead to companionship and learning:** A great number of websites, self-help books, memoirs, blogs, documentaries, and YouTube videos exist about BPD—many from the point of view of the person with BPD. If your child is unaware of their diagnosis, they won't be able to access these helpful resources.
- **You won't lie by omission:** At some point, perhaps in adulthood, your child may learn they have BPD. Like many people who have discovered this from a new therapist, from their case file, from an insurance company,

or by accident, they may ask you why you never told them.

Cons of Disclosure
- **Stigmatizing information online:** Before you tell your child, do an online search for BPD, because your child certainly will. There is a lot of depressing and stigmatizing information out there. That's mostly because, in our experience, the majority of people with BPD don't think anything's wrong with them. They think their problems are someone else's fault, and they project all their pain and self-loathing onto other people. Family members who are the target of this blame are traumatized, and some of them make no bones about it online because they're angry about being the target of abuse, and they want to tell their stories.
- **Psychiatric diagnoses are not fixed:** Diagnostic resources like the *ICD-11* and *DSM-5* are routinely revised, and what we know about psychiatric disorders and their clusters of symptoms changes regularly. Thus a psychiatric diagnosis is not as stable as some medical diagnoses. On top of that, psychiatrists and clinicians often disagree about how a diagnosis is confirmed. So, what you

tell your child may be out of date in a few years.
- **Secondary gain:** Children can use BPD as an excuse not to take responsibility at home, school, or work.
- **Overlabeling:** When one is diagnosed with BPD (or any disorder), it's easy to see behavior, emotions, and thoughts as "belonging" to the disorder when they may be perfectly natural reactions to situations, or symptoms of something else entirely. For example, your child may get angry at being cheated by a friend but dismiss that anger as "being borderline." Or they may see mood swings as being related only to BPD, when in fact they might be indicative of a different psychological problem, such as bipolar disorder.

As we've said before, you know your child best, and you need to make your own informed decision about whether or not you want to tell your child. Many parents struggle with this, so you are not alone. Here's a sampling of how some mothers responded when a different mother asked if she should tell her thirteen-year-old daughter about her diagnosis.

Janice: I wouldn't tell her. She's so young. There's plenty of time.

Edith: We told my fourteen-year-old daughter in conjunction with her therapist. We all told her, "You are *not* this diagnosis. This does *not* label you. There is so much more to you than this diagnosis, and we are here to support you. You can get better. DBT therapy can help you to not even meet the qualifications for this diagnosis. This does not change how we love you."

Nichelle: We held off until my daughter was nineteen and mature enough to process it. I felt like giving her that info too soon was throwing gas on an already blazing inferno. She struggled with the info even then, but at twenty is finally doing the best she ever has.

Majel: We had a talk with my eighteen-year-old daughter, my daughter's therapist, and my husband and myself. The therapist went through each BPD trait and asked if she ever felt that way, did it, or thought about it. After she went through all the traits, she talked about the diagnosis. My daughter had been diagnosed with depression a couple years before. So she was open to a BPD diagnosis also.

Kathryn: Hubby and I told my thirteen-year-old daughter. Our son, ten, has autism. We explained that just like her brother, her brain is going to see and feel the world differently. Different doesn't mean bad or less. Just different. We told her that we need people like her in this world, because if everyone were the same we would have a boring world. We told her, we're not always going to agree or get along, but we love her and we will walk alongside her.

Seska: We didn't tell her because of her penchant to latch on to a diagnosis, overeducate herself, and then blow up the behaviors and make the behaviors even worse, mainly for additional attention. She had done that with her bulimia, PTSD, and anxiety diagnoses. For us, it was the best decision. You just can't put the genie back in the bottle, so it is a very important issue to carefully discuss with your child's treatment team.

Annika: The hospital told us to tell her about the symptoms—the dysregulation rather than the name of the diagnosis—because we treat the symptoms. If you do decide to tell, I think it is important for you to communicate that this is not a life sentence. And it's a very treatable disorder and within their control to overcome or control. They just have to *want* to get better.

Convincing Your Child to Go to Therapy Sessions

Once you've chosen a therapist, getting your minor child with BPD to go to sessions may be the next big hurdle for you. If they are dead set against going to therapy, and you make them anyway, they probably won't get much out of it. If they're cautious, that's understandable. Processing emotions and looking at parts of yourself you don't like is very hard work. And yet, when the therapist is good, a trusting bond develops, and if your child is willing to do the work, they most certainly can improve.

So what can you do when you're struggling to get your child to try therapy? You might say something like:

- I wonder if it would be helpful if you had someone to talk to besides me?
- You appear so unhappy and sad sometimes. It breaks my heart. Maybe talking to someone will help you feel better.
- Why not give it a try? You have nothing to lose, and it could help.
- Yes, therapy can be hard. Sometimes the therapist will ask you to talk about painful things. But if you don't talk about them, they will stay with you and keep you miserable. When you process these things in therapy they lose some of their power to hurt.

- If it turns out you don't like the therapist or the type of therapy, you can try someone else.
- Lots of people go to therapists. It doesn't mean that something is wrong with you. It only means you need someone who will be there for you and only you to help you figure things out.
- Lots of people go to therapy, even celebrities and athletes.
- We will keep the fact that you're in therapy private, between you and me. No one else has to know.

If you're trying to convince an adult child, you might try:
- I have a few limits if you want to live here. One of them is that you find a good therapist—I'll help you find someone—and work hard in therapy. To be able to determine that you're working at it for real, I'll need your permission to talk to your therapist every so often.

Actions speak louder than words, so you could also:
- Take the lead and go to counseling yourself.
- Negotiate and say that if a certain behavior changes in specific and measurable ways, you'll put therapy on hold. If you do this, be

prepared to again insist on therapy if the child resumes the specified behaviors.
- Go to family counseling, where there is no designated "problem person." Be willing to admit to your contributions to any problems.
- Create a contract with your child stating that they will go to a specific number of sessions, say six, but they have to participate wholeheartedly. After that, it's their decision whether to continue.
- Consider online counseling. Help them pick someone out.
- Put therapy as a must-do to get certain rewards. This is not the best strategy since they need to work in therapy, but if getting them there is a matter of overcoming the unknown or fears that can dissipate, this can be a productive method.

Residential Treatment Centers

Residential treatment centers (RTCs) offer longer-term placement for children with behavioral or emotional problems that parents cannot manage at home, and for when alternatives have not worked. Here are some examples of when an RTC might make sense:
- The child is not safe at home, perhaps because they are self-destructive.

- The family is not safe at home with the child, perhaps because they are acting out.
- You can't provide an environment that is safe and supportive of the therapeutic work, including being unable to set and maintain boundaries.

RTCs offer care 24/7 with counseling, therapy, and trained staff that may include psychiatrists, psychologists, nurses, social workers, and mental health counselors. Keep in mind that not all RTCs specialize in BPD and may serve children with a wide variety of issues.

Pros and Cons of Residential Treatment

Many parents who have used residential treatment will tell you that there are pros to this form of full-time treatment. One pro is that experts will be watching your child and keeping them safe. Another is that if your child can tolerate the therapy, when they leave the facility they'll be more capable of leading a healthier life.

There are also cons to RTCs. Some parents regret sending their children to residential treatment because they lost control of the child's therapy, as well as of when (or even *if*) they could see them. Some report that counselors didn't understand BPD and used therapies that are often not effective for treating BPD, such as complicated reward-punishment point systems.

One parent said the RTC population they used mainly consisted of people with drug addictions who talked to her daughter about the pleasures of getting high.

As with choosing the right therapist, or whether or not medication is appropriate for your child, you will need to evaluate an RTC before sending your child there. Here are some things to consider (American Academy of Child and Adolescent Psychiatry 2016):

- If possible, find an RTC close to your home or near enough that you can visit your child periodically.
- Learn what you can about an RTC online. Parents in support groups may have had experience with a facility you're looking at, and they may share insights with you.
- Ask RTC staff whether they treat children with BPD symptoms. If they mainly treat children with substance abuse problems, your child may learn unwanted behaviors.
- Ask staff if they provide individual and group therapy. Their answer should be yes.
- Learn whether the facility provides academics as well as therapy, so children don't fall behind in school. If they do, are the teachers certified by the state?
- Ask if the facility is accredited. Then check with the accrediting agency to verify that the accreditation is current.

- If your child is willing to participate in their treatment, ask to do an on-site visit or tour of the facility. Try to determine how much freedom residents are allowed.
- Know that lock-down facilities are for involuntary admission, or patients who don't want to be there. A lock-down facility may be safer for children who are self-harming.
- Get all promises and policies in writing.
- Ask about the credentials of the staff and whether the facility performs background checks before hiring.
- Ask the director what provisions they have for emergency care, such as if a child gets a sore throat or breaks an ankle.
- Ask the director how they define success with a child.
- Ask how staff handles discipline.
- Ask about their visitation policy and if children are allowed to call home.
- Ask about costs, and check with your insurance company about coverage.

CLINICIAN'S CORNER WITH DANIEL LOBEL

Your child may not want to go to residential treatment, which may cause short-term conflict because they may feel betrayed or abandoned. In the long term, though, if the treatment is successful, your child will realize that you were acting in their best interest—and in fact, the choice to keep them at home would have been worse parenting. To minimize the traumatic aspects of transitioning to residential treatment, your child should know as far in advance as possible that you're considering an RTC. You may want to suggest it as a possibility as soon as possible, but not in a threatening way. Frame it as an option that's in their best interest if treatment at home is not successful.

Inpatient Hospitalization

Hospitalization may be necessary as a last resort in serious cases. The goals of inpatient hospitalization are not to treat your child or to cause lasting change. The goals are to keep your child and family safe when your child is at risk for suicide, and to stabilize the child, so they are no longer in imminent harm. During your child's stay, they will go to group sessions with people who have a variety of mental health issues. In the sessions they'll learn skills to help them manage their mental health or to improve their mood. A staff psychiatrist will probably see them every day. Staff will monitor them closely for suicidal feelings, depression, anxiety, and other mental health concerns to see if they are getting better, worsening, or staying the same. Individual psychotherapy sessions are generally not helpful in an inpatient setting because the focus is keeping the patient safe, not exploring the details of their disorder. However, patients are often referred to a therapist upon discharge.

When should you consider hospitalization? When your child's suicidal thinking becomes chronic or when it becomes a suicidal *plan* the child intends to carry out, or when self-harm has been severe enough to require medical attention—especially if the child is also experiencing an episode of major depression or if a substance abuse problem gets worse.

Paul: *When my daughter was fifteen, I was able to get her admitted to a state-run pediatric psychiatric hospital, and she remained there for a year and got the intensive help she needed, including DBT. My daughter is now twenty-four. She has a job, which she has held for nearly a year, and is saving money to buy a car. The change in her behavior is profound.*

Lisa: *My daughter Angie had extreme self-harm and suicidal thoughts. I put her in all kinds of therapy: inpatient, residential, and partial hospitalization. At one point, she had twenty-five hours of therapy a week. Once she realized she wasn't getting out without putting in the work, something switched and she participated. Hospitalization was wonderful and helped adjust her to real life. I'm happy to say that she is doing so much better now. She has* *now been self-harm free for four months. I am so proud of her.*

Top Takeaways from This Chapter

Every child is different, and a particular treatment—a therapy, a therapist, a medication, or a treatment facility—that works great with one person may not work well with another. Do your research, ask questions, and take notes. And trust your gut! You've got this! Here are some key points to keep in mind as you read on:

- Treatment works! But your child must be willing to work at therapy and be dedicated to making life worth living—including taking some accountability for their own misery. These attitudes are probably more important than the type of therapy you choose, because if a therapist doesn't work out, your child will be motivated to try another. Sadly, you can't control your child's attitude, but you can influence it by not reinforcing unwanted behavior—a topic we'll cover later.
- Although treatment works, it is not a cure. There is some debate about whether people can be cured of BPD. People's symptoms can decrease to the point that they can live a normal life, work, and have happy relationships. And people can improve to the

point that they no longer formally qualify for the BPD diagnosis. But as people with heart disease will always have to live a healthy lifestyle, people with BPD will need to be cautious about their triggers, have skills to use when things get dicey, have a support system in place, and most likely see a therapist.
- It's vital to ask lots of questions about medications: what they do, what the side effects are, and if they interact with other medications. Keep them locked up, and keep track of how your child is doing while taking them.
- When selecting any kind of treatment, trust your gut. If you don't like the therapist you chose, choose another. If you have an inkling that you may need a hospital or residential treatment center, start your research now. Don't wait until there's a crisis.
- If your child needs an RTC or hospitalization, that doesn't mean you're a bad parent. It means your child's BPD is more severe. You are even allowed to be relieved at getting a break from your child.
- Remember, once your child turns eighteen you no longer have any control over whether they seek therapy or what happens if they do seek treatment. You can only make

therapy and treatment a requirement if they want something from you, such as housing, but if they're not working at it, you may be wasting time and money.

CHAPTER 5

Improving Your Mental Health

Elena: *Before the crisis I didn't prioritize self-care because I felt all my time and energy was needed for my BPD/anorexic daughter and my family. Being a good parent and wife was paramount. My own needs could wait. I couldn't let anyone down. I worked the night shift so I could be there for my family. I was doing penance because I felt somehow responsible for my daughter's illness.*

Then my daughter became suicidal, and I found watching her suffering unbearable. I decided that if my daughter was successful in her suicide attempt, I wanted to die too. According to my faith we would both be in a better place. Ultimately, I was hospitalized for three weeks—this was exceptionally difficult for me as I felt indispensable.

My psychiatrist told me I was burned-out from caring and was trying to give from an empty cup. He insisted self-care was a priority. It took some time, but I finally recognized that it was essential to my well-being. Now I do Pilates, swim, and meditate. I see a therapist and meet with friends for coffee. I do not allow myself to feel guilty about needing help or support. I find the time to do self-care because I have learned the hard way what happens if I don't.

The fact that you are reading this book means that you cherish your child who has BPD and feel anguish that they experience such pain. Watching someone you love in physical or mental pain makes you desperate for a magic spell that will take the pain from them and give it to you. Your love, however, doesn't change the fact that raising a child with BPD comes at a huge cost. It can provoke discomfort, anger, discouragement, sadness, emotional pain, and disturbing practical consequences for the whole family. Families get run down, overwhelmed, and fall apart. So do parents.

Families are less likely to fall apart when parents are willing to make their own mental health a top priority, right next to that of their child with BPD. You need to be at your best to learn and implement the communication strategies and parenting techniques you'll learn about in chapters 7 through 9, not to mention the techniques you'll find in all the other chapters. While some who are parenting kids with BPD can hold it together (the more educated on BPD they are, the better off they are), far too many are treading water or drowning in the deep end of the pool. Some find themselves suicidal at some point, whereas others have given so much to their child that they literally have nothing left to give and no longer desire to be in contact with their adult child.

If you've ever flown on an airplane, then you know that in the case of an emergency, you're directed to put your oxygen mask on *before* helping others. Have you ever wondered why? Because if you help others first, you're likely to run out of oxygen—and find yourself unable to help *anyone*, let alone yourself. Parenting a child with BPD is a lot like that. In this case, administering oxygen to yourself means taking some *me* time so you can replenish yourself *before* you've given everything you've got and passed out.

Think you don't have the time? Make it. *You* are by far the most important component to your child's healing. Not only that, you are the most important person in their world. If you give, give, give and get nothing (or hostility) in return, there's a chance you'll enjoy your child less, become a more bitter person, or have compassion fatigue, which is feeling burned-out because you're not giving yourself enough attention. Your ever-alert child, who practically feels rejected if a parking meter refuses to take their coins, will be able to sense when you've run out of energy and compassion for them.

In this chapter, we're going to talk about the big mental health issues for parenting kids with BPD: trauma, grief, and stress. Then we'll discuss three measures to deal with these issues: seeing a therapist, practicing radical acceptance, and grieving your losses. And finally, we'll cover some techniques you can practice to help reduce the trauma, grief, and stress you experience while parenting a child with BPD.

Trauma

Witnessing self-injury and suicide threats or attempts and being the focus of BPD-impulsive aggression and rage can cause complex post-traumatic stress disorder (CPTSD). CPTSD is like PTSD, except that it results from smaller incidents over many years (for example, domestic violence) instead of just one traumatic incident (such as a car crash).

Tanya: *The shame of what my child has done stops me from reaching out to others. I feel sad and scared. All I do is go to work and come home. I have pushed away friends because I never know what will happen if someone comes over, and I am so exhausted mentally and emotionally that I want to scream.*

Ken: *I don't know how you can not feel traumatized by this. It takes every ounce of energy you have and then some. I started having panic attacks and my doctor put me on medication.*

Fran: *My sixteen-year-old daughter will attempt suicide without warning or will completely destroy our home and cause serious injury to family members. We've had to have police officers physically restrain her to prevent* *her from kicking, biting, and scratching us with her long fingernails. We love her dearly, but that love comes with a constant side of fear.*

Tammy: *Our family has a certain dread because we don't know what kind of mood my son will be in and how he might sabotage any given situation. This extends to a constant state of hyperalertness and, in my case, high blood pressure, as well as chronic insomnia for both myself and my partner.*

Delfina: *I told my therapist that I feel like I'm in an abusive relationship that I am not allowed to leave. There is no way I would put up with this behavior from anyone else on this earth.*

Trauma changes areas of the brain that play a big role in both our memory function and how we respond to stressful situations. Because of this it's important to address trauma at once—if not for yourself, then for any other children in the house.

Signs You May Be Experiencing Trauma

The impact of trauma can be subtle, insidious, or outright destructive, with both physical and mental repercussions. How do you know if you're experiencing trauma? You may feel one or more of the following symptoms to one degree or another (Center for Substance Abuse Treatment 2014).

Emotional Symptoms of Trauma	Physical Symptoms of Trauma
• Denial	• Headaches
• Anger	• Digestive symptoms
• Fear	• Fatigue
• Sadness	• Racing heart
• Shame	• Sweating
• Confusion	• Impaired memories
• Anxiety	• Lack of sleep
• Depression	• Difficulty concentrating
• Numbness	• Feeling jumpy
• Overreactions	• Hyperalertness (that is, walking on eggshells—this releases cortisol, a stress hormone, which damages your body over time and creates mild to severe physical or mental illness)
• Guilt	
• Hopelessness	
• Irritability	

Remember, don't be hard on yourself if you're experiencing any of these emotional and physical symptoms. They are *normal* responses to an *abnormal* situation.

Grief

When a child dies, family, friends, and their community comfort parents, but parents grieving the many losses associated with having a mentally ill child do not get any flowers. This grief is often not addressed by mental health professionals either. As a result, you may not recognize your grief or allow yourself to process it. And that may make things worse.

One mother says, "The stress and trauma is foremost in your mind. The brain has to deal with it, but the grief is buried deeper. It is a heavy, sinking feeling that floats around the edges of your thoughts. You try to ignore it and hope it goes away, but it is always there like a rock in your heart. The grief lies quietly in the background, popping up when you least expect it, like when you first wake up in the morning or you see other moms post about their child's success on social media. But it gets better with time, and I will never lose faith!"

Parents in your situation grieve a number of things, but their grief generally falls into two categories: grief for their child with BPD, and grief for themselves or other family members.

Grief for Their Child

- **Mourning the life they wanted for their child.** "My child may never have a functional marriage and children. No prom, friends, or football games."

- **For some, mourning the child they had before the disorder took effect.** "What happened to the sweet little boy he was? I look at old photos and cry. I love him but now he is into drugs and hanging out with the wrong people."

- **Mourning the fact that their child feels such pain.** "I feel like she will never know true joy, happiness, or empathy for others. I would give anything to take that dark space away. I have no choice but to watch her suffer."

- **Mourning their child's lost potential.** "He's a great musician who could rival anyone. He wants to play concertos with all the great orchestras throughout the world. But he'll never go to Oberlin Conservatory. I'm dealing with it better, now, after coming to grips with the fact that no amount of distress will change things, and readjusting my expectations, and helping him identify and work toward new, more realistic goals."

Grief for Themselves and Family

- **Mourning the everyday family life they wanted.** "I grieve the 'job' I've done as a mom. I had high hopes for our family. I hoped our two boys would be friends instead of one lashing out and being violent and the other hiding out in his room. I will miss the moments of learning to drive and negotiating curfews, seeing his excitement and joy, and making memories. I feel like we have lost him again and again, death without dying, pain without end, and unconditional love without reciprocity."

- **Mourning the life they wanted for themselves.** "I grieve that I can't retire and travel the world with my husband. We expect our child will always be living with us." Also, "This may sound selfish, but a lot of grieving has to do with the loss of my family, the loss of my friends, and my loss of peace. I am the collateral damage to her illness. But as others have said, it does get better over time, although it is never really gone."
- **Grieving the fact they'll never have the kind of relationship they wanted and expected to have with their child.** "I cried on and off for a year. Now I have accepted and embraced the relationship I have with her. It's not what I expected it to be, but it still fills my heart."

Dealing with Grief

If the above passages resonate with you, consider these tips for handling grief (of either type):

- Get grief counseling: many parents said this was valuable.
- Name that feeling *grief* and allow yourself the time and space to feel it.
- Change your expectations and help your child work toward new, more realistic goals that they can actually achieve.
- Talk to trustworthy friends and family members. You might also try talking to other parents of children with BPD in online support communities.
- Advocate for children with BPD. Make a difference.
- Don't feel ashamed for your self-interested grief. It is perfectly okay to mourn your own losses as well as your child's. Do not judge your own grief. That will only make the feeling worse.
- Keep in mind that everyone grieves differently and there is no timetable. Be patient with yourself.
- Know the signs of depression, and get early treatment if it happens to you.
- Take care of yourself as best you can.

Stress

Stress is your constant companion when you have a child with BPD, either because something just happened, something is happening now, or you know something—God knows what—will happen in the future. When you experience acute stress—that is, you see a prowler or a bear—chemicals flood your body to prepare you for fight or flight (the "stress response"). The stress response is supposed to be temporary. Once you've fought off or run away from the bear or prowler, it's supposed to dissipate.

But when your child has BPD, every day is a "God knows what crisis will happen today" kind of day. You're hyperalert and feel like you're walking on eggshells. You're living in a perpetual stress-response state. When stress-response chemicals like cortisol are constantly in your bloodstream, they can cause or exacerbate stress-related illnesses like heart disease, obesity, diabetes, depression, anxiety, immune system suppression, headaches, back and neck pain, sleep problems, and more.

As with trauma, the signs of stress come in two varieties: physical and mental. You're probably familiar with these (American Institute of Stress 2019).

Emotional Symptoms of Stress

- Depression or anxiety

- Anger, irritability, or restlessness
- Feeling overwhelmed, unmotivated, or unfocused
- Continually being in a bad mood or feeling emotional
- Sleeping too much or too little
- Racing thoughts or constant worry
- Problems with memory or concentration
- Making bad decisions

Physical Symptoms of Stress

- Tight muscles
- Headaches
- Musculoskeletal problems
- Overeating or undereating
- Constipation or diarrhea
- Nausea or vomiting
- Getting sick more often
- Reduced sex drive or impotence
- Changes in heart rate and blood pressure
- Inflammation of the arteries, leading to cardiovascular problems
- Addiction to things intended to reduce stress, such as drugs, alcohol, tobacco, sex, gambling, or gaming—anything that's mind numbing

You Need Your Own Therapist

There's good news about traumatic stress. Unlike BPD, it has been the focus of major research for a long time, and we know how to intervene to reduce its effects. Let's start with the intervention of therapy. In my work, it has become very apparent to me that parents who were seeing a therapist felt more confident and healthier than those who weren't, which translated into better parenting.

Beth: *I see a therapist for issues I already had, plus some for caregiver complex post-traumatic stress disorder. Having someone validate my feelings about my child helps a lot because when I try to explain my child to someone else they just say it's "typical teen behavior." My therapist has also helped me to stop overthinking my daughter's issues, to get outside of my head, to accept things, and to even learn to somewhat predict what my kid was going to do next.*

Lanelle: *The most valuable thing I learned from my therapist is that I was making myself miserable. She gave me ideas on how to draw limits, when it was okay to help my child, and when I should let her be independent.*

Scott: *Seeing a therapist is the best form of self-care for me. She helps me set boundaries, pay attention to my inner critic,* *and validate my attempt at being a parent of a mentally ill child. It has really helped me realize I can't control what she does, no matter how much I worry and stress over her.*

Carlie: *My own therapy helps me keep things in perspective because I can say all the things to my therapist that I can't say to my child. I can just rant and be all sarcastic and get it all out of my system.*

Having my own therapist also gives me an opportunity to pick a professional's brain for ideas to help my daughter and myself. It's been invaluable for me.

You can find information about finding a therapist in chapter 4.

Radical Acceptance

Along with therapy, radical acceptance is another way for parents to cope with trauma and stress. What is radical acceptance? It's accepting something so deeply that you feel it in your little toes. Marsha Linehan, the researcher who created dialectical behavior therapy (DBT), looked closely at how people react to misfortune and categorized their responses into four general types (1993):

1. **Trying to change the circumstances.** For example, let's say your child has tickets to a great concert but has to work that night. The first thing they would try to do

is switch shifts with someone else or get the night off—that is, change the circumstances.

2. **Trying to change emotions about the circumstances.** If they can't switch shifts or get the night off, they can think about all the money they'll make that night working. Your child decides there's no use fretting about something they can't change and downloads a bunch of new music instead.

3. **Continuing to be miserable.** Your child complains about the situation to anyone who will listen for two weeks after the concert. They remember this incident as one of the worst things that happened in their life *ever*.

4. **Accepting the circumstances without judging them.** Your child can't go. They wish they could, but there's really no way to tell what might have changed in their life if they had gone. For all they know, they could have gotten wasted, driven home in a drunk friend's car, and crashed. There will be other bands and other concerts. This isn't going to ruin their life.

You've probably heard that the definition of insanity is doing the same thing over and over again and expecting a different result. Well, radical acceptance comes when you stop banging your head against the wall because your hopes and reality refuse to intersect.

Radical acceptance *does not* mean:
- Liking the reality
- Agreeing with the reality
- Being happy about the situation
- Forgiving a person who wronged you

Before we explore radical acceptance further, we want to introduce you to a philosophy of hope. This metaphor was originally crafted for adult partners, not children, but it applies to readers with adult children who have shown for a long time that they're not going to change (which applies to at least one third of readers). This type of hope resides in parents who, against all the evidence they've been presented, think one day their child will spontaneously get better. It doesn't apply to children who are learning, growing, in treatment, and finding their way. Such actions indicate that they have the potential to recover.

Catfish Hope

Catfish is a reality-based documentary TV series that explores the world of online dating. A "catfish" is a person who creates fake profiles on social media sites with the intention of luring unsuspecting "hopefuls" into falling in love with them. In each episode the show's hosts investigate—at the behest of a hopeful—the catfish to determine whether or not the person is real. In almost all of the episodes, the hopeful ends up crushed by the truth and cries when they find out that the photos—and the phantom internet person—they've told "I love you" to is a fake who has been deliberately fooling them.

For most hopefuls, the red flags about their "relationship" are everywhere. For example, if somebody doesn't want to meet you in person or talk on the phone in five years of online courtship, it's a good sign that they are not who they say they are. Deep down each hopeful knows this, but they *need this person to be real. They have planned a future with this person. They are emotionally vulnerable with this person.* So they miss or ignore all the red flags that most people would see. They believe every excuse of the catfish because their need for the relationship to be real is so deep.

After the big reveal, the hopeful is in much pain and anger. At first, they're angry at the catfish. But eventually they come out of their trance and wonder why they fell for the lies. They say things like, "Everybody in my life told me not to trust this person, but I went ahead and did it anyway." This is the essence of *catfish hope: My story looks bleak, but, in the end, my situation will be the exception. I will live happily ever after.* People who have a family member with BPD can become the victims of their own catfish hope.

I am so depressed and sad. I have denied the fact that my son has BPD. I struggle with how to accept this. I kept thinking that if I paid off his debts again, he would learn and get better. I gave him lots of positive feedback and support. And yet he continues on his nonstop relationships with the wrong kind of women ending with unexpected pregnancies and children he can't support and rarely sees. He gets into bar fights and goes to the hospital demanding pain pills—I think he has prescriptions from doctors all over the city. His finances have been a mess forever—bankruptcy, judgments, loans at high-interest loan places. My husband and I have paid off tens of thousands of dollars in payday loans only to watch him go right back to those places and get himself into the same mess. Collection agencies keep calling our house because he puts us on the forms. We keep expecting him to learn his lesson and change. But so far he hasn't. I'm starting to wonder if he ever will.

Giving Up Catfish Hope

Radical acceptance comes when you can look at the situation, not through the hopeful's eyes, but through those of an unbiased onlooker who can assess it, including the history that led up to it, and see it for what it is. *Once you can radically accept the truth, you can take the proper action.*

The truth: Your daughter has BPD, at least for now. Don't expect her to always act in ways that seem logical to you, any more than you would expect your two-year-old to put together a bookcase.

The upshot: You're going to have to quit denying reality and learn how to parent a child with BPD. Without radical acceptance, you wouldn't educate yourself about the disorder.

The truth: Your son says he will move out, but he hasn't in a year. It may have something to do with his free room and board, not to mention the cleaning and laundry service. The truth is, your son is not going to move out because he gets free room and board plus all his freedom, and if he moved out he would have to pick up after himself.

The upshot: It's your house, so you make the rules. Charge for room and board, and don't provide free laundry and cleaning services. If you hadn't radically accepted the truth, your son would live in your home until it came time to bury you.

Fighting and railing against a painful reality actually causes more suffering than just accepting the undesirable reality. In other words, suffering is an emotion that we, ourselves, layer on top of our pain. If we accept an unwanted reality, no matter how unwanted it is, we can avoid suffering. That's radical acceptance. Pain is unavoidable. Suffering is optional. When we resist radical acceptance, we stay miserable. (Remember Marsha Linehan's third type of response mentioned earlier in the chapter?) We are constantly disappointed and grieve each time another "surprise" crisis happens. What might happen if you choose to accept your reality instead of continuing to rail against it?

Margret: *I am proud of myself for radically accepting that my daughter will not respond to things in the way I would. She was angry with me for some nothing reason, so she punished me by not returning my phone calls for a month. Normally I would get very hurt, angry, and frustrated. Radically accepting that that's the way she deals with conflict has freed me from being constantly disappointed that she doesn't act differently. When I practice radical acceptance, I am saying, "I am not going to suffer because of what has occurred." It helps you stop feeling like a victim.*

You might wonder, *How can I radically accept my truth? How do I radically accept a daughter who repeatedly self-harms and threatens suicide?* The same way that we learn to accept everything else. Some people must accept that they or a family member has a terminal illness, that a family member is going into a war zone, or that their parent is being deported and they don't know when they'll ever see them again.

Leo: *Radical acceptance is not about looking on the bright side or staying positive.*

It's seeing exactly what is, accepting the fact of its existence, and, yes, sometimes, seeing the beauty in the ugliness and the teeny-tiny sparks of light in the dark.

Destiny: *I learned that learning how to practice radical acceptance was like learning anxiety-busting techniques. It was relatively easy to learn the nuts and bolts of how to do it, but it was far more difficult to master it. It took a lot of practice to really get the hang of it, but once I got there, I knew I never wanted to go back to my old way of being. It definitely felt strange and foreign at first. I just had to remember that it was all about acknowledging my current reality. Today I see radical acceptance as going hand in hand with mindfulness, being in the moment and being present where I am.*

You can't radically accept everything all at once. You have to start with the small things. Picture radical acceptance as a highway with lots of exits. You try to stay on the highway, but then you feel nonacceptance and you take an exit and feel grief, anger, or some other emotion. When you're ready, get on the highway again. Get on and off as many times as you need to. It's more of a process than a destination. Just keeping getting back on the highway and practice.

Sophie: *Practicing radical acceptance has been big for me. Not that you have to like it, of course, but there are things you cannot change, and the past is one of them.*

Additional Coping Techniques

Besides the three main measures we just covered, there are many other techniques you can practice to cope with stress, grief, and trauma. We only have room to explain two: mindfulness meditation and self-compassion. We chose the former because it is backed up by a lot of research, and parents regularly mention it as being a useful coping tool. We chose the latter because you can't have compassion for your imperfect child if you don't have compassion for yourself as an imperfect being.

Mindfulness Meditation

Mindfulness is awareness without judgment. It involves becoming aware of your emotions, your physical sensations, and what you are currently doing in the present, while at the same time, withholding all judgment. The opposite of mindfulness is often called "monkey mind." When you're in monkey mind mode, you perform daily activities with a multitude of different things clattering around in your brain: a problem at work, an issue with your child with BPD, what you're going to have for lunch, where you're going, and so forth.

Other Beneficial Evidence-Based Activities

Here are some other ideas for reducing trauma, stress, and grief in your life.

Art and other creative endeavors: Just forty-five minutes of a creative activity can reduce stress and distract you from your problems (Scott 2020). Paint a picture, knit, plant a garden, dance, or do batik.

Decluttering: Clutter can make you feel stressed, anxious, and depressed. Decluttering can help you improve focus, process information, and increase productivity. It's also good exercise and can give you a sense of accomplishment (Sander 2019).

Exercise: Moving your body improves mood, sleep, and your ability to do everyday activities. Exercise boosts energy, can be fun, strengthens your muscles, combats health conditions and diseases, and improves your sex life. Choose something you like that you're most likely to do (Mayo Clinic 2019).

Friendships: Close relationships with others increase your sense of belonging and purpose, boost happiness, reduce stress, improve confidence and self-worth, help you cope with trauma, and encourage you to change unhealthy lifestyle habits (Mayo Clinic 2019). Do not isolate yourself because of your child. Your child's behavior says nothing about you as a parent other than that you need support from the very people you're avoiding.

Meet your friends someplace other than your house.

Typically men's friendships are based on doing things, so finding a friend to talk with can be harder for them. Men may need to take a risk and really talk with a best friend from high school, work, or college. Telling their friend that they don't need them to problem solve, that all they need to do is listen and keep what is shared to themselves, can be an ice breaker that might lead to a helpful conversation.

Gratitude: Taking time to think about all the positive things in your life rather than ruminating on the negatives is the single most positive thing you can do for your happiness.

Nature: People who spend two hours a week in nature can see a boost in mental and physical (if they're walking) health. Go for a walk in the woods. Visit a park. Take a long bike ride on a city trail. Listening to nature sounds can have a similar effect (Denworth 2019).

You can practice mindfulness as a form of meditation, which involves sitting quietly, breathing deeply, and concentrating fully on your present awareness. For example, when your mind zings to the birthday cake you need to make for the party tonight, pretend the thought is a cloud and let it float on by. Come back to the meditation and continue to focus on the present moment. Keep focusing on your breath, in and out. When other thoughts come up (*Boy, I really suck at this!*), continue to let them float on by. It takes practice.

Let's try a loving-kindness meditation, which is a timeless way to practice mindfulness. This script is based on a meditation by Buddhist monk and mindfulness teacher Jack Kornfield (2008).

1. Sit in your chair in a quiet, private place and belly breathe. Take deep breaths from your diaphragm in and out. Focus on the present moment and let everything else fall away: your burdens, problems, and so forth. Imagine sunshine flowing down like honey through the top of your head, continuing down through your facial muscles and neck, relaxing each part of your body down to your toes.

2. Close your eyes. Call up the face of someone alive or dead whom you love or loved. Call up that love and compassion and let it flow through you. Imagine that person right beside you, sending their love. Repeat in your head, *May you be filled with loving-kindness. May you be well in body, heart, and mind. May you be at ease and happy.* (You get the idea. You can write your own script if you prefer.)

3. Now call up a picture of yourself, the competent and confident adult who can handle what's thrown at you. Repeat the phrases: *May I be filled with loving-kindness. May I be well in body, heart, and mind. May I be at ease and happy.* (Some parents find it hard to wish themselves compassion. If you have a hard time, start small. Wish yourself a good day at first and go a little further each day.)
4. Think of your child and repeat the phrases using their name.
5. Think of someone else, repeating the phrases with their name. If you feel bold, try this step while thinking of someone you don't like. Wish them well. You may very well feel better afterward.
6. Open your eyes and come back down to earth. Do this meditation once a day and keep track of your moods in a journal to see if it's helping. You might be surprised.

I heartily recommend that you practice some form of meditation daily for at least five minutes. Meditation can improve your outlook tremendously. Research has shown that mindfulness meditation reduces rumination (obsessively thinking about something), boosts working memory, improves focus, makes us less emotionally sensitive, allows us to think more flexibly, and helps our relationships be more satisfying (Davis and Hayes 2012). It is also commonly reported to reduce stress, insomnia, anxiety, pain, depression, and high blood pressure.

Georgia: *My loving-kindness meditation has helped me truly have good, kind, and loving thoughts going my daughter's way, and I believe she is picking up on this. The biggest change is that I stopped asking so many questions: "Could you clean your room? What time is work? Could you change the cat litter?" My questions were logistical with zero heart-to-heart connection. Now I sit and listen and try to reflect back her underlying feelings, which is exactly what all the experts recommend that you do.*

Self-Compassion

When you think you've made a mistake, do you have an inner critic who bullies you? Most people have an inner critic who lives in the back of their mind and says things like, *See, you can't do it,* or *You're stupid,* or *You'll never get what you want.* Would you believe that your inner critic can do the same amount of harm to you as someone else saying it to you? It's true.

The essence of self-compassion is treating yourself like you would treat a good friend who is experiencing a problematic situation (Neff 2011). Self-compassion turns that inner critic on its head. When we practice self-compassion, we tell ourselves that no one is perfect, to be gentle with ourselves, and that not everyone gets what they want—but it's not their fault. A self-compassionate person understands that there are times everyone feels like they're not good enough, and that's part of the human experience.

If you can't accept your own imperfections, how can you accept the imperfections of those around you—especially your child? Not only that, but the inner critic also does not motivate us to perform better. It tears us down in the same way it would if someone else said those unfair, accusing things to us (Neff 2011). Even if it's difficult at first, cultivate self-compassion. Because you're raising a kid with BPD, you likely already have more compassion than most people. All you have to do is turn it toward yourself.

Gather People to Support You

You'll need others to support you as you parent your child with BPD. If you have a partner, try to configure things so that at a minimum they're not doing any harm or taking away from your ability to parent—you don't need to parent another adult. Some support people may offer practical help, such as running errands or making a meal, whereas others can offer emotional support or a shoulder to cry on. Others may have expertise in a helpful area, such as the law or working with schools.

Top Takeaways from This Chapter

We covered some crucial topics for self-care in this chapter. Parents who are raising a child with BPD often overlook how important it is for them to take care of themselves. If they don't, their journey will be a lot more difficult than it has to be. Here are some key points to take forward with you:

- You need to help yourself before you can help your child. Sometimes you are the priority. Otherwise, you're no good for your child.
- When you accept what can't be changed, and that things are as they are, you're freed up to start changing the situation or yourself in relation to it. This frees up much time and energy for you to start taking care of yourself.
- Trauma, grief, and stress are likely three large issues you'll need to deal with as the parent of a child with BPD. Seeing a therapist, practicing radical acceptance, and grieving your losses will help you deal with them.
- Over time the loving-kindness meditation (and mindfulness meditation in general) will become your new best friend that will be with you on your journey.

- Be as compassionate with yourself as you would be with a close friend going through a similar problem. Treat yourself with the same kindness you treat others with.

CHAPTER 6

How BPD Impacts the Whole Family

Like alcoholism, a personality disorder is a family disease. With an alcoholic, everything revolves around them and their drinking. When someone in the family has BPD, everything revolves around their moods, desires, behaviors, and so forth.

When our daughter moved out, suddenly there was more room in the house. It was strange to be in the living room just to relax or watch TV. When she was here, all our energy had been spent trying not to set her off—who sat where at the table, who showered in what order, and even road trips all revolved around her idiosyncrasies.

Studies have found that family members (mostly parents) of people with BPD experience the following problems (Kay et al. 2018):
- Uncomfortable feelings
- Significant distress
- Social humiliation
- Financial strain
- Marital discord
- Difficulties in caretaking

- Feeling overwhelmed
- Feeling unable to cope
- Feeling exhausted by stress
- Feeling devalued and unsupported

Research has also found that (Kay et al. 2018):
- The burden experienced by family members with a relative diagnosed with BPD is greater than those with other mental disorders.
- Psychiatrists hold negative attitudes toward patients with BPD.
- Family members of individuals diagnosed with BPD sometimes experience challenges and discrimination when attempting to engage with health services, enhancing their burden.

The burdens for family members are very real. For example, clinical psychologist Kristalyn Salters-Pedneault points out that clinicians rely heavily on family members to help manage the person with BPD (2020a). Family members organize the treatment schedule (with its many clinicians and different levels of care), keep track of how the disorder is affecting their loved one from day to day, and help the child with BPD take medications and get to therapist appointments on time. This takes its toll on the entire family, not just one caregiver, causing a great deal of stress and even trauma.

Watching a family member in pain, having suicidal feelings or actually making a suicide attempt, threatening to harm themselves or actually harming themselves, and destroying objects or the house itself is another source of stress and trauma. Salters-Pedneault reports that watching high-risk activities such as these can cause very severe psychological trauma (2020a). We concur; many parents we've worked with and encountered believe they have PTSD.

We've only just begun to talk about the effects of a BPD diagnosis on the family, and you may already be feeling overwhelmed. As you read on, keep in mind that the rest of the book is going to help you manage this burden. For example, you'll learn how to reduce arguments, improve your limit-setting skills, and reduce your fear and guilt. Also, a big part of improving your life and feeling better will be making self-care a habit, which we discussed in the previous chapter. You need self-care like a person jumping out of an airplane needs a parachute. Even if you think it's not important or you're too busy, pick a self-care technique we went over or find another one and put it in your daily schedule. Otherwise, you'll run out of energy and won't have anything to give your child.

We're going to look at some major ways that BPD can disrupt family life, including how it affects siblings and marriages directly. And we're going to look at ways to deal with others judging you and your child with BPD, and talk about the drama triangle and ways to avoid it.

The Household

Claudia: *Our house is like being in a war zone. Even when you know their pain is making them act this way, the constant yelling and violence has an effect on your well-being, which lowers your capacity to deal with other basic issues. We literally have no idea how our lives will be from one day to the next.*

Stan: *I am shocked at how difficult it is to focus on work, marriage, and quality time with my other children, or even have a conversation with my wife, after five years of living with a mentally ill child.*

Jill: *There's no way around it: a child with BPD is a major disruption to the household. It may feel like there's no place to escape to, given that your home—your safe space—feels like a war zone. What can you do?*

It may sound like heresy to suggest that you should try to be happy when your child with BPD is not happy, but you should. Jumping on the roller coaster with your child will not make you a better parent. It will make you a worse parent. Their upset is catching, so you have to make an extra effort to not let their emotions affect you. Just because they're angry or sad or elated doesn't mean you have to be as well.

Your job is to model balanced emotions—and to be happy, to *be* there for your other children, and to work on your marriage (and we mean doing something other than talking about your child with BPD). You still need to have a fulfilling life, regardless of the BPD that's in it. This goes for every member of your family. You're not being mean or irreverent by trying to be happy or to feel good just because your child doesn't feel the same way.

This book will give you more than enough ways to help your child. You could spend years learning and implementing parenting strategies for kids with BPD, but if you let everything else in your life—the household, your marriage, your work—fall apart, you'll have learned these strategies for nothing. The better off you are emotionally, the more you bring to parenting not just your child with BPD, but their siblings as well. The more you bring to your marriage. The more you bring to life.

Siblings

As one might expect, growing up with a sibling with BPD is not easy. Your other children are experiencing the same behavior as you are, but without any perspective or adult coping skills. Pamela, who had a sister with BPD, believes that she would have been a very different person had she not had a borderline sister. She writes:

Growing up with a borderline sister shaped who I am today. I started out as a happy, trusting, energetic baby but became an anxious, depressed, codependent, and traumatized adult. Most of my parents' focus was on my borderline sister's well-being and her next crisis. Any leftover energy was put toward my father's career (where he went to escape) and my mother's struggle to manage what was going on at home.

Due to their own overwhelm, my parents failed to really appreciate that I was a child with a brain that was still forming, and I had absolutely no coping mechanisms for living with an increasing amount of chaos with very minimal support.

As a result, I grew up very quickly and became an over-responsible teenager. I earned good grades, never got into trouble, worked jobs, and had a lot of after-school activities. This was, in part, due to my desire to stay out of the house as much as possible. Additionally, I intuitively felt a lot of pressure to not cause any additional stress for my parents, who clearly did not have the energy to deal with anything else. Whatever problems I had, I did everything I could to minimize them and solve them on my own.

I also knew that my best option was to not have any problems in the first place, which resulted in me becoming an anxious overachiever. I don't remember anyone telling me this, but I did feel an inherent responsibility to "make up" for the fact that my sister was gravely disappointing my parents, so I'd better do something extraordinary.

My parents always tell me proudly, "We never worried about you! You were never a problem and always did so great!" The reality was that my internal world was falling apart, and not only was I becoming increasingly traumatized, I also wasn't learning the life skills I needed to function well in the adult world. Additionally, as the "little adult" in the house, my parents often looked to me to help with my sister.

Without any authority or parenting skills, there was an expectation that parenting my sister was a "group effort," and I was expected to look out for her and manage things when they weren't around or were too overwhelmed. This is where my lifelong struggle with codependency began, and my sense of responsibility for my sister extended long into our twenties and thirties. While I became a professionally high-achieving adult, I have struggled interpersonally and lost a lot of years trying to save my sister who really did not want to be saved. I have spent two decades in therapy and have been diagnosed with generalized anxiety disorder as well as PTSD.

As you can see from Pamela's story, siblings are affected by BPD even if they don't seem to show it. And most of the time, that trauma can affect them long after they've grown up and left the house. It's important to keep your other children in mind, so here are some ways you can help them.

Periodically check in. If you feel stressed and traumatized by what's going on in your family, your other children are likely feeling all of that and then some, but may not be showing it. Your non-disordered children may not offer this information unsolicited, but they need to know that you can and will make the time to help them or get them help.

Offer to get them their own therapist who is knowledgeable in BPD. If they turn you down, continue to offer it from time to time. If you think they need therapy, insist on it. Early intervention is key for trauma.

Put together an adult support system. Enlist aunts, uncles, grandparents, friends' parents, coaches, teachers, and so on to look out for your non-disordered children. You are not a superhero, and as much as you want to, you will not always have the ability to be there for all of your kids when they need you. They need other trusted adults whom they can turn to. Sometimes, it really does take a village.

Be mindful of concealment or overachieving. Your other children may feel the need to conceal their own struggles or overachieve to "make up" for or escape from what's going on with their sibling with BPD, or both. Just because they seem to be doing well doesn't mean they're okay.

Reassure them. Regularly let them know that you will make time for their struggles. Expressly tell them that, even if their problems are not as "big" or "dramatic" as those of their sibling with BPD, they are still important.

Don't use your child as a "helper." Don't involve them in the adult parts of dealing with your child with BPD. They are not their sibling's parent at any age, nor are they your confidante. Making them in any way responsible will set them up for taking on inappropriate responsibilities in other people's lives later in life.

Validate their concerns. If your children come to you with concerns about their sibling with BPD, validate their concerns, but reassure them that you are responsible for what's going on and will consult professionals if you need more support.

Encourage them to live their best lives. If you see your other children intervening or trying to help their sibling with BPD, praise them for their kindness and concern, but reinforce that it really is okay for them to focus on themselves and leave the parenting to you—and the mental health work to the professionals.

Encourage hobbies and sports. Help your non-disordered children find something outside the home that is important to them and doesn't involve any other family member. Hobbies and sports can offer a reliable and regular place to escape to, where people are interacting in healthier ways. Hobbies and sports can offer your children a sense of control over something in their life.

Maintain an open-door policy. Keep in mind that your other children may actually know far more about what is going on with your child with BPD than you do. They know the dynamics at school, in the neighborhood, and with friends because they often see their sibling when you don't. Your child with BPD may be using them as a confidante, or they may be bullying or cajoling them into being a coconspirator. Don't ask them to betray their sibling, but make sure they know that they can always come to you with concerns. Take any concerns they have very seriously, even if they sound outlandish. There is a good chance that you're only seeing a portion of your BPD child's reality, and that their siblings are seeing or hearing about the worst of it.

Be on the lookout for trauma. If your children are being exposed to suicide threats or attempts, eating disorders, violence, verbal abuse, extreme rages, drug or alcohol addictions, or self-harm, they are likely being traumatized and will need professional help to work through it.

They may feel survivor's guilt. Your child with BPD may have negative reactions to the success or celebration of their siblings, which can cause nondisordered siblings to feel guilty. It's important for you to stress that they have nothing to feel guilty about, and that their BPD sibling's feelings are not their responsibility. Make sure you celebrate your other children's successes; don't inadvertently deprive them of their need to be recognized for their own achievements in an effort to keep the peace. This may take some creativity.

Beware of "splitting." Children with BPD sometimes try to "split" their siblings. One sibling is all good and becomes the trauma-bonded secret keeper, whereas another sibling is all bad and becomes the sabotaged target of their angst. Sometimes the child with BPD will split the same sibling and vacillate between the two projections. This can be incredibly traumatizing, and your children will need support in navigating this dynamic.

Be honest. Don't pretend that what's happening in your household is normal and nothing to worry about in an effort to not scare your children. They know that what's going on is scary. By downplaying this reality you're gaslighting them and teaching them to not trust their own perceptions.

Don't expect your non-disordered children to babysit your child with BPD. Also consider not allowing the sibling with BPD to babysit your other children. Using responsible adult sitters will keep your entire family safe.

In the case of divorce. Consider splitting the kids up so that the child with BPD lives with one parent, and the other children live with the other parent. Leaving one parent to deal with all of the children alone on a full-time basis is too much and will likely further destabilize your children's home lives.

Have a contingency plan. Who is going to be the new go-to for your child with BPD if you're unexpectedly incapacitated, or after you pass away? If the child relies on you for financial support, how will they survive without you? When they are age appropriate, communicate your plan to the other siblings so they aren't living in fear of being forced to take over your role one day.

Intervene in their arguments as appropriate. It takes a skillful eye to discern what's really happening between your children. Sometimes they will fight just like any other siblings. Other times, your child with BPD may be starting the fight and setting up their sibling to take the fall. There may be a lot more going on under the surface, and it's important to take note of when things seem off to you.

Once all of your children are adults, relationships will change. Here are some important things to keep in mind.

Don't get involved in adult sibling arguments. It is important to transition to a neutral position in the family once your children are adults. When they were children, you were the referee and the peacemaker. If you play these roles with them as adults, you'll be seen as taking sides. If they come to you with complaints or problems about one another, maintain a neutral, empathetic, and appropriately validating position with all of them. Instead of rescuing or mediating, redirect them to other resources (therapists, DBT skills, books on BPD and boundaries, support groups, and so forth) that can help them deal with the issue on their own. They will learn valuable and much-needed skills, and you will remain a safe person for all of them. Also stay neutral on the outcome of any argument.

Don't pressure your adult children to maintain a relationship. If you're unable to have a healthy relationship with your child with BPD, it's likely your other children won't be able to either. They need the freedom to take care of themselves, and any pressure from you (explicit or implied) will teach them that they should maintain relationships with people who might be abusive. You may have a lot of reasons to keep your family together, but it's not your other children's responsibility to make that happen at a cost to their own well-being.

Don't vent your frustrations or fears on your children—at any age. Only talk to your adult children about their BPD sibling if they bring them up, and keep the conversation validating but neutral. Don't deny or cover things up, but don't volunteer things that will only cause them more worry or create problems between them and their sibling. Regardless of the quality of their relationship with their BPD sibling, your other children are likely losing sleep over them also.

Explaining BPD Behavior Without Using the Diagnosis

Talking about BPD with your child poses challenges. For starters, using the phrase "borderline personality disorder" may make them feel *labeled*, which can complicate how they view themselves and their potential for recovery. However, there is merit in discussing behavioral aspects of your child's BPD and pairing them with consequences. For example, "When you yell at people, they back away from you, and then you end up feeling abandoned. If you don't want to feel abandoned, you might stop yelling at people." Here's a script to consider that explains BPD symptoms without using the actual diagnosis terminology. You can also use it to explain your child's behavior to siblings.

Everyone's brain is wired a little differently. Some people are more intense than others. Your [your sibling's] feelings are more intense than most people's.

Everyone has a different way of looking at things. It's like some people have an Apple operating system and some a PC. Many people think in lots of shades of gray all at once, but some people, including you [your sibling], can only think in black and white. [Your sibling thinks in black-and-white terms, so even when they act like they don't like you, the love is still there. It's just that they can only cope with one color, or feeling, at a time.]

Everyone has different coping skills, and we all struggle with some coping issues more than others. Sometimes you [your sibling] act in extreme ways, like getting upset over things that most people might not think are so important, or becoming very angry or loud [or whatever your child does]. We are going to help you [your sibling] to learn better ways of managing your [their] emotions, and a therapist is going to help also. [We understand that being around this can be difficult, so if you need more support, come to us right away.]

Your [Your sibling's] illness isn't anyone's fault, and you [they] can make changes to get better. We will help you [them] with that, and in time things won't feel so stressful.

It's a whole lot more difficult for you [your sibling] to be as responsible as others are about some things, and you [they] need to make an extra effort to be responsible, even if it's hard. You'll [They'll] probably make mistakes at first, and that's okay! You'll [They'll] get better with practice.

We will be spending a lot of time with you [your sibling] to help you [them] with your [their] extreme thoughts, feelings, and behavior. [But we will schedule one-on-one time with you too. If you ever feel like you

> need more time or support from us, we want you to let us know. We will make the time.]
>
> We are going to work with you [your sibling] on getting better, but it's going to take time. Progress can be slow, and sometimes it's two steps forward and one step back. [It may not look like they are working hard, but they are.] If you [they] put in the effort, you'll [they'll] make mistakes at first, just like everyone else. But over time, you'll [they'll] get better and better. We will be here to support you [them].

Being Judged

It would be nice if neighbors, extended family members, and the world at large understood the reasons behind the cognitive, emotional, and behavioral dysregulation of kids with BPD, but generally they don't. People judge children with BPD, and their parents—no bones about it. Many people find the parents of kids with BPD wanting in the parenting department, *because everything is the parent's fault, isn't it?* This judgment happens with mental illness in general, but it's particularly challenging with a heavily stigmatized disorder such as BPD. We live in a "buck up and everything will be fine" society. As a result, parents with kids with BPD learn to isolate themselves.

> *Protecting my extended family from my son and my son from them has become a way of life. Every day I live with the isolation one feels of even close family not understanding what we go through every day. People don't have a clue that their opinions are so off base and unhelpful, and that they make me isolate myself even more.*
>
> *We hear, "It's just a teen being a teen. She'll grow out of it." Or, "Yes, my teen is a handful too." I want to scream, "You don't get it!" They think our daughter is this way by choice.*

Unfortunately, neighbors gossip. Did you see how their daughter dresses? I saw an ambulance pull up to their place just the other day. Nosy neighbors who make it their business to know the business of others increase the tendency of parents with BPD to isolate.

> *My sixteen-year-old daughter is famous in the neighborhood because we feel like we have to keep calling the police when she gets enraged and violent. She also flirted with a grown man next door who has a wife who saw the whole thing.*

From our many years of experience working with BPD, we can wholeheartedly state that everyone—partners, adult children, siblings, friends, stepmothers, and so on—thinks that no one really understands what it's like to have someone with BPD in their life, unless they've experienced it firsthand. Even some clinicians don't really get it. Parents often say that explaining what it's like to live with a child with BPD is like trying to explain being a parent to people who are childless. So don't take it personally that your family, friends, or neighbors don't understand what you're going through. This is easier said than done. Here are some concrete ways to help you cope with gossip and judgment.

You *can* easily find people who walk in your shoes every day. The online BPD community and, to a much lesser extent, in-person groups contain hundreds (maybe thousands) of parents who will not judge you because they know exactly what you're going through. They can answer questions, offer input, or just be there to listen. There are online support groups, such as Support for Parents of Children with BPD on Facebook and MovingForward@groups.io, which hosts several Zoom support group meetings a week. Life is so much easier when you are supported by a caring community of people who truly get what you're going through.

You can't control what other people think. You've probably heard this one from your mother: what other people think about you is their problem, not yours. It's true! What matters is what *you* think of yourself. When others say something judgmental, don't JADE (justify, argue, defend, or overexplain—see chapter 7). Instead, change the topic. People will get the hint very quickly that you're not going to talk about something. It's very hard to respond to nothing. Who knows what you'll be able to set.

The Drama Triangle

In a household with a child with BPD, the family quickly learns to either give in to the needs of the child, which makes the disorder worse, or to not give in, which can provoke temper tantrums, rage attacks, symbolic violence (throwing things, punching holes in walls, destroying property), and actual violence (see chapter 14). According to Margalis Fjelstad, author of *Stop Caretaking the Borderline or Narcissist* (2013), family members often design the rules and roles of the family around the needs of the person with the disorder, making daily interactions for them comfortable by removing any anxiety, pressure, or frustration they might feel. This leaves other family members to deal with those uncomfortable emotions, and consequently they have to give up something of themselves.

One way to reduce this dynamic is for parents to learn to recognize and then avoid the "drama triangle" (called the "Karpman triangle" in psychiatric circles) (Bansal 2020).

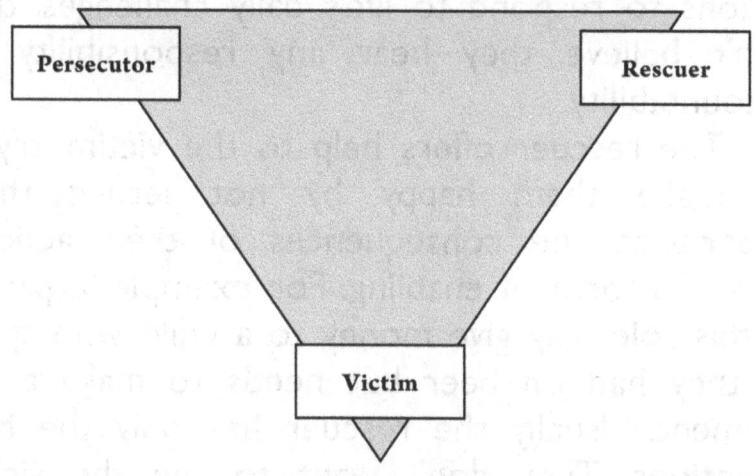

Figure 1 illustrates the different roles (victim, persecutor, and rescuer) in the drama triangle that family members take on according to their own perspectives and the situation in question. For example, your child will probably see themselves as the victim most of the time and you as the persecutor, whereas you may see it the other way around.

The persecutor is the supposed villain. They are perceived as being angry, critical, controlling, and rigid. They have the attitude of "It's all your fault." Their role is to blame and criticize the victim. For example, your child may see you as the persecutor when you don't give them what they want.

The victim usually imbibes the stance of "Poor me." Most of the time, they see themselves as hopelessly and helplessly lost and powerless. They convince themselves there is nothing they can do. Because they don't take actions to respond to life's daily challenges, they don't believe they bear any responsibility or accountability.

The rescuer offers help to the victim, trying to make them happy by not letting them experience the consequences of their actions. This is a form of enabling. For example, a parent in this role may give money to a child who spent all they had on beer but needs to make a car payment. Usually the rescuer has only the best intentions. They don't want to see the victim suffer. However, the rescuer keeps the victim dependent while giving them an excuse to fail.

Not every conflict will result in a drama triangle, but it's good to understand how the dynamic plays out. Let's look at a highly simplified example.

> Janet and Jeff have a seventeen-year-old son with BPD, Sam. Janet, Jeff, and Sam agreed that he could go to summer camp if he got at least a C in all his subjects. At the end of the year, he gets several Cs, but fails one class. Sam writes a list of two dozen reasons why he should be able to go to camp anyway and slips it under his parents' bedroom door. It ends with, "You'll be the worst parents alive if you won't let me go." (Sam is playing the victim and sees his parents as the persecutors in advance.)
>
> Jeff and Janet read the note and discuss it. Janet knows that if she and Jeff reward Sam with camp (a positive reinforcement), every limit

they set in the future will be twenty times harder to observe, and Sam will lose the incentive to get good grades. "No camp for Sam," she tells Jeff. "We had an agreement. He doesn't even take responsibility for his bad grade. He has learned nothing."

Jeff, who wants Sam to think well of him (and wants some time alone this summer with his wife), is more inclined to agree to let Sam go. Jeff wears Janet down with reasons their son should go until she finally capitulates. In doing so, she gives up what's best for Sam's education, gives up something of herself, and makes it harder to set limits in the future. (Janet becomes the bad guy, Sam the victim, and Jeff the rescuer.)

The next morning, she says nothing to Jeff. He pleads with her to tell him what's wrong. She explains why she feels like a victim. In her mind, Jeff is the persecutor. They argue some more, and in the end Sam goes to camp, and they don't get to enjoy their time alone together like they should have.

Nobody wins in a drama triangle because everyone is pitted against each other. That's bad for the entire family. Keep in mind that despite its name, the drama triangle doesn't need three people. For example, if Janet was parenting alone, she could serve as both persecutor and rescuer, if she first tells Sam no and then changes her mind.

Let's pretend that Janet and Jeff had a chance to redo this entire interaction, this time managing to avoid the drama triangle and handling the situation in the right way.

Upon receiving Sam's note, the first thing Janet and Jeff do is consider each other's needs and desires so that they can determine if they have a drama triangle in the making. They can see that they do, so next they identify their roles, which are easy to spot. If Janet holds firm with the agreement they'd made with Sam, she'd be the villain, and if Jeff swoops in and lets Sam go to camp anyway because he wants time alone with his wife, then he'd be the rescuer in Sam's eyes.

Janet starts the conversation by noting that she too wants some time alone with Jeff. Then she calmly explains that if they give in, she's concerned that Sam will never respect their limits again, and that that will set them up for a terrible future: both because he will no longer respect their limits, and because they will be powerless to affect his grades.

Jeff thinks about that and acknowledges that she has a point. Still, he needs a break, badly, and he wants to spend time on their marriage because he feels they're growing apart. (In the first example they fought before he could mention this.) Each acknowledges that the other has valid and important points.

Working together, they come up with a compromise. Rather than let Sam go to summer camp, they'll let him stay with his favorite uncle, aunt, and cousins on their farm on a lake (which he loves) and, as a reward for all the Cs he received, pay for a trip to his favorite amusement park. By not paying for camp, they have enough money left over to stay at a bed-and-breakfast that is ninety minutes from Sam's uncle's house, in case of emergency.

It takes practice to get good at recognizing the drama triangle and the roles different participants play, and it's hard work getting good at avoiding the triangle altogether. Here are some tips for avoiding the drama triangle (Bansal 2020):

- Refuse to be inferior or superior; better than, worse than, right, or wrong; or deserving of blame or of defense. Don't argue about who gets more or less, or does more or less. These are all black-and-white, splitting kinds of ways to look at things. The truth is usually found in a gray area.
- State expectations without taking a tone that is blaming, criticizing, lecturing, scolding, threatening, preaching, or overreacting. A child with BPD can detect any of these undertones at one part per thousand in your voice, body language, and facial expressions (remember, they're looking for it), so don't overdo it.
- Realize that the disorder may be so entrenched that you may not have the kind of relationship you want with your child until

they're in recovery. You won't be the first parent this has happened to, and you won't be the last. Still, no matter how unpersecutorial you are, your child may still try to thrust you in the persecutor role. That doesn't mean you have to play along. They may also try to place you in the role of rescuer. You don't have to form that point of the triangle either. You can change the dynamic all by yourself.

Top Takeaways from This Chapter

Here are a few key things from this chapter to keep in mind as you read on:
- Having a family member with BPD affects *everyone* in the family. Not only all the things I mentioned in this chapter, but also finances, taking the child to appointments, finding doctors, filling prescriptions, managing medications, keeping track of limits and observing them, using new communication techniques (chapter 7), learning more about BPD in general, and making decisions.
- If you are a mother who wants your husband to be more involved, show him appendix A. Realize you are a person under much stress, and take care of yourself. Treat yourself as you would treat a friend going through the same thing. If your child broke their leg,

family and friends would show much concern. They might even send cards and flowers. That doesn't automatically happen with a mental illness. You have to explain why you need support and then ask for it. If you feel shame—which you have no reason to—you may not do this. Remember that it's not your fault your child has BPD, and it isn't your child's fault either. Reach out and ask for help.

- You will be a better parent if you don't match your emotions with your child's, letting them go up and down. Your role is to stay calm, steady, and good-natured for the sake of the rest of the family, especially siblings. I'm not saying you should repress your feelings, which you should know from the last chapter. I'm saying it's okay to be happy. Self-care will be a vital part of you accomplishing this balanced nature.
- Speaking of siblings, they are just as affected by your child with BPD as you are, only as children, they don't have a mature brain or the experience that can help them handle it. Remember to make time for them and to be attentive to their needs.

CHAPTER 7
Life-Changing Communication Techniques

> *It's important to understand that people [with BPD] can't just turn off their emotions because they "make no sense." It's easy to believe that if they can't put their finger on the reason they're feeling the way they do, it must be because there is no reason—and that once this is pointed out to them, they should easily be able to stop feeling the emotion. It doesn't work that way. The fact that the trigger is unnameable doesn't mean it doesn't exist.*
> —Shari Y. Manning, Loving Someone with Borderline Personality Disorder

Learning new ways of communicating with your child is key to your relationship with them. Communication is the biggest arena in which relating "happens," and when it goes wrong, explosions can happen and the relationship goes south. When communication goes well, the relationship improves.

With most communication, you just say what you want without too much thought. You can't do that with people who have BPD. When you speak, you need to think through how you want to initiate a conversation or respond to your child. In this chapter, we're going to discuss these helpful communication tools, and one "tool" you shouldn't use:

- Validation: How to make your child feel heard and understood. Validation is like a verbal hug; for example, "I hear you are very depressed."
- SET-UP (*s*upport, *e*mpathy, *t*ruth–*u*nderstanding, *p*erseverance): This communication tool starts with a verbal hug (support and empathy) and ends with a truth. For example, "I understand that you feel like your teacher hates you, and you still have to go to school."
- BIFF (*b*rief, *i*nformative, *f*riendly, and *f*irm): This is the most stern of the communication tools; it can help you remind your child of your limits and say something firmly in a way that indicates you're not in the mood to argue. This tool can be either written or verbal.
- JADE: This initialism stands for something you should *not* do—*j*ustify, *a*rgue, *d*efend (yourself), or *o*verexplain. Using these four communication styles is called "JADEing," and

learning to refrain from using them is an incredibly useful skill.

Before we get into more details about these communication tools, let's cover some important basic communication skills.

Healthy Communication Skills

Remember, people with BPD have a special built-in radar for detecting any word, tone of voice, or facial expression that could signal real or *imagined* abandonment, rejection, or feelings of worthlessness. So let's review six ways to avoid these triggers.

1. **Be aware of your voice inflection, facial expressions, and body language.** When body language and verbal communication don't match, nonverbal communication takes precedence in the mind of the listener—and this is all the more true for people with BPD. For example, if your voice sounds happy but you're frowning and your arms are crossed, the listener is going to think you're upset—regardless of what you're saying. A simple phrase like "Could you clean your room today?" could have a multitude of connotations depending upon how it is said. Don't cross your arms. Don't stand if the other person is sitting. Have a relaxed posture and a neutral or leaning-toward-positive facial expression.

2. **Stay focused on your message.** While you're talking, your child may try to change the

subject. That's a sign that the issues you two are experiencing are not related to what you're fighting about, but about the fact that you're fighting. Your child is probably hurting for some reason and taking it out on you, probably because you're a safe place to do so. Ignore the attempts to distract you. Just calmly continue making your point and come back to the other subject later, if doing so is appropriate.

3. Simplify. Earlier in this book, I wrote that trying to think logically while experiencing an onslaught of emotions is like trying to do a math problem while waiting for news about a cancer biopsy. Keep sentences short, simple, clear, and direct. Leave no room for misinterpretation.

4. Have a mutual "take a break" signal. When one or both of you are feeling overloaded, or it appears that the conversation may escalate out of control, stop the cycle of conflict by signaling that you want to take a break. In our experience, once your child reaches an emotional high of 6 on a scale of 1 to 10, they can no longer reason. Either person can signal that a break is a good idea. You can agree on a verbal or nonverbal signal. My husband and I have a code word: "banana."

> **Chen:** *My child turned on me the instant I said no to something. I suggested a time out: "Let's speak when I have time to think about things."*

"Why do you need to think about things?" she responded.

"Because I like to pause a bit these days," I explained. She gave me a sheepish apology half an hour later.

The following morning we spoke about the previous night's argument, and my daughter said, *"It wasn't about you not giving me what I asked for. It was all about my feelings."* In the light of day, they are able to better understand themselves.

5. Stay away from black-and-white thinking and the word "but." Minimize your use of words like "always" and "never." Avoid "but" altogether. Use "both" or "and" instead. For example, if you say, "I appreciate that you got all Bs, *but* you failed English," the "but" extinguishes the compliment. Try, "I appreciate that you got all Bs. That's really great. I'm so proud of you! I see you also got an F in English. What happened there?"

6. Make "I" Statements. When responding, describe what happened, then, using the word "I" instead of "you," tell the person how what they did made you feel. These are called "I statements." So rather than saying, *"You are a selfish person for eating all the peanuts,"* say, *"When I went looking for the peanuts, they weren't there. I was really disappointed to find they were all gone. I had really been looking forward to eating them."* This style of communicating is less blaming.

Now that we've reviewed some simple communication tools that can help keep conversations with your child on track, and before we break down the main topics of this chapter, let's go over a skill you can practice for yourself—when you're feeling anxious or in need of a break.

Belly Breathing

When you're going to have a difficult conversation with your child, the first thing you'll want to do is soothe yourself and your own emotions. Before you say anything, belly breathe a few times. "Belly breathing," or diaphragmatic breathing, is an all-purpose tool, like a multitool pocketknife. You can belly breathe when you're anxious, stressed, needing to sleep, meditating, in the car, or in need of a break from a stressful day.

Find a comfortable position, either lying on your back or sitting. Place one hand on your stomach and the other on your chest. Imagine your stomach is a balloon, and sip in air so that your belly button rises toward the ceiling or the wall you're facing. Then let the air out. Take a few breaths as you normally would. Your belly should rise and fall with every breath in (inhale) and every breath out (exhale). Then repeat the process. Do this for as long as feels good to you or is helpful.

Belly breathing fights the stress response and anchors you to the present moment (Bergland 2017). It will calm you down and slow down the pace of the interaction, so you have more time to think about which technique you want to use and what you want to say. Practice this tool until it becomes second nature. Try it at work when you become frustrated, impatient, or angry. Try it at the dentist's office when they're drilling. (I did, and it helped.) When you're having a disagreement with your spouse, belly breathe. Then you'll be prepared during a BPD crisis.

Validation

Validation involves listening to your child's emotions while being fully present, reflecting the emotions back in your own words, and asking questions to make sure you fully understand their internal experiences. When you validate your child's emotions (feelings, *not* thoughts or actions), you not only radically accept the emotions, but also your child. You are saying, *I understand you have this very powerful feeling. This must be very difficult for you.* And perhaps, if true, *if I were in your position, I would feel that way too.*

For a child who feels unconnected, isolated, and worthless, being heard and understood can be life altering. One mother told me that her child cried the first time she tried validation because her daughter finally felt understood. People with BPD are continually frustrated because nobody understands the depths of their pain or the degree of worthlessness they feel. Invalidating remarks make your child feel invisible, misunderstood, unappreciated, and unloved.

> ### Validation When You Don't Agree
>
> You don't have to agree with a person's thoughts or actions in order to validate them. To *validate* someone's experience of an incident doesn't mean you'd feel the same way if the same thing happened to you. *Validation* means listening to your child's emotions (both those displayed and discussed) while being fully present with them, reflecting the emotions back in your own words, recognizing that their emotions are real to them, and saying that it's okay for them to feel the way they do. You may not agree that your child *should* feel the way they do, especially when it's about you, *but they do*, and feelings don't have IQs. Reach across your reality and grasp their hand in comfort, because they have a disorder and can't come to your reality without treatment.

One important note: If you feel uncomfortable with the way your child is talking to you (raising their voice, calling you names, otherwise creating a lot of stress), wait until they are calm and willing to meaningfully engage to have a conversation. Say, "I care about your feelings, and I want to talk with you about your concerns. However, I don't feel comfortable doing that until things are calmer." Notice I didn't say, "When you stop shouting." Your child will take finger pointing as a challenge, and your goal is to end the conversation and let things cool down. You might also try saying, "Let's touch back with each other in an hour. I can hear about your concerns and feelings then."

The Three Steps of Validation

To simplify things, try these three steps for practicing validation with your child (Manning 2011).

Step 1. Be present and listen with your whole body. Give your child your full attention and be mindful of your body language. Sit if they're sitting; stand if they're standing. Be aware of the expression on your face; it should show care and concern. As you listen, it is critical that you withhold any judgments. Your child is letting you into their life, so be respectful.

Step 2. After you've listened closely, reflect your child's emotions back to them using slightly different language. Ask about other emotions they may be having, if you can guess what they are based on the situation. Ask questions to learn more and to show that you're listening.

Step 3. Normalize your child's emotional reaction as being one that others would have, if this is true. Consider whether you might feel the same way. If you would, say so. If you

wouldn't, but you know this event or situation would upset your child, you can say, "I can see this is just the kind of thing that would really upset you." (This is always true.) The key is to find a way to say that your child's behavior makes sense without pathologizing them or making them sound defective. Here are some examples of normalizing comments:
- We all have times when we feel that way.
- Lots of people would feel that way.
- Anyone would feel that way.
- That is an understandable reaction.

Let's look at an example of validation in action. Say your daughter Carrie is upset because her brother Josh was asked to go on a special outing with his friends, and she wasn't invited. She feels left out, rejected, lonely, and miserable. She responds by locking herself in her room for four hours instead of clearing the dishes off the table, her chore for the evening. When Carrie comes out, she's half angry, half despairing, and complaining about Josh.

The fact that you support Josh in having his own friends and having adventures with them without Carrie is irrelevant to validating your daughter's feelings. *Validation is not about whether she should have gone, the degree to which she responded, or whether she should have locked herself in her room. It is only about the emotions she is having right now and your response to them.*

So what do you do? When she comes out of her room, ask her if she'd be willing to take a moment to tell you what's wrong. Have a seat in the living room if that seems appropriate. Then:

1. *Be present and listen with your whole body. Withhold any judgments:* "I am so angry at him!" Carrie says. Tears roll down her cheeks. "It's so unfair I couldn't go. Now I have nowhere to go, and I'm bored and unhappy stuck at home, and my friends already have plans, and I already told them I was going to the lake!"
2. *After you've listened closely, reflect Carrie's emotions back to her using slightly different language. Ask her about other emotions she may be having, if you can guess based on the situation:* "Oh, honey, I can tell you're really disappointed and upset that you couldn't go. It sounds like it would have been a fun time. I'm so sorry that happened to you."
3. *Normalize Carrie's emotional reaction as one that others would have, particularly someone with her history:* "If that happened to me, I would have felt disappointed too. How about I help you clear the dishes, and we can listen to that band you like. Then maybe we can watch a movie. It's the third of the month and all the streaming services

released new movies." (If she says no, say, "I'll check back in an hour." Don't clear the dishes for her, but do give her a break on time, as long as she clears them in the same day.)

Validating Questions and Statements

Some of these questions and statements were drawn from Amanda Smith's blog post "37 Validating Statements (A Quick Cheat Sheet for When You Are Stuck)" (2020) on https://www.hopeforbpd.com.

Validating Questions
- What happened then?
- What are you feeling?
- What happened exactly?
- Are you safe?
- Can you tell me more?
- Are you upset with me?
- I don't understand. Can you help me understand?
- What can I do to help?
- Have you ever felt like this before?
- Then what happened?
- Would you just like me to listen or do you want my help?
- Was that difficult [upsetting, horrible, tough] for you?
- Did that make you feel disappointed [lonely, sad, worried, angry]?

- Was that really frustrating [disgusting, surprising] for you?
- You sound sad [embarrassed, annoyed, anxious, afraid, bored, apathetic]. Are you feeling that way? Are you feeling depressed [resentful, amused, confused, jealous, guilty, ashamed, depressed, loving]?

Validating Phrases
- Wow, how hard that must be.
- That really stinks!
- That's messed up!
- How frustrating!
- What a tough spot to be in.
- Darn, I know how much that meant to you.
- I can see you are making an effort.
- I can see how hard you are working.
- I can see this is important to you.
- I can see right now you're not feeling so great about your older sister.
- Tell me about what you're thinking.
- I can hear/see that you're feeling mad [glad, sad, scared].
- So, what you're telling me is, when this happened, you started feeling mad [glad, sad, scared]?
- I can tell from your voice [tears] that you're feeling mad [glad, sad, scared].
- It must feel terrible for you to believe that. I am so sorry this feels bad for you.

Phrases for Offering Love and Support
- I believe in you.
- We are going to get through this.
- Thank you for being in my life.
- We're in this together.
- It makes sense that you feel mad [glad, sad, scared].
- It makes sense that you think _____.
- I want to hear about your morning [afternoon, day, night].
- I've noticed that you _____.
- I need your help with _____.
- Thank you for being someone I can trust.
- It meant a lot to me when you _____.
- I value your ability to _____.
- I believe we can figure this out together.
- I'm proud of you.

Common Validation Mistakes

As you try out validation techniques from this chapter, watch out for the following common mistakes.

Leaping into problem solving. It is almost irresistible for parents to start solving their child's problem. Unless they say so, that's not what they need from you. First, you're not validating, and second, it implies that your child can't solve their own problems. If you have a tendency to do this, pay less attention to the situation they're talking about (for validation purposes, it doesn't matter) and listen closely for their emotions, expressed or unexpressed.

Not talking about their child's emotions. Many parents miss the point of validation entirely and skip right to responding. *When validating, forget about the exact situation.* Imagine yourself as a detective searching for just the right emotions your child is having. Search online using the search phrase "list of feelings and emotions." That will help you rephrase what your child says so you're not using the same words all the time.

Thinking they have to "validate" things they don't agree with. Again, validation has nothing to do with thoughts, opinions, and behaviors. Validation is about your child's inner reality, not the empirical truth.

Getting emotionally triggered and adding that emotion to the conversation. Sometimes your child is going to be angry or upset with you. It takes practice to respond to your child's emotions instead of explaining, defending yourself, or correcting their assumptions. If your child is off base and says something like, "You don't love me," or "You're never there for me," try saying, "If I thought that were true, I would be very [emotion] too." You will have time to correct their impressions later, such as saying, "I do love you." When you contradict your child, it comes off as invalidating. It is as if you are saying that they have no right to their feelings. For an easy rule, just remember to use the phrase "If that were true..."

Not using the right tone of voice. Be careful not to sound too mechanical, even though validation can be hard at times. You want to sound concerned and caring, even when your child upsets you. Sometimes that will be difficult. Practice.

Never Invalidate Your Child

To "invalidate" someone means that you deny their emotions, you tell them they have no reason to have those emotions, or you don't take them seriously. Here are some examples of invalidating statements (Hall and Cook 2012):

- Don't be rude. Give grandma a hug.
- You'll get over it.
- Why aren't you happy about _____?
- You can't be hungry yet.
- Don't be silly, lots of people like you.
- You should be more _____.
- It's not such a big deal.
- Your sister can do this by herself. Why can't you?
- I understand. (Don't say this unless you have BPD—you haven't been in your child's shoes.)
- Stop being such a baby about this.
- You do like mustard on your hot dogs.

- No, I'm not mad (when you obviously are).
- You shouldn't be so upset about this.
- I can't believe you're scared of _____.
- Just calm down.
- There's no reason to feel that way.
- You're too _____.
- Stop being so negative.
- You'll feel better tomorrow.
- Here's what I think you should do. (Instead, wait for the person to ask for help or your opinion.)
- You should feel _____.
- Don't say that, you don't mean it.
- You're so _____.
  You should also avoid:
- Explaining how they should have acted
- Switching the conversation back to you
- Giving them advice
- Laughing at their ideas or feelings or acting condescending
- Ignoring them when they are present
- Telling them what they can or can't do
- Being philosophical ("Life isn't fair.")
- Using logic and reason to counter their emotions ("It's not that big of a deal.")
- Speaking as if they aren't present
- Talking about your child's feelings with others without permission

Remember, you don't have to agree with your child's feelings, thoughts, or actions in order to validate them. All you need to do is to convey the message *I see you. I hear you. I care. And I empathize with you.*

Validation Tips from Other Parents

Susan: *You have to set your ego aside so you can validate instead of getting upset and reacting.*

Christine: *Validating someone means fighting the impulse to tell them they're wrong when you think they're wrong, and it's hard not to defend yourself and your actions. But my experience is that it works 100 percent of the time. Nothing takes the argument out of my son like validating how he feels.*

Grace Lee: *Even when it feels ridiculous, do it anyway. Even when they're acting like it's the end of the world because you asked them to set the table. Validate the feeling, not the action.*

Diana: *My biggest hint is to be sincere. Believe in the fact that your child needs validation. I saw a huge change. She no longer escalated her conflicts. Validation was a real game changer.*

Gates: *The hardest part of learning to validate was regulating my own emotional reactions to my children and my own triggers regarding parenting and children so I could* learn to focus on my daughter and her emotions.

Fran: *My communication with my daughter improved when I wrote down what I wanted, then rewrote it taking her listening/hearing/comprehending abilities into consideration. Needless to say, the two versions are very different.*

SET-UP

The SET-UP (support, empathy, truth—understanding, perseverance) communication tool can help you when you need to think on your feet and want to avoid being dragged into emotional and unproductive interactions (Kreishman 2018). If the dash confuses you, think of the acronym as *s* upport, *e* mpathy, and *t* ruth in an atmosphere of *u* nderstanding and *p* erseverance. This tool acknowledges the reality your loved one lives in, but it brings them into your reality. As with the validation tool, SET-UP clearly conveys to your child *I care about you, and I empathize with you.* But unlike with validation, the T ("truth") part of this tool also communicates *I have a reality too, and it is XYZ.* The truth part of this method employs "truth statements," which can also imply *This is how it is going to be,* or *This is the way we are going to do things.*

The SET-UP tool has three steps, and it's vital that you do them in order; otherwise the practice is meaningless. Before employing this tool with your child who has BPD, you may want to try it with friends and family members until it becomes natural. Get feedback and become comfortable with the tool. Use it in low-stakes interactions with your child until you're comfortable with it.

Step 1: Support. A support statement usually begins with "I" and demonstrates concern and a desire to help. It should imply *It's important to me to try to help you feel better,* or *I care that this issue is important to you.* Let's use the example of a child wanting his mother to drive him to work because he missed the bus and is late, but she can't. The mother says, "I see, you want me to drive you to work. I know your work is important to you, and I agree it's important that you get to work on time."

Step 2: Empathy. Express empathy using a "you" statement, which signals that you can put yourself in their shoes and look at the world through their eyes. Continuing with the example above, the mother says: "I can imagine it feels frustrating that you missed the bus and you're worried about being late to work."

Step 3: Truth. Truth statements address the practical options of what can be done to deal with the current situation and are best expressed in nonjudgmental ways. The mother's truth statement might be, "But I only have thirty minutes to get to work, and I can't be late today. I'm sorry, I can't take you [truth]. Perhaps you can wait for the next bus and make the time up at the end of your shift."

The truth point of the SET-UP tool will be the most challenging for your child because it will confront their attempts to avoid the situation. It also demands practical problem solving (covered in chapter 9). You are stressing accountability, and that's not easy for someone with BPD because it puts shame on top of shame. That's why the "support" and "empathy" statements are so vitally important.

BIFF

The BIFF (*b*rief, *i*nformative, *f*riendly, and *f*irm) communication tool is one to use when there is a goal afoot (Eddy and Kreger 2011). When we need to remind someone of a limit, BIFF is there to help. When SET-UP hasn't gotten the point across and we need to say, *Sorry, that's the way it is,* in a nice way, BIFF is there. When someone is more interested in being right than in coming to an agreement and is only listening just enough to argue with your point, BIFF can close the discussion. Here's a breakdown of the method:

> **B**rief—BIFF statements are short so that your child can't pick them apart and find something to argue about. They are also about one issue, and thus are more understandable for your child.

Informative—We use BIFF because we have information we need to get across: "I will be at the movies from two to five." Make it simple. (Remember, they are waiting for those biopsy results and can't take in too much information at once.)

Friendly—Say the informative part of BIFF in a friendly and respectful way, even if you don't feel it. Use the usual pleasantries, even if they don't. For example, "Please," "Thank you," or "Nice to talk with you."

Firm—Make your "truth" statement crystal clear so there is no room for interpretation: "I told you that if you did drugs in the house, you would have to leave. You did drugs yesterday, and now I'm asking you to leave by the first of next month."

If your child objects to something (and it may be quite a vociferous objection), you can say, "This isn't a power struggle—it's about me making what I feel is the right decision," or "This isn't about me trying to control you, but about doing what I feel is right as a parent."

I was on terrible terms with my twenty-four-year-old daughter, but I missed terribly my fourteen-month-old granddaughter, who had lived—until recently—her entire life with her mother in my home. So, I invited them both to lunch.

My daughter replied with vitriol and rebuke. I'd just learned BIFF, so I came up with a decent BIFF response: "I hear you. How you feel matters to me. I would enjoy seeing you. Let me know if Sunday lunch works for you." To my surprise, she replied pleasantly and offered a time and place they'd meet me that Sunday! It worked! Magnificently! I was sold on it and so happy.

Let's look at the BIFF method in a real-world scenario:

You see your child watching TV in the living room, and you sit down and ask if you can talk with him a minute. He agrees and turns down the volume. You say, "Honey, as you remember, I asked you not to leave food in your room because it attracts ants [informative]. You didn't do that for a week, which I appreciate [friendly, and it acknowledges something the child did well, which is very important]. I see there is a plate with food on it in your room right now [informative]. Can you please take the plate back to the kitchen and clean it now? It is very important that you remember not to keep food in your room [two informative statements]. If you don't, we're going to have to consider not allowing you to bring food to your room at all [firm and informative, and the whole thing is brief].

However he responds, keep BIFFing him. Whatever you do, don't JADE him (which you are going to learn about shortly).

You can also use BIFF in written form. Let's start by imagining a nasty email. Elizabeth is estranged from her daughter Alynna for reasons she doesn't really understand, and the two haven't talked to each other for months. One day Elizabeth gets this email:

> Hi. I can't believe I am writing to you after all you've done to me. But I need you to give me the pearl necklace you said was going to be mine one day right now. I'd like to wear it. I can pick it up tomorrow. Is morning or evening better? Don't get into the rest of the money that I owe you. I will give it to you when I give it to you.

Elizabeth couldn't be angrier. She knows her daughter wants the necklace so she can sell it. The necklace has been in the family for three generations. She can't believe Alynna would do this. She writes a furious email message, then deletes it because she realizes her goal is not to shame her daughter but to simply tell her a firm no. She ignores the issue about Alynna owing her money to simplify the matter. That's another issue. She writes a BIFF response:

> It was nice to hear from you. I hope you're doing well [friendly]. It's true that I talked about giving you the pearl necklace one day. When I did, I made it clear that I was leaving it to you in my will (living trust, really) for when your dad and I are gone. That may be a detail you forgot [informative]. We are sticking with that [firm]. If I don't see you by

the holidays, have a Merry Christmas and Happy New Year [friendly and brief].

JADE

Sometimes during conversations, people are not really interested in hearing your side of things, playing fair, or negotiating a solution. They want to get you to talk so they can shut you down, argue your points, overcome your objections, and point out how you're wrong and they're right. During these kinds of conversations, especially, take some guidance from the acronym JADE, which has its origins in Al-Anon. Horde your words like silver dollars and do not JADE: *j*ustify, *a*rgue, *d*efend, or *o*verexplain.

Let's look at a phone conversation between Becky, a twenty-seven-year-old woman with BPD, and her mother, Mary Kay. Take note of how Mary Kay uses validation, SET-UP, and BIFF.

Becky: Mom, can you take care of Janie [Mary Kay's granddaughter] in an hour for about four hours? I have some of her toys and a peanut butter sandwich. Tracy from the restaurant called in sick just an hour ago and the manager called me to come in, and I need the extra hours because I had to get a new tire. I get off at midnight and can pick her up by 12:30a.m.

Mary Kay: Hi, honey. Nice to hear from you [friendly]. I won't be able to take Janie this time. I have other plans [firm, however she doesn't *justify* by giving a reason that Becky can argue with, suggesting her situation is more important]. I hope you find another babysitter at the last minute though; those extra hours sound great [friendly]. [Notice how she put "firm" within two "friendly" slices of bread to make a BIFF sandwich.] I know how important work is to you. What a shame it is that you are having this difficulty [support from SET-UP]. However, I can't babysit today [firm; Mary Kay could have used only SET-UP in this scenario, but she used BIFF because she knew Becky would need something stronger].

Becky: What are you doing that is so important, more important than taking care of your granddaughter?

Mary Kay: [Doesn't fall into the JADE—justify, argue, defend, overexplain—trap] I can see you're getting frustrated and maybe a little angry [validation], but to answer your question, I have other plans.

Becky: But what?!

Mary Kay: Other plans. [Repeat as often as needed.]

Becky: What about Daddy? I'm sure he will do it! [Dad always dropped everything for Becky, until he learned about the need for parents to stick together, especially when it comes to limits.]

Mary Kay: Dad is standing next to me. He is shaking his head no. [Repeat no more than once and move on.]

Becky: Let me talk to him!

Mary Kay: He is still shaking his head no. I know that is hard and disappointing for you [validation]. We are getting ready to go now. I know this must be very frustrating. On the one hand, you need money; on the other hand, it's hard to get last-minute help [empathy]. You're in a bind, I can see. That's no fun [validation]. Why don't you try Sylvia and Tom? They may be able to help. I'm sorry that we're busy. I know you had no notice [friendly], but today we can't do it at the last minute [firm].

Becky: [Getting panicked] Mom, I need the money! What do you have to do that's so important?!

Mary Kay: We had plans in advance [not justifying, arguing, defending, or overexplaining]. Maybe next time, honey. I hope you find someone. I have confidence in you [friendly].

Becky: Do you want me to leave Janie with a stranger? Maybe someone who uses drugs? Don't you love her? What kind of parents and grandparents are you? [Uses emotional blackmail and its triad of tools: fear, obligation, and guilt—FOG, covered in the next chapter.]

Mary Kay: [Ignoring the FOG] I really do care that you find someone so you can pick up some extra cash [support]. I can see that you're upset about this [empathy]. The manager will understand that you cannot make it without notice and will not hold this against you [more support]. However, we can't do it, and we have to leave now [truth]. See you soon. Love you [friendly]. You'll be okay. [Hangs up and turns off ringer.]

Handing Your Child's Rages

Rages are always terrifying for the people being raged at, but BPD rages can reach another order of magnitude. One woman describes an enraged person with BPD this way:

> When in a rage, it seemed like she was channeling an evil spirit. Her eyes had no life in them: just a blankness. She didn't see who I was or how she was hurting me. There was no way to negotiate, no way to reason or argue. She did not understand rational arguments. Her voice would become more rapid, accusatory, demeaning, patronizing, irrational, and paranoid. Her tone was very fast—rata-tat-tat—like she was offensively firing at me. She would pace and become very menacing, growing closer and closer as I became more and more afraid. She was no longer someone I knew, though I tried with all my power to talk her out of the fog. But it never worked. The rage seemed to need to run its course until she felt relief, no matter how much it killed me. (Kreger 2008, 30–31)

A child in a rage is a child in pain. Still, you need to be able to get yourself out of the path of the tornado, whatever lengths are required. Don't minimize the effects of this behavior on your well-being. That's like not locking the doors of your house and car when you live in a busy city. It's also important to note that a child who copes with frustration by raging at others may graduate from verbal abuse to physical abuse.

First, do not let yourself be abused. If your child is that angry, you need to immediately remove yourself and any other family members (especially children) from the situation. That could be another room, but if the person is in a rage and out of control, it probably means leaving the house. Keep a "safety kit" handy with an extra car key, some money, and anything else you might need if you can't immediately get to your wallet or purse. Beforehand, think through where you might go. Call a close friend and ask if you might go there if something happens.

And what about calling the police? We consider it a last resort—sometimes unfortunately necessary, but always to be approached with caution. As a parent of someone with BPD, it's important for you to know that, according to the Treatment Advocacy Center, a nonprofit "dedicated to eliminating legal and other barriers to the timely and effective treatment of severe mental illness," people with untreated serious mental illness are sixteen times more likely to be killed while being approached or stopped by law enforcement than other civilians. And these risks are most likely amplified by racial disparities in police violence. For example, in 2020, a Harvard School of Public Health study found that Black Americans were, on average, more than three times more likely to be killed by the police than white Americans. Calling the police can also escalate a conflict that might be lessened using some of the communication techniques in this chapter. So, whenever and wherever possible, we recommend that you consider non-police emergency responses and organizations (acknowledging, of course, that for some of us, non-police resources may be limited), if they exist in your area, and try deescalating the conflict before it gets to a level 10 out of 10.

Let's say that things are not that serious and, on a scale of 1 to 10, your child is at a 5 or below. Try these tips for engaging an angry child in a conversation.

Step 1. Soothe yourself by belly breathing (chapter 7) and telling yourself positive messages. Some suggestions:
- I can handle this.
- These are just words.
- This is the BPD talking.
- My child is feeling great pain and misdirecting it at me because they feel safe with me.

Step 2. Make sure your body language is relaxed, including your voice and face. Your child will pick up on any tension, dislike, anger, or frustration you bring to the conversation. Practice this skill in low-stress situations before you're facing your raging child. You need to practice because your body's automatic response to a crisis will be fight, flight, or freeze.

Step 3. Validate, validate, validate. Use the communication technique SET-UP (support, empathy, and truth in an atmosphere of understanding and perseverance) from earlier in this chapter and BIFF (brief, informative, friendly, and firm) if needed, but don't JADE (justify, argue, defend, or overexplain). After validating your child's feelings, ask them what the issue is. Be sure to tell them that they need to speak more softly and respectfully—be specific about what you want—before you can listen to them, because the way they're talking to you is making you uncomfortable, upset, and so forth.

Step 4. If your child's rage level doesn't go down, say, "I'm going to have to talk to you when things are calmer. (Or, if you've agreed on a timeout code word, which I suggest you do, use it.) Note how this phrasing takes advantage of passive construction. Don't say, "When *you* are calmer." When your child is aroused emotionally, avoid any kind of criticism or invalidation. If your child is safe without you, leave—go to another room, go to another floor, go outside to the garden, or take a drive to someplace fun.

Step 5. Your child will try to keep engaging you, so stay firm about waiting for your child to calm down: "We will talk about this in an hour." The timeframe is up to you, but remember that an hour is an eternity to them. Then leave.

Step 6. When your child is calm, talk about the issue that was tied to the raging. Ask questions. Perhaps it wasn't an event that triggered your child, but their *interpretation* of the event. For example, maybe someone ignored them at school or work, and they assumed the worst. If you can, coach them to think of alternative explanations. For example, "Have you considered that perhaps they didn't see you?" Now is the time to reward your child for calming down with positive words or maybe extra privileges, not to criticize them for the rage. Always give positive feedback when you can. If you had a limit and they didn't observe it, wait until the next day to discuss that during a problem-solving session.

Step 7. Congratulate yourself. When you take these steps, you are teaching your child to develop frustration tolerance, accountability for their actions (the rage), and self-soothing (they need to calm themselves without you). You are also teaching them that people everywhere will not be spoken to that way, including potential partners and coworkers. That's a lot of learning for just walking to another room or out the door. You're practicing good BPD-savvy parenting.

Setting Boundaries

If your child is an adult and living with you, I suggest your contingency be that, if their rage continues, they will have to leave the house. If their rage occurs on phone calls, hang up and don't talk with them on the phone

> anymore (or for a set period of time). If they rage again on the phone, double that set period of time. If they are a minor, their punishment can be no privileges—just three meals, a bedroom, and their homework checked every night.

To deal with rage attacks, parents should put on their detective hat and search for the unknown events or actions that led to their child's rage attack, if possible. Gather data on when the attacks occur and look for common factors or anything that seems to set off your child. You may also have no idea. Track these rage attacks as soon as possible after each one and write down what may have contributed to the attack, if you know—for example, you talked to your child right after work or school (Aguirre 2014).

> "The first step is prevention. Most importantly, BPD adolescents need to know which factors make them vulnerable to such [rage] events. Do these rages occur at night with lack of sleep? Under the influence of drugs? During arguments with certain friends? During final exams and high stress? Recognizing early signs of irritability and mood changes can be critical in preventing further escalation. In some ways, parents need to become scientists, noting data about these factors" (Aguirre 2014, 42).

Here are some other tips for dealing with a raging child:
- If your child is willing, you can teach them the relaxation skills you learned in chapter 6. When you notice them getting twitchy, suggest they use them.
- As you know, don't feed the disorder, or give in to your angry child when it's not in their best interest long term. Giving in will only encourage your child to pitch another fit the next time they want something.
- Consider medication. Talk to a psychiatrist specializing in BPD.
- Use distraction. Talk to your child about something that has nothing to do with what's going on or involve them in some activity. This must be done carefully because it can make them even madder. Sometimes a stupid pun or silly joke may help break up the tension.

Handling One Son's Rage

When my son is raging at me and screaming obscenities, I used to leave the house first thing. Now what I do first is validate, validate, validate. I tell him that I can see that he is terribly angry with me, and then I am quiet and let him talk. But if the rage has gone too far and validation hasn't worked,

> I just leave to give him time to regain control. He might break a few things, but at least he won't break *me!* Then later, I sit and listen to what he has to say in a calm way. If the situation ever escalated to physical violence, I would call the police as a last resort. I have never had to do that so far, but I would do it to protect myself.

Name Calling

If your child calls you names, constantly criticizes you, or says nasty things that you wouldn't tolerate from anyone else, you need to put a stop to it, for your child's sake as well as your own. If they learn that they can get away with treating you in this manner, you can bet they'll treat others the same way. Your child will not go far in life treating people poorly. When it comes to name calling and similar behavior, the "form before content" rule applies: do not acknowledge the content of communication that has poor form—in this case, where the form is abusive.

Even if you're a BPD-savvy parent, you might think that name calling, criticism, or general nastiness have no effect on you. That's not true. Feeling depressed, frustrated, confused, hopeless, and like you're a terrible parent, along with having a hard time taking care of yourself, are signs that your child's abuse (and yes, it is abuse) *is* having an effect on you. If your child is verbally abusive toward you, reread chapter 5, and promise yourself you'll try at least one of the self-care techniques, such as the loving-kindness meditation. You are at a fork in the road: the one labeled "self-care" leads to a better future, whereas the other, labeled "do nothing different," leads to a parental breakdown in which you have nothing left to give your child and you don't like being around them.

Paula: *I exhausted others with my search for help and support for my child with BPD. Health care professionals seemed to think I was handling it well. My child was very aggressive, and the professionals didn't understand the abuse I was suffering. No one ever asked me if I felt abused. Maybe I hid it well. There is an element of shame attached to admitting that you are the victim of parental abuse. It is an admission of inadequacy, of failure, of hopelessness. I feel very alone and I feel guilty, but for what? It doesn't make sense.*

After all, why can't I parent, since I see tons of others around me who seem (on the surface) to be doing a superb job? I think I carried a fear of judgment from my community (we lived in a small, affluent part of town). There was a certain expectation (standards) that permeated the environment. And even when I mentioned it to a counselor, they brushed the abuse aside. I even had one praise me for my stoicism. I think their focus was on child abuse, and they had little or no idea that parental abuse is a very real thing. And I'm still alone. Very alone.

If you feel alone, as Paula did, seek out the support of others. Don't face verbal abuse alone, and don't stand for it. You can use the steps outlined in the preceding section, or other techniques in this book, to deal with it.

CLINICIAN'S CORNER WITH DANIEL LOBEL

Your child communicates with you using both form and content. "Content" comprises the words they're speaking (for example, "Can I go out with my friends?"). "Form" is how politely and respectfully they speak to you (for example, not shouting, swearing, or name calling).

When a child is talking to you with unacceptable form, ignore the content and say, "When you're ready to discuss this in a calm tone of voice, we'll talk." If your child continues to act abusively, go to another room, go outside, drive away, or, if this happens all the time and your child is an adult who is very toxic, you could get a restraining order. These same guidelines apply to conversations over the phone. If you employ these methods continually without backing down, your child

> will be forced to vary their tone when they want or need something. (We're going to talk about limits in chapter 9.) Keep in mind that when it comes to communicating with your child, form always trumps content (2018).

Top Takeaways from This Chapter

We covered several helpful techniques in this chapter that can help you better communicate with your child with BPD. Remember, communication is where the relationship "happens." Study these communication methods until you have them down pat. You can't look at a book in the middle of a conversation, so *practice in advance* with someone you trust. With your child, start with a mild situation before moving on to a more complex one. When in doubt, or when things get heated, validate. You really can't do this too much. If validation were a word, it would be nearly as common as the word "the." When you need to make a point, use SET-UP. That should be your next most common tool. When you *really* need to make an important point (and probably need some action taken or not taken), use BIFF. Finally, don't JADE.

Here are some other key takeaways from this chapter to keep in mind as you continue on:

- Practice good communication skills.
- Don't invalidate your child. It's worse than doing nothing.
- Stay focused on your message. Repeat yourself if necessary. Use the "broken record" technique—repeating yourself over and over again.
- It's always "form before content." Tell them you will listen to them when they can discuss the matter in a calm way. If your child gets away with yelling at you, they may increase the frequency and intensity of these behaviors.

CHAPTER 8

BPD-Savvy Parenting Techniques Part I

Avoiding Enabling and Handling Fear, Obligation, and Guilt

It's Saturday, family day for the Anderson family: Pat and Joe and their children, Don, thirteen, and Amy, eleven, who has BPD. Last week, Amy got to choose the outing, a Disney movie. Don was looking forward to his choice because he thought the movie was sappy, although he sat through it anyway. "Today I want to go bowling," he happily declared, diving into his pancakes. His parents said yes. But Amy's eyes got stormy. Everyone looked at each other. They knew that facial expression.

"I don't want to go bowling," Amy bawled. "My arms aren't strong enough and everyone always beats me! I'm no good at that. Don just wants to do that because he's better than me." Her parents tried reasoning with her, and when that failed and Amy started to go into tantrum mode, her parents knew no one was going to go anywhere unless Amy got on board. "Don, can you pick something else, something

Amy wants to do too?" his mother asked. Don's face was expressionless. "Whatever," he mumbled.

"An eleven-year-old is running our household," Pat said to a friend a few days later. "It is always Amy's way. When she wants something, she backs us into a corner until we give her what she wants. Otherwise, there is absolutely no peace in the house. She is impossible to discipline. Traditional things like shutting off her allowance don't work. So giving into her demands is easier."

This story illustrates a key concept one must understand before they can become BPD-savvy parents. We call it "feeding the monster." Pat and Joe have become experts at "feeding the monster," which is the exact wrong way to parent a child with BPD. It's important to be clear that the "monster" is BPD itself, not the child.

CLINICIAN'S CORNER WITH DANIEL LOBEL

Children with BPD often tell their parents that they are bad parents. This is because the child holds the parent responsible for their happiness. Associated feelings of guilt often cause the parents to give in to their child against their better judgment. Or sometimes the parents give in because they are worn down by extensive conflict and mistreatment.

Capitulating to the unreasonable demands of a child's BPD—or feeding the monster—only causes the disorder to grow (2018).

How can you tell if you've been feeding the monster? Parents who feed the monster tend to have kids who exhibit the following characteristics:

Short tempers: This trait develops because parents don't let their child experience frustration by waiting for something. When they demand an answer right away or want something *now*, make them wait until it is convenient for you. This teaches them frustration tolerance.

Unusually aggressive: This characteristic develops because temper tantrums or rages in the past have gotten your child what they want. Remember the "form before content" rule. An aggressive approach (anger, tantrums) should never result in your child getting their way.

Little empathy: This characteristic develops because your child has never had to consider anyone else's feelings. For example, in the opening story, Amy doesn't consider her brother's feelings and the fact that it's his turn to choose an activity. It's up to you to stick to your limits and explain what it's like to be in another person's shoes.

Self-absorbed: This characteristic develops because your child has been allowed to always be the center of attention. Don't let your child hijack other people's celebrations (birthdays, weddings) and don't overreact to their bids for attention when they've done so in a negative way. For example, don't make a really big deal out of your child wearing inappropriate clothing to school. Discuss what is proper, but don't make what they've done a crisis because they're likely doing it to provoke you. Pay more attention to your child when they are acting in a neutral or positive way, which reinforces those behaviors.

Vulnerable: Your child is more fragile and more vulnerable to self-loathing and self-harm. This characteristic develops because they haven't had the opportunity to develop coping mechanisms such as self-soothing or flexibility. Deep down, they feel less competent because they doubt they can fend for themselves.

Least functional: In a similar vein, compared to children with BPD whose parents do not feed the monster, they are the least independent and the least functional. That's because they are so skilled at getting other people to do things for them that they can't do it on their own.

When the child with BPD sees that abusive or toxic behavior is successful in getting what they want, they will use the method more often.

This is the basic behavioral principle of positive reinforcement. In other words, the parents positively reinforce the behavior by giving in, which increases the frequency of the behaviors (tantrums, whining, pleading, rages). When you give in to your child's hurtful behavior, you greatly increase the chances that your child will use this behavior in the future as a primary tool to get their way.

But that's not the whole problem. The behavior will become more hurtful over time, while the parents' will to resist feeding the monster (BPD) will diminish. This downward spiral leaves parents feeling more and more helpless and hopeless, and ever closer to the breaking point when they no longer wish to spend time with their child, because everything associated with them is extremely painful.

There are four main techniques you can use to avoid feeding the monster. We'll discuss the first two—stop inadvertent enabling and don't be taken in by emotional blackmail—in this chapter, and the remaining two in chapter 9. With a firm grasp of these techniques, you can become a BPD-savvy parent and stop feeding the monster, which will help you and your child with BPD live fuller lives. Let's start with enabling.

Stop Inadvertent Enabling

Enabling is a way that parents prevent their child from dealing with the negative consequences of their actions. It's different than supporting, which is helping your child do something that they are incapable of doing for themselves, such as tying their shoelaces; or facilitating them in gaining control of their behaviors or life, such as encouraging them to go to therapy. Enabling is a form of feeding the monster because it prevents your child from learning from their mistakes. They don't mature and grow, develop a sense of accountability, or want to become independent because you—dear mom and dad—are there to get them out of trouble.

Enabled children are those who don't leave home, who don't get a job or who quit them, who marry someone who's willing to take care of them better than their parents, or whose parents worry that they will never get along on their own. *No good comes out of enabling your child.* Enabling is a one-way ticket to supporting that child financially and emotionally for the rest of your life—not to mention worrying about what's going to happen to them after you die. That may sound dramatic, but it's true.

Most children like feeling more and more independent as they grow older. But when you suggest to a child with BPD that they do something for themselves, they feel as if they're being pushed out of the nest only to fall thirty feet onto a flatbed truck full of manure. So they may complain, act like a victim, rage, tell you that you're a "bad parent," or otherwise mistreat you. All they know is that your request makes them feel bad, hence you must have caused it. Of course, that isn't true: you've triggered their fear of abandonment and rejection. The disorder caused this fear; you were merely the trigger and designated target of your child's emotions. So don't take it personally. If your child reacts negatively to you suggesting that they do something themselves, you're doing the right thing.

Parents should be able to guide their children in such a way that they're increasingly able to figure out how to be responsible for their life, and then gradually give them greater freedom as they prove they can handle greater responsibility (while still being able to ask for help). For example, if a teen is able to stick to the amount of screen time they're allotted, the parent can be more flexible when they need an extra thirty minutes for whatever reason.

> **Julie:** *My thirty-one-year-old son has lived on the streets. He has busked for a living. He has walked around looking disheveled all the time, all the while wanting to change the world with really good, progressive ideas that he just couldn't put together.*
>
> *Now he works full-time. Owns a car that he got on his own. Is able to hold a job, get up early, and all that. When one job didn't work out, he had another one within days. I couldn't believe it, because the "old" Rob would have been in bed for who knows how long if something didn't work out.*

I'm not saying things are perfect and normal. I am saying that there is hope. BPD to me is something that has to be managed, like diabetes. There is no instant fix. They will have their ups and downs. We all do—only theirs seem much bigger. Our job is to learn how to be the best emotional support without enabling. It's the hardest thing that I have ever had to learn how to do! I try to stay strong and stay hopeful with faith. And most of all, to love him and let him live his life his way.

A prime characteristic of a BPD-savvy parent is that they don't depend on their child with BPD for their feelings of self-worth—as either people or parents. Children with BPD have unstable perceptions of themselves (identity problems). When other people (particularly their parents) meet their needs, they see themselves as lovable. When other people don't meet their needs, they feel self-loathing. If you let your child's binary feelings about you affect how you feel about yourself, you will say yes to everything—even if it's bad for your child. You'll become an enabler and thus feed the monster. The same is true for emotional blackmail.

Don't Be Taken in by Fear, Obligation, and Guilt

Emotional blackmail is a powerful form of manipulation in which people close to us threaten, either directly or indirectly, to punish us if we don't do what they want. Many people with expertise in BPD would say that people with the disorder never manipulate; rather, they're only doing their best to survive. It is tough to separate your child from the disorder when they apply emotional blackmail.

Whatever the circumstances in your child's life, often they are experienced as a life-or-death struggle. So your child will pull out the big guns, a combination that Susan Forward terms FOG: fear, obligation, and guilt (1997). These are the tools of the emotional blackmailer, just as paint and brushes are the tools of the painter. The FOG can drift in, making everything cloudy, confusing you, and leading you to feed the monster. Your child may emotionally blackmail you purposely or unconsciously.

Here are some examples of emotional blackmail using fear, obligation, and guilt:
- You'll do this [not do this] if you love me.
- I thought you were a good parent, but I guess I was wrong.
- I'll cut my wrists if you don't do this for me.
- If you don't let me go, then you're for sure the crummiest parent on the face of the planet!
- My friend's parents would do this [wouldn't do this]. Why can't you be more like them?
- You owe me.
- How can you do this to your own child?

Kids with BPD who use emotional blackmail usually don't know a better way to get what they need. They use their knowledge of you—your hot buttons, vulnerabilities, and intimate details—to get what they feel they desperately need to feel safe and loved, and to not feel abandoned. If emotional blackmail is a major component of your relationship with your child, I recommend seeing a therapist and reading Forward's book, *Emotional Blackmail: When the People in Your Life Use Fear, Obligation, and Guilt to Manipulate You*.

When it comes to dealing with the emotional blackmailer who is your child with BPD, Forward recommends the following tactics (1997).

Stall: Don't make quick decisions, no matter how much your child is pressuring you. Now is the time to bring forth your diaphragmatic (or belly) breathing, because neither you nor your child will find the delay easy. To give yourself some breathing room, you might say:

- I need some time to think about this.
- I don't have an answer for you right now.
- Let's discuss this a little later.
- I'm not sure how I feel about this. I need some time to think.
- You're asking an important question. I want to give it the thought that it deserves.
- I need to talk to your father.

Your child will want to know how much time you need to make a decision. If you're not sure, answer, "As long as it takes." If you do know, add some cushion to that timeframe, both for your sake and to help your child develop a tolerance for frustration. If the issue they've brought up has an actual deadline, make sure it's real. *Time is on your side.*

Research: Do some information gathering about the request, if needed. Consider the following:
- Was the request made in a respectful way?
- Is it good for your child?
- Are they emotionally and intellectually prepared for this?
- Have they done something like this before? If so, how did that turn out?
- Will you be available by phone if something goes wrong?
- Will there be other dependable people there, people you don't know, or people you don't think are a good match for your child?
- Will this help teach your child something valuable, like independence or accountability?

Inform your child of your decision: Do so nondefensively, anticipating their response if your decision is counter to what they want. Validate their disappointment first. If you need to, use the communication strategy SET-UP (support, empathy, and truth in an atmosphere of understanding and perseverance). If you're still not getting your message across, use the stronger

BIFF method (brief, informative, friendly, and firm). Don't JADE (justify, argue, defend, or overexplain). (All of these strategies are covered in chapter 7.) If you need to, walk away. Leave the room or house if you have to.

> **Amrita:** At age five, my son Dev had symptoms of BPD. The pediatrician said to lock him in his room, and he destroyed his room. By high school, things were so bad we homeschooled him.
>
> When he was fourteen, I saw a therapist. She said, "You can't control another person." I said, "You must be crazy, because that flies in the face of everything I have been taught of what a parent is supposed to do—control their kids." She said, "You can't control another person, and that's what is making you crazy. You can't fix or rescue anyone either. As long as your peace and happiness are based on another person, you have no control over your peace and happiness."
>
> Things changed. Not with him, but with me.
>
> Our son now struggles with addiction. He lives on the streets. It's a long story, but we can't permit him to live at home, and he won't go to sober living. We looked up every resource in the city for him and gave him a long list. It was very important that we did that for our peace of mind. But he chooses not to use them. I had to quit letting my son be a razor

hanging over my head, and to know that if he dies, it was from his choices.

When it got cold, one day he called and asked for his winter coat. I brought it to him where he was waiting on some intersection, and he looked dirty and disheveled. It just about killed me to not bring him home. He said he would commit suicide before going to sober living. But he has been using that as emotional blackmail for a long time. I said, "Dad and I can't give you what you need at home. Call the numbers I gave you. You need more structure, and we don't like playing the warden." Then I got home and sobbed.

We made the right choice. Three days later he called and said he would either go to sober living or jail on outstanding warrants. He learned—really learned—that we were not going to rescue him like we usually did, and he had broken bridges with every friend.

To get to this point, I listened to codependency books on tape instead of panicking and worrying, read about detaching with love, and joined a support group for parents of addicted children so I didn't feel alone. I have an excellent therapist and I take antidepressants. I paint watercolors and acrylics. I submit my fiction to writing contests. It helps to have something else I have a commitment to. I also have a blog.

He could die because of what he is choosing. Or he could really work at it this time and have a great life. We will see. Maybe this time he will make it.

We've covered the basics of what emotional blackmail entails, as well as tactics for dealing with your child when you feel like you're being manipulated. Let's take a closer look at the elements of FOG (fear, obligation, guilt). Because these are the weapons employed in emotional blackmail, it's a good idea to shed some light on them.

Feeling Fearful

Boy, do parents of kids with BPD have a lot of fears:
- Fear their child will commit suicide
- Fear of the effects their child with BPD will have on siblings
- Fear that their child will never have a normal life full of real love and happiness
- Fear that their child will end up addicted to some substance or in jail
- Fear of putting their foot down and observing limits
- Fear that they are bad parents who caused their child's BPD
- Fear that they're abandoning their child, combined with fear that they're doing too much for their child

- Fear that their child will never be able to live independently and take care of themself
- Fear that the child will alienate extended family who might have cared for them
- Fear that their child will self-harm
- Fear that their child won't graduate from high school
- Fear that they'll give up on their child
- Fear of losing a say in their child's treatment when they turn eighteen, or of not being informed about their treatment
- Fear for their grandchildren, who may not be living in a good environment or who may be neglected or emotionally abused
- Fear of being emotionally or physically abused with no one to help them or take them seriously
- Fear that their marriage won't survive
- Fear that their child will not learn to be loving and compassionate
- Fear for their own mental health
- Fear that their child won't be able to get or keep a job and will end up homeless
- Fear that their child will become pregnant or get a sexually transmitted disease
- Fear that their child will not be independent before they die, and that the burden of taking care of that child will pass on to siblings

Surely most of these fears resonate, and you carry some of them with you a lot of the time. If you carried all of them in your head all of the time, you'd never get anything done. Dwelling on fear, anxiety, and worry will not make it less likely that your fears come true. What fear *will* do is activate the stress response we described in chapter 5. During the stress response, cortisol and adrenaline flood your brain, and, as explained in chapter 5, living in a constant state of stress can make you physically and mentally sick. So what can you do to manage your fears?

As hard as it is, radical acceptance is the best way forward (see chapter 5). Radical acceptance takes time—maybe even years. Just keep getting on the radical acceptance highway and remind yourself that you did not cause it, cannot control it, and cannot cure it—whatever "it" is. As much as you love your child, you cannot be at the wheel in control of their life. They own their car and can drive too fast and run through stop signs.

Here's another exercise that you can practice to rein in your fear:

> Imagine the worst possible outcome for your child with BPD. Write it down on a piece of paper, and how you'd handle it. Keep in mind that, however much this outcome would traumatize you, you would survive this. You'd have no other choice. Now, consider what you can do for your child, perhaps jotting it down. For example,

you *can* be an advocate for your child, and, if they agree, try to find them the best treatment possible.

Concentrate on what you can do for your child, not on what you can't do. This mind-set will help ward off your fears.

Feeling Obligated

Jessica: *I'm exhausted by the sheer number of angles my twenty-one-year-old son takes to get something from us. He said his car broke down and he needed $300 to fix it. We said we would pay half. Then we found out his car was just fine. Big argument. Two months later it was like it never happened. He begged us for a security deposit to move into an apartment because he couldn't stay with friends anymore. We didn't want him living on the streets, so we paid it directly to the landlord. We spent a lot of time crafting a letter setting strong, detailed boundaries, including paying back the $300, what we will give him, what he will take care of, and so forth. Now he emails us again to help him pay for car insurance because it's hard to get when you've had three accidents and two speeding tickets in a year. My husband told him we'd help him before talking to me. He thinks it's "our duty." When does it stop? Does it ever stop? I'm exhausted.*

Parents feel obliged to do a lot for their children with BPD—things they would never do for healthier siblings. As a result, they end up feeding the monster. Your obligation, as a parent, is to do your best to raise your child to live independently in the world so that they can pursue a job, engage in healthy relationships, afford a place to live, and so on.

Keep in mind that while your child is growing up, part of your responsibility is to help them learn how to handle daily life, like handling money, cleaning up after themself, and so forth. However, once your child is an adult, you are not obliged to let them live with you, give them money, clean up their messes, do their laundry, listen to how you wrecked their lives, drive them everywhere because they lost their license or totaled their car, or let them smoke pot in your house. Obligation is one of the weapons that kids of any age can use to try to blackmail you; only you have the power to unarm them—by not giving in to your sense of obligation when it seems that you're being manipulated.

Feeling Guilty

The final element of FOG is guilt, something we're all too familiar with—but especially parents who have a child with BPD. Let's do a simple exercise that explores different forms of guilt to see if we can put our guilt into a useful

perspective. Divide a sheet of paper into four columns and add the following heads to each:
1. Things I feel guilty about that never were under my control
2. Things in the past that I feel guilty about and cannot change
3. Free-floating guilt I cannot pin to a source, or guilt on steroids
4. Things I am doing now that make me feel guilty

Once you have your columns set up, start filling them in with all the things you feel guilty about. For example, column 1 might include "invalidating my child before I knew they had BPD." Column 2 might include "an ex-partner who may have contributed to the development of my child's disorder." Column 4 might have "worrying about the effect of BPD behavior on their sister." The columns may overlap a bit, and that's okay.

Now have a look at your list. Feeling guilty about anything in columns 1 through 3, no matter how justified you believe your guilt is, is detrimental to your child. First and foremost, such guilt leads to you feeding the monster—enabling your child or giving in to emotional blackmail. Secondly, this guilt robs you of time and energy you could use for problem solving the guilt items found in column 4—the only problems you really can do something about. You need to protect the energy that's required for the creativity, research, and out-of-the-box thinking you need to solve these problems. The guilt items in columns 1 through 3 also rob you of time and energy you could spend with your child or their sibling, or on practicing self-care.

What if this exercise draws forth something huge for you? What if you really did something to feel guilty about? How are you to find perspective on such guilt? Consider Gayle's story.

I am guilty for allowing physical, emotional, and mental trauma to happen to my son—by his father—and for being apathetic during his childhood, therefore undermining his feelings. I handle my guilt by changing my parenting style to help undo what was done and regain his trust. I've learned how to "pause" as a way of coping, because sometimes it's overwhelming. The guilt is still there, but I know that I'm doing all I can, so it's not as strong as it was some years ago.

In hindsight, Gayle may have done the wrong thing when her child was young, but how many years should she remain in "parent jail" before she forgives herself? Gayle's story doesn't belong in group 4, "things I am doing now that make me feel guilty." It belongs in group 2, "things in the past that I feel guilty about and cannot change." Parents make mistakes, and Gayle made mistakes *before* she knew her child had BPD. She can't change those mistakes, but she can choose to change her parenting in the present—which she's doing.

As you reflect on the types of guilt you feel, remember that there is so much information (books, websites, blogs, videos) about BPD available today, that there are established treatment methods that have been proven effective, and that there are numerous nonprofit organizations available to help you (see appendix C). When *Stop Walking on Eggshells* came out in 1998, most of this didn't exist. If your child was diagnosed with BPD then, there would have been *no one* to help you. Now there are clinicians who specialize in it, as well as parent support groups. So instead of dwelling on the past that you can't change, focus on the good and the present moment; you will feel better.

Hope: *I was at my daughter's school and a bunch of kids were preparing for their senior year. I talked to a few of the parents I knew and went home and cried. I felt like such a failure as a parent because my experience was so different. The next day we had a retreat at work, and I shared a room with someone I knew, but not well. She started talking about one of her daughters who had put her through years of hell. I asked, "Does she have BPD?" and the answer was yes. And I lost it, because it felt like this huge weight lifted off my shoulders. I'm not saying I've never made mistakes, but I felt all my self-blame melting away.*

Parenting Techniques from Savvy Parents

Cassie: What I have learned is, Don't try to do this alone. My son had two major meltdowns back-to-back. Each time I had to radically accept that I could not handle this alone. I trusted that the professionals at the hospital could handle him better than I could. When he was gone, I practiced self-care and wrote up a list of house rules he had to agree to. This way there would be no back-and-forth between us.

The next day when he called to ask if he could come home, I said yes, but only if he agreed to follow the house rules. He agreed. Surprisingly, he has been following them 85 percent of the time for three months. I feel better knowing I will no longer be ashamed to call for help, because it helps me support him and it helps him get the help he needs. I will no longer try to do this all on my own.

Isabella: For myself, first I had to radically accept that my daughter was different. Second, with DBT and lots of research, I found more effective ways to communicate that reduced conflict. Third, I accepted that my child has emotions on steroids and that she is going to overreact to everything; she can't help that. And third, if none of that works, pretend an alien has invaded your child's body and that that is who you are dealing with.

Paula: We don't use the word no—it's a big trigger for anger. We have found other ways of saying it, like "That's very expensive, I'm not sure we can afford it," or "That would be better to do in the summer—it's freezing this week." Or we get our daughter to think about things overnight to see if it's still a good idea (she's impulsive).

Mei: I use humor a lot. When my daughter asks for something unrealistic or expensive, I typically respond with "Marry rich" or "When did we become the Kardashians?" This approach works okay for us when she's asking for things or slacking on her chores and homework.

Christine: I found that making things conversational rather than making a request gets better results. Instead of "Go clean up the dishes," I say, "Hey are you busy? Can you help me with the dishes?" It makes my daughter feel she has a choice rather than just "Mom says do this."

Tamara: Patience has helped. I consider it my most advantageous quality. I have a lot of it. I also have a very accepting nature.

Jean: I model self-compassion for my kids. When I make a mistake, I do not criticize myself or call myself "stupid." This communicates the idea that self-criticism is not a valued and an appropriate response—it *actually makes things worse. I don't want my child with BPD to develop an inner critic any more than BPD gives her.*

Bella: *Don't take your child's behavior personally. Depressed, anxious, and impulsive kids in overwhelming pain do and say many hurtful things. Even though you are the target, this is usually more about their pain than it is about you. Take a few deep breaths and separate the disorder from your child. Slowly repeat to yourself,* My love is deeper than your pain, *and respond to your child as calmly as you can.*

Top Takeaways from This Chapter

Have you ever been to a farm where you can pet the animals, and as soon as you feed one sheep or goat all the others come running? When you run out of feed, they greedily sniff your pockets and lick your hand until the next person with food comes along. The animals have been positively reinforced to run up to people, something the animal probably wouldn't do in its natural environment.

That very principle of positive reinforcement is at work when you feed the monster. Your child wants more, and they run to the person who has something to offer. Over and over again they will perform the behavior that got them what they wanted in the past. So, you have to be very careful about what kind of behavior you reward. If you're a BPD-savvy parent, you'll positively reinforce *desired* behavior, such as getting good grades and setting the table, and *not* having a meltdown or punching a hole in the wall. Both you and your child will come out winners.

Here are some other key takeaways from this chapter to keep in mind:

- You need to learn to forgive yourself. Carrying guilt about things that you can't control or that happened in the past is inhibiting your good parenting, not helping it.
- You and your child are on opposite sides of the autonomy and independence issues: you want them to develop those two attributes, whereas they see your efforts to instill these qualities as you abandoning or rejecting them. This dynamic makes it harder to not feed the monster with enabling or emotional blackmail. Reassure them in other ways, such as through validation and by spending time together, among others. Even though your child was scared of going to first grade, and you weren't happy about being apart from them, you still made them go because you had their long-term well-being at stake. You knew that this was a crucial first step in your child gaining independence. Toeing the line with a child with BPD is more challenging, but you must encourage them to spread their wings

(and support them when they do), even if they'd rather sit in the nest and wait for you to bring them worms. Otherwise, how will they ever know they can fly?

CHAPTER 9

BPD-Savvy Parenting Techniques Part 2

Limit Setting and Problem Solving

In the last chapter, we introduced the concept of feeding the monster (the monster being BPD, not your child). Parents feed the monster when they give in to their child against their better judgment to avoid any of the following (Lobel 2018, 88):
- Mistreatment
- Conflict
- Feelings of guilt and inadequacy
- Being shamed in public

In chapter 8 we discussed two vital techniques to ensure you don't feed your child's disorder:
1. stopping inadvertent enabling, and
2. not being taken in by emotional blackmail and its triad of tools—fear, obligation, and guilt, or FOG.

In this chapter, we're going to cover two others:

1. setting and consistently enforcing limits (boundaries), and
2. helping your child problem solve so they can do things for themselves.

Setting Limits

Children with BPD, with their changing identities and shifting moods, need limits, structure, rules, and expectations—even if your child doesn't initially follow them. Setting limits and telling your child what those limits are allows you to state your views clearly, avoid battles about things you can't control, and back up your views with consequences and rewards when possible.

Unconditional love does *not* mean unconditional tolerance. Always keep that in mind.

Azumi: *Setting boundaries and following through was one of the biggest challenges I ever had. I read about how it needed to happen, but when it came down to it, I failed again and again. I thought, What if she cuts herself? What if she attempts suicide again? What if she runs away? What I found instead was a child that desperately needed me to be consistent. I thought by enabling her I was keeping her safe and loved, when what she saw was a mom who didn't care what her daughter did because she "got away" with anything.*

Was setting limits easy? Absolutely not! It took a good month of fighting, yelling, crying, and talking to her to understand that I loved her too much to continue parenting her out of fear. We both now have a clear, expected understanding of rules and consequences.

Rewards and Consequences

Just about every parent of a child with BPD who we've interviewed tells us that punishments have no effect on their child. This is probably because the unwanted behavior is part of the mental illness. Expecting punishment to extinguish borderline behavior is like expecting punishment to extinguish manic episodes in those who have bipolar disorder. You can't prevent a manic episode through punishment, but, using rewards and consequences, you can try to affect what they do (or don't do) once they're having an episode. In the same way, you can't stop your child from feeling what they feel by using punishment, but you can have an effect on the damage they cause themselves, their relationships, and property when they have those feelings.

So, when it comes to setting limits for your child, think in terms of *rewards* and *consequences* rather than punishments. If your child proves trustworthy in a certain arena, then you can trust them with more important things. If they abuse your trust, there should be consequences, such as not allowing activities that require a high degree of trust. For example, if your teenager meets their curfew for a certain length of time, reward them with a later curfew. If they do the opposite, don't let them go out at night or set an earlier curfew. The specifics are up to you. Just as each child has unique DNA, so too do they have a unique bundle of rewards and consequences that matter to them.

Of course, you need to take control of the rewards and consequences, which you can do much of the time as a parent. For example, if you pay for your child's phone, you can close the account or take it away. The stronger and more numerous the rewards and consequences are, the better. Notice the behavior when your child of any age does something you like; for example, remembering to take the garbage out. Also be sure to acknowledge positive behaviors, such as remarking on when your child dresses in appropriate school attire. Everyone likes to feel that when they do something right, it gets noticed. It also makes the person more likely to do more of these good behaviors.

Use Genuine Positive Reinforcement

People with BPD are terrified of abandonment, which often makes them feel the need to do anything they can to get attention—and if positive attention is hard to come by, children with BPD may have learned that acting out is the more reliable way to get what they need (Aguirre 2014). So, it is of utmost importance that you catch your child doing something positive and reward them for it. You can also reward them for changing a negative behavior. Just noticing the behavior and saying thank you with a smile is a great starting point. Make sure your body language (facial expressions, tone of voice, posture) matches what you're saying, and give them your full attention. If your child isn't doing anything positive, reward them for neutral behavior. Here are some examples of rewards:

- A hug and a "Thank you," "I'm proud of you," "Great job," and so forth (use specific details to show that you really noticed what they did)
- Extra time to spend with people they like or to do something they like to do
- Add an extra half hour to curfew
- Cook a favorite meal or go to a favorite restaurant
- More access to the car
- Longer sleep time on the weekend
- Extended screen time
- Movie night
- Something new for their room
- Concert tickets
- Having friends over for a sleepover
- New clothes
- Gold stars on a calendar
- An app

- A game

When your child tries to get attention by doing unwanted behaviors, pay minimal attention to these and don't overreact—as long as your child isn't in danger or putting anyone else in danger. Sometimes it's obvious that they're acting in a bothersome way purely to get attention from you, such as dressing inappropriately for a family function. Their intention is to get a rise out of you, embarrass you, and argue when you ask them to change their behavior. In this example, you might point out to the child that they may feel embarrassed dressed as they are, but then let them choose how to dress for themself. If you choose to not react, they'll be less likely to try to get attention that way in the future.

The Limit-Setting Process

Setting limits is a *process*, not something you do once. You never can tell what your child might do, but some things are rather predictable. So don't wait until there's a crisis; anticipate what your child might do and set limits beforehand. The following steps will walk you through the limit-setting process. Do this planning process with your spouse when you have quiet time and privacy. You may need to *make* time for this.

Identify Your Limits

Determine what your limits are, both large and small. Your limits should be tied closely to your needs, values, and wants, along with what is best for the whole family. Your number-one priority should be safety in your home for yourself, other children, and your child with BPD. If your child is disruptive, aggressive, or demonstrates risky behavior, you have to carefully pick your battles. You want to avoid a power struggle about anything that's less than critical. Don't make your initial limits too difficult. You want your child to have some early success to build on.

To create the safest environment for everyone, you might consider some of these limits:
- No physical aggression in the house
- No bringing strangers to the house without permission
- No discussions of inappropriate topics around younger siblings
- No illegal substances or alcohol in the home
- No emotional, verbal, or physical abuse of any kind
- No going into someone else's room without their permission

Once you're clear on the scope of the limits you want to address, it's time to consider rewards and consequences.

Set Rewards and Consequences

First, consider the rewards you can give your child for hewing to a limit you've set—or for doing any positive behavior you'd like to reinforce. For example, if your daughter washes the dishes five nights this week, thank her each time. If she avoids getting into a fight with her brother for two weeks, you might take her to a restaurant of her choice as a reward. And the rewards can grow in size, as the limits prove more challenging. For example, if your son struggles with physically violent outbursts and he's managed to avoid them for a month, you could reward him with something that's really important to him.

You also need to come up with appropriate consequences for your child when they don't observe a limit. Whenever possible, consequences should flow naturally from the limit. For example, if your child lies, the result should be that you no longer trust them. That will be a bummer for them when they want you to trust them with something. Or, if they're not at the designated pick-up spot after school when they said they would be, and you had to wait fifteen minutes for them, no more picking them up. When the child doesn't comply with the parent, the parent doesn't have to comply with the child.

Consequences should be appropriate for the infraction and the age of your child, and should be spelled out in advance whenever possible.

They can be a privilege you take away, chores they can do, or something else important to your child. You might want to give your child an allowance for no other reason than being able to use it as leverage. You're going to need to "observe" (or enforce) the limits you set every single time, so make the consequence something big enough to matter, but not so big that you're not willing to implement it at 10p.m. even when you have work the next day.

Plan for Countermoves

Countermoves take place when your child tests your limits or acts even worse to make sure you're serious about a consequence and will really follow through. For example, you ask your child to shut the front door and they do—by slamming it as hard as possible. You should plan for *when* countermoves occur, not *if* they occur. Keep in mind that the maturity that you're endeavoring your child to internalize feels like abandonment to them. So expect to go two steps forward and one step back.

Of course, the minute you set a limit, you child is going to test it to make sure you really mean it. For example, if curfew is at 11p.m. and they usually drift in at mindnight, after you've set a limit, they will come in a 1a.m. This is why you have gone through the limit-setting process. You have already outlined what the consequence will be, considered what they might do in response, and planned for various eventualities.

This limit testing is so universal that it has a name: "countermoves" or "change back" behaviors. In her book *The Dance of Anger,* a book that mentions the need to set limits, Harriet Lerner writes:

> "Making a change, however, never occurs easily and smoothly. We meet with a countermove or 'Change back!' reaction from the other person whenever we begin to give up the old ways of silence, vagueness, or ineffective fighting and begin to make clear statements about the needs, wants, beliefs, and priorities of the self. In fact, Murray Bowen, the originator of Bowen Family Systems Theory, emphasizes the fact that in all families there is a powerful opposition to one member defining a more independent self. According to Bowen, the opposition invariably goes in successive steps:
> 1. 'You are wrong,' with volumes of reasons to support this.
> 2. 'Change back and we will accept you again.'
> 3. 'If you don't change back, these are the consequences,' which are then listed...
>
> Countermoves are the other person's unconscious attempt to restore a relationship to its prior balance or equilibrium, when anxiety about separateness and change gets too high ... Our job is to keep clear about our own position in the

face of a countermove—not to prevent it from happening or to tell the other person that he or she should not be reacting that way. Most of us want the impossible. We want to control not only our own decisions and choices but also the other person's reactions to them. We not only want to make a change; we also want the other person to like the change that we make. We want to move ahead to a higher level of assertiveness and clarity and then receive praise and reinforcement from those very people who have chosen us for our old familiar ways" (2014, 34–35).

Talk with Your Child

Once you and your spouse have landed on some limits, rewards, and consequences, sit down with your child and—together, using plain, simple language—write down the limits, some of the more formal rewards, and the consequences. Discuss the limits and consequences with your child, as well as the rewards for compliance. If they come up with what you feel is a reasonable compromise, consider implementing it instead. For example, you might want your child to get a B in math class, but the two of you negotiate that, in exchange for getting a higher grade in English class, they can get a C in math. Put the written contract in a place where everyone can see it, such as on the refrigerator. Both parents and the child should sign the contract.

Observe Your Limit

When your child observes your limit, give them positive reinforcement, such as a genuine smile and a thank you. This can motivate your child to keep acting that way. Rewards have been known to lead to your child exceeding your expectations. For example, they might set the table four days instead of three. When your child wants to do something outside the limits you've set, point right to them.

As you probably know, when you have a child with BPD you're always waiting for the other shoe to drop. Sometimes, children with BPD sabotage themselves when things start to get too good. They worry that if they seem too self-sufficient, you'll walk away (Lobel 2018). Be aware of this tendency. Be excited for their accomplishments, but not *too* excited.

If your child doesn't observe the limit, implement the consequences *every single time*. Your ability to observe limits and withstand countermoves will make or break your ability to succeed at setting not just this limit, but also any future limits. If you show that you're not serious about limits, your child won't take them seriously. This is why it's so crucial to think carefully and choose consequences that (1) will have an effect and that (2) you will observe every time.

When your child transgresses a limit, which they will, remain calm. Take a deep belly breath.

Relax your muscles. Using BIFF (and possibly SET-UP and validation later), remind them of the limit and the consequence (both in writing); this should be a natural consequence for overstepping a limit. Try not to sound judgmental or critical. They already feel self-loathing. You don't want to add to that. You'll get a chance to talk about the incident later when things are calm. The best policy is to simply explain the connection between your child's behavior and the consequence.

Setting Limits—An Example

Let's look at an example of how two parents went through the process of setting limits for their daughter. After reading our recommendation for a zero-tolerance policy for abuse, Irina and her husband, Paul, decided they needed to set a limit for their thirteen-year-old daughter Miranda. She had recently screamed at her mother: "Why did you have to be my mother? I hate you! I wish Dad had married someone else!" So, the limit was easily identified: form before content. Miranda needed to speak to her mother in a respectful way.

Set rewards and consequences: Irina and Paul decided to reward Miranda with a smile, and perhaps a thank you, whenever she treated her mother respectfully. As for consequences, Miranda's most prized possession was her cell phone, which her parents paid for. They decided that reducing its function (they could remotely limit the phone to only call them or 911) was the ultimate consequence. They decided that they would reduce its function for one week. If Miranda spoke disrespectfully to her mother again in that timeframe, and reminding her of the limit with SET-UP or BIFF didn't change her attitude, they'd add another day to the consequence.

Plan for countermoves: Irina and Paul knew that Miranda would try to enlist her grandmother (Paul's mother) to soften or eliminate the punishment. So, they called Grandma, explained what was happening, and received her assurance of noninterference.

Talk with your child: They asked Miranda to talk to them. She was wary that she'd done something wrong and was going to be punished, or that her parents had bad news to give her. When it turned out that they wanted to discuss how she spoke to her mother, she was relieved. She thought that "taking her phone" was *way* overdoing it, but due to her BPD Miranda isn't able to put herself in her parents' shoes to feel what it must be like to be spoken to so harshly. They explained that if she disrespected her mother again, another day would be added to the consequence. She signed the contract and they put it up on the refrigerator.

Miranda broke the agreement later that night when she yelled at her mother.

Observe your limit: Irina decided to call Paul into the living room so he could back her up. She informed him of what had taken place.

Using SET-UP, they reminded her of the agreement. Miranda, of course, erupted. Paul reminded her, "If you continue this, we're adding another day to the consequence." Miranda went silent and ran to her room and slammed the door.

This scene repeated itself several more times during the week, adding several more days to the term of the consequence. When she signed the limit agreement, Miranda hadn't realized how difficult reining in her temper would be. Her parents offered to go through dialectical behavior therapy (DBT) skills training (via videos and workbooks) together, or to give her other tools to help her soothe herself when she got upset. They offered this several times before Miranda said yes. Setting and maintaining the limit wasn't easy; it wasn't fun. But going through the process gave them something they didn't have before: influence.

Limit-Setting Tips from BPD-Savvy Parents

Idina: *We make our daughter earn her privileges daily, using labor as a consequence. For example, if she doesn't clean up her dishes and food trash from the living room before she goes to bed, she has dish duty the following day. Making her do something in response to her bad choices has been effective.*

Alessya: My daughter responds much better to incentives than punishment. The trick is to find their currency, what dangling carrot will motivate them. I set limits and behavior expectations, and set consequences for when said behavior doesn't occur. Period. It does work. Why? Because I don't take crap, I don't waver, I follow through, and I'm the boss, not my children.

Zoey: After we caught our daughter with pot, we put together a written agreement that we could search her room, phone, or backpack any unexpected time. She could have gone to jail.

More Parenting Techniques from Savvy Parents

Josefina: We have one-on-one dates once a month, with both girls. We go to lunch or dinner, their pick. Then we go shopping or to an activity of their choice, so they can spend their allowance money. We also make dinner at home together every Thursday, have regular movie and game nights, and do some kind of activity at home one-on-one, weekly. It's usually some kind of art project. That way we make sure both girls have our attention.

Susan: I call out my daughter's lies, every single one, big or small, and explain why *it's harmful behavior for both her and the person involved.*

Sam: *The most valuable thing for my own sanity was realizing that my daughter's emotions were her own emotions. I didn't need to be part of the roller coaster ride, and the less emotional I am, the quicker she calms down. I tell myself that if I, as an experienced adult, can't control my own emotions, how can I expect my hormonal, mentally ill teenager to manage hers?*

Juan: *I have had some success by creating a daily schedule of sorts. When my child gets depressed, I put together a basic list like showering, eating, and tidying as you go. When she feels better, I plan on adding activities like baking, walking our dog, anything outside, or coloring (you can find phone apps). Luckily, my child likes to write, take photos, and do art. You can do an online search for "borderline personality disorder" and either "art" or "poems" and get a tremendous amount of material.*

Problem Solving

Your child probably comes to you with many problems that other children their age without BPD could probably learn to fix themselves. But your child spends a lot of time in survival- and pain-management modes and hasn't learned enough problem-solving skills. Work with them through problem-solving steps enough so that they learn how to solve problems on their own, but not so much that they fear you're not going to help them again.

Step 1. Determine from them what kind of help they need. When your child asks for help, ask what the issue is and what kind of help they want. For example, do they want you to listen, give advice, or help them figure out what to do? If your child is too emotional to answer, validate them: "It may seem like things seem hopeless right now, but when you get to the point where we can sit down and talk about it, I'll do my best to help you." Wait until they are ready and communicate your belief that it's okay to feel lost right now, and that they can and will get control of themselves in their own time: "I've seen you do this before."

You may or may not want to be involved in your child's problem, or only be involved up to a certain point. For example, if your child's having financial problems, you may want to limit your involvement. You can explain that they can call creditors to set up payment plans, but refuse to make those calls yourself. Your child may propose a compromise, such as listening in on the phone call and giving feedback.

Step 2. Ask questions. If they're looking for more than just listening and validation, ask enough questions to assess what's going on. Keep in mind that your ultimate goal is not to solve this one problem, but to help them learn how to problem solve for themselves. Show them how you approach problems. Perhaps you break big problems down into smaller pieces, so share this method with them. *Make sure you are getting the whole story.* Some children with BPD tend to omit details that make them look bad. Without that information, the information you do receive may be useless.

Melania: *I was taught that when focusing on problem solving, family members should assume that their child has good intentions unless shown otherwise, that there is no one truth, and that everyone is doing the best they can—although things could improve.*

Ask your child what the desired outcome would look like. Does the problem have an interpersonal component (involving a relationship), involve following a number of steps (like getting the heat turned back on), or have components of both? If your child can't describe the problem or what the solution would look like, do what you can to help clarify things. You might ask what the main problem is and then break it down into smaller, more manageable pieces. Remember, you can't solve a problem you don't understand.

Step 3. Brainstorm and troubleshoot solutions with your child. People approach different kinds of problems in different ways. Some problems take time to solve, are delicate, and involve other people, whereas others need firmness, research, and promptness. If your child has problems coming up with solutions, find something good to say about the ones they do come up with, even if they won't ultimately work. Help them think through the risks and rewards for each possible solution. But make sure *they* are accepting responsibility for the solution, not you. You advise, they decide. Otherwise, they may blame you if the solution fails.

Reward their effort and tell them you have faith in them, which will lead to more effort and eventually better solutions. Shari Manning, author of *Loving Someone with Borderline Personality Disorder*, writes:

> Telling your loved one you have faith in her may be a little helpful but not sufficient. In reality, only the repetition of solving problems with success will breed confidence. Remember also that if you give in and solve the problem for her, you are undermining her confidence in the long run. If the problem is something like going to a bank or calling someone, you might offer to be with her but tell her she is going to do all the talking. If the problem is at work or somewhere that you cannot be, you could offer to role-play the situation. (2011, 141)

Look at the pros and cons of various solutions and anticipate the different possibilities that could occur. These are things you know intuitively, but your child may not. Between the two of you, decide on a course of action. Your level of activity in this decision making depends upon the problem, your child's age and abilities, and what's at stake.

Step 4. Define your role. Do you have a place in the plan for solving the problem, or is your child going to get back to you after they've attempted to resolve it. You may discover that your child lacks confidence in their ability. You may wish to coach them a bit, but don't take over. Manning writes:

> Don't withhold a solution to the problem if you have it ... but don't try to "fix" things without asking if your help is wanted. Don't say anything you don't mean sincerely. Don't say, "We need to..." Say instead, "Would it be helpful for you to...?" This puts the onus on your loved one. Communicate your hope and belief in your child's ability to get in control. (2011, 111)

Choices Can Be Game Changers

Everybody loves choices. Even if you always want a chocolate ice-cream cone if you go for a treat, you still like the thought that you could get one of those weird new flavors, if you felt like it. Children love choices too, because so many people—teachers, friends, and yes, parents—are telling them what to do.

For example, let's say you need your three-year-old to get into the car right now, but he doesn't want to leave the party. He wants to be the last one to go. You have a different agenda. So you ask him, "Do you want to hop, skip, or run to the car?" You've changed the game. Instead of, "Get in the car now or you're in big trouble, mister!" you've offered a choice. Your child forgets that he didn't want to go to the car and considers which method of getting there would be the most fun.

Using another example, it's time for your ten-year-old to get dressed, but she's delaying. You could ask, "Do you want to dress up, wear old clothes, or wear something of mine?" That's an intriguing choice for many children, especially the part about wearing something of yours, which could be a scarf, a watch, or a necklace. Again, you've changed the game.

Let's say your adult child lives at your home with his two kids. Extra people means extra work, and you want him to do some of the work. You might consider offering him a choice: "Do you want to vacuum the house, clean the bathroom, or do the laundry?" If you really want him to do a particular task, offer choices that make the thing you want done the most desirable choice. Also, since nobody really likes to do housework, you might offer a reward once the job is done, such as going out for coffee or ice cream, or whatever your adult child likes.

Giving choices can get more challenging as children get older, especially with teenagers, who think they know everything, or with adults, who may not think they know everything but are quite certain they know more than you, the parent. So put on your thinking cap and consider what choices you would have wanted as a teenager or adult—choices that don't involve using illegal substances, of course. Here are some examples of ways to ask for (and not ask for) something you'd like from your child.

What you want done: You want the dishes washed by a teenager or adult child.

Old way to ask: "It's your turn to wash those dishes. Do it now!"

Offering choices: "After you wash the dishes, do you want to watch that show you were telling me about, or call one of your friends?"

What you want done: "You want your adult child to get up on time for work."

Old way to ask: "Get out of that bed right now or you're going to be late!"

Offering choices: "If you get up on time for work tomorrow, I'll make your favorite breakfast."

What you want done: You want siblings to stop fighting.

Old way to ask: "Both of you, stop this bickering right now! I don't care whose fault it is!"

Offering choices: "I have an idea. How about we do some role-playing, and I can be one of you and one of you can be me? Everyone will get a turn to be somebody else!"

What you want done: You want a teenager or adult child to stop playing video games and go outside.

Old way to ask: "You are getting addicted to that damn device! It's affecting your brain!"

Offering choices: "I am thinking about giving up the internet because people spend too much time on it. But I'll keep it if you spend more time on other things, such as..."

More Advice from BPD-Savvy Parents

In interviewing parents, it quickly became clear that educating themselves about BPD was key to them becoming BPD-savvy parents. Also important are experience, healthy limits, and overall confidence in yourself. Before we close out this chapter, we thought we'd let some BPD-savvy parents offer more advice.

Connie: *I think the number-one thing parents can do to become BPD-savvy parents is to stop blaming themselves for their child's illness and start cultivating self-love. When people value and love themselves, the limits come naturally. Knowing DBT concepts and language is also important.*

Katherine: *I've always been a parent who had no tolerance for disrespectful behavior, regardless of mental illnesses, and a parent who has always valued myself. So, limits have always been easy for me to establish and keep. I have never subscribed to parenting out of fear or making sure my children like me. That's not my job as a parent.*

Lori: *I believe that everything I'm doing for my daughter is in her best interest and that mistakes are learning experiences for both of us. I don't waver with her in the heat of the moment. Since she was a toddler, it's been clear that she was the kid who would test boundaries, so I feel like she got me practicing early.*

That being said, I've had my share of sleepless nights worrying and feeling fearful. Books, support groups, and therapy have helped bring me more confidence and calm to those rough nights. It also helps to know it's my adult child's responsibility to manage their illness. Always learning and always growing.

Sheri: *I think that recognition of learning how to parent differently is key. I am in the process of having to tell both of my own parents to keep their mouths closed—that they may not agree with what I do or do not do, but it has to be that way in order for me to be the parent my child needs. My borderline child needs to be parented completely differently* *from what I was taught. It is a steep learning curve.*

Carol: *I'm definitely a BPD-savvy parent. My mantra when I first became a parent was "Always follow through on what I say." So if I set a consequence or a limit, I stuck/stick to it no matter how hard it is. It's exhausting. But I know if I don't do it, the whole ship sinks.*

Pearl: *What has helped me grow into being a BPD-savvy parent is reading books on parenting children with BPD, therapy for myself with a clinician experienced in working with people with BPD, and the unfailing support of two good friends who have excellent boundaries, who don't judge me, and who have helped me to learn to forgive myself for my perceived failings and move on. I was raised by a person with BPD, so it's been a very long road to learning what's healthy and not healthy in a parent-child relationship. I finally feel like I've got a decent handle on it. I still have bad days and make mistakes, but it's so much better now than a few years ago.*

Jackie: *I am a BPD-savvy parent. My job was to teach my daughter how to survive in this world, not be her friend. That doesn't mean I was strict, but I was firm—no always meant no debate. Thanks to attending DBT group therapy with my daughter, I learned how to better communicate with her. I learned how she perceives situations, and it's much different than the way I do. I have always wanted to* be "helpful," but when I discovered my "helpful" ways were not helpful at all, I learned to stop and help her become more independent. That has helped me with my daughter as well as my other relationships.

Right now, taking all these actions may seem overwhelming. And it will be at first. In a way, you're learning to parent all over again. But what worked well for your child's siblings won't necessarily work for your child with BPD—you know this already. In time, you too will be a BPD-savvy parent.

Top Takeaways from This Chapter

The top takeaways you should remember for this chapter:
- Setting limits and telling your child what you can—and cannot—tolerate will decrease the number of battles
- But it's important to follow your own limits. One deviation—you said the child had to be in by 9p.m. and she shows up at midnight, and you think, oh well it's only one time—no, no, do not do this! With this one act, you destroy the whole program. So set rules you can and will enforce
- Talk with your child about your limits and the rewards and consequences for adhering to them. Make a written plan together.

- Catch your child doing something positive and praise them. Everybody does something right once in a while. When you praise good behavior, you'll get more of it.
- Expect your child of any age to test your limits, such as not complying with your rules or acting especially annoying, often to see what you will do in response. Stick to your limits, and your child will learn that you really mean it.

CHAPTER 10
Parenting a Preteen with BPD

In my experience working with parents, the following story about a preteen is not unique by any means. Yet it's amazing how many clinical professionals can hear such a story and still maintain that a person cannot be diagnosed with BPD until they reach age eighteen.

By the time my son Brandon was eighteen months old, he would tense every muscle in his body and his eyes would look at me crazy, like he wanted to devour me, and he would wrap his chubby arms around my neck and squeeze so hard he would shake. He would press his head so hard onto my belly that it would hurt. One time he hugged my friend's older dog Spanky and squeezed until Spanky yipped in pain. We rushed in and pried him away from the dog. After that, we always kept Spanky in another room.

As he grew, he had long, passionate tantrums that couldn't be soothed in less than half an hour or more. He could be so passionate or so clingy or so tantrum-y, and then immediately transition to being perfectly fine, independent, and happy. His moods were like walking on eggshells from a very young age. Even then I could never quite tell if he was going to nonchalantly set the table or if he would have a total meltdown and throw the plates and silverware on the floor.

Sometimes when I dropped him off, he would run into his school just fine, and sometimes he would kick and scream and flail his body until the teachers pulled him off of me. He did that until third grade. His moods and tantrums just got worse as he got older. By eleven, he was refusing to go to school, which he had previously loved. Then he started talking about wanting to be dead. I was frightened to death.

By twelve, he was making suicidal gestures and getting arrested for domestic violence against me. He was hospitalized in the psych unit twice at age twelve. He was diagnosed at twelve with bipolar disorder. Over the next two years, I kept telling his psychiatrist that something was off, it wasn't just bipolar disorder. I understand that's the typical misdiagnosis for kids who really have BPD. Especially boys.

A new psychiatrist heard me and spent several appointments talking to Brandon, and then concluded that, while he wouldn't officially diagnose him with BPD because he's a minor, he would add "meets clinical criteria for BPD" next to his diagnosis of cyclothymic mood disorder.

When asked when they first noticed BPD traits in their own children, and what those traits were, here's how some parents responded.

Victoria: My child had problems in school from the first week of kindergarten. She was always very needy, but she couldn't bear to be separated when she went to school. She had low self-esteem, and I had to prepare her a long time ahead for all upcoming events, even things like trips to the grocery store. She also had unnecessary fears and anxieties—more than normal.

Maria: At age twelve, my son had risky behavior, obsessed over relationships, and had a very pessimistic attitude. He lied and blamed others for things that he did more than ordinary children. He was super, super needy. No matter how much love I gave him, it was never enough.

Samuel: My daughter is seven and we are on the waiting list for a psychiatrist for suspected BPD (her mother also has it, putting her at increased risk). She has crippling anxiety and major tantrums with dissociative episodes, and one small letdown leads to an hour-long rotten mood. I need to tell her every single plan/detail for every minute of the day. She acts like an adult, not a child.

Azumi: At age five, my son wanted us to hurt him. He would say, "Punch me in my tummy—just punch me hard." He had never been exposed to any kind of violence or *physical discipline. By age eight, we worried about his severe depression. He struggled with making friends. He would ask to come home on every playdate because he was offended by something, and he would go into his room and sulk and play the victim. Also, around that time he started eating to "fill the hole."*

Hiro: *At a very young age—and still today—my daughter has zero ability to handle disappointment. She could ask us what's for dinner, and I could say "Spaghetti," and if she wasn't in the mood for Italian, her entire day would be ruined and she would be miserable and maybe even have a raging tantrum.*

We surveyed parents of preteen children, and the following lists summarize the BPD traits above and beyond those recognized by the psychiatric community that they noticed in their children. Fear of abandonment, probably the most universal BPD trait, is demonstrated in preteens as separation anxiety.

CLINICIAN'S CORNER WITH DANIEL LOBEL

One of the earliest signs displayed by children at risk for developing BPD is exaggerated separation anxiety. It is normal for children to experience some level of anxiety or discomfort, but children at risk for developing BPD cannot calm themselves or allow themselves to be calmed by others when separated from their parents. They continue to protest and resist efforts to be calmed. These children may become so upset that they throw up or experience headaches or stomachaches from the stress, often requiring the parent to stop whatever they were doing and come to the child's aid. The resistance to separation and the anger associated with it are the prototype for later exaggerated fears of abandonment that are characteristic of BPD (2018, 11).

Other Frequently Mentioned BPD Traits
- Low self-esteem
- Difficulty sleeping
- Difficulty making transitions
- Trouble making friends
- Huge variances in maturity
- Sensory-processing issues
- Small things (to the parent) sparking a major crisis
- Great upset at a change in routine
- The need to have time strictly scheduled
- Constant lying and blaming
- Internalization of problems
- Can't let go
- Attention deficit disorders
- Separation anxiety
- Rules are flouted and punishments don't work

Clearly, as any parent can tell you, a child exhibiting BPD traits has a "personality." And, as you've probably discovered, most therapists and other mental health professionals will not diagnose BPD in adolescents, let alone children younger than twelve. But as Fran Porter puts it in the foreword, if your youngster had a broken leg, would you wait until they turn eighteen to treat it? Of course not!

There is a scientific basis for treating children with BPD traits as early as possible, regardless of whether they have an official diagnosis or not. A child's brain develops more slowly than their body and doesn't mature until one reaches their mid-twenties (more about this in the next chapter). To simplify greatly, a child with BPD who's dysregulated has a brain that is putting down pathways in a dysregulated way. The longer those pathways are connected in a dysregulated way, the harder they will be to change. (It's possible, but difficult.) So, what is a parent to do if they can't get a BPD diagnosis, and thus the help they and their child need?

The therapist of Dolores's ten-year-old told her that her child had BPD symptoms, but that she wasn't "allowed" to diagnose a child this young with BPD. Fortunately, the therapist taught Dolores basic techniques that often help children with BPD, such as how to validate a child's emotions (chapter 7), and this helped enormously.

Dolores: *I had been downplaying her emotions to try to help my child. And that was* *a huge mistake! I was invalidating her, the opposite of what I should have been doing. Now I know how important it is to validate her feelings. I am emotionally present for her, and I also guide her on how to recognize her emotions—even if I think her emotions are over the top or make no sense. Naming these feelings and talking about them really helps.*

We realize that it can be difficult finding the help you need for your preteen because many therapists won't diagnose a preteen with BPD. In fact, many erroneously believe that young children *can't* have BPD. So, with that in mind, we're going to go over some techniques in this chapter that you can use with your child if they exhibit any of the traits mentioned above, or if they've actually been diagnosed with BPD, as well as look at some common problem areas for them. If you haven't already, be sure to read chapters 8 and 9; they offer the foundation of skills that we'll build upon in the coming chapters.

Speak in a Calm Voice

At ages nine or ten, interactions between kids can become heated. Maybe during a playdate another child finds your child's toys fascinating (because they are new to them), and your child may decide their toys are too exciting to share. Some parents yell at their children to tell them to share and be nice. No kid likes to be yelled at, but for a child with BPD traits, a loud voice is likely to trigger a meltdown. (Also, you don't want to be the kind of role model who raises their voice when they're angry. Your child is always watching you for indications about how to behave.)

So, what's a parent to do? When your child is loudly arguing with a friend or gets upset, and you know it's time to intervene, ask the children how things are going in a quiet and calm voice. This may stress you out, so pretend you're a calm and collected 911 operator! (Practice this voice in your bedroom or bathroom before you need to use it, because you will need to use it eventually.) Genuinely listen to their complaints while conveying care (or at least neutrality) with your face and body language. After validating both kids' emotions, see if the children have any ideas for solutions, or determine yourself if there's anything you can do to smooth things over. Use the communication tools from chapter 7.

Sometimes there isn't anything to be done, and the other child is angry and wants to go home. And that is okay. You have done well by modeling calm behavior and—whether you realize it or not—your child noticed your behavior. You have also revealed, by your behavior, that conflict can be managed without hysterics. If that child will no longer play with your child, you can teach your child that the argument at the house resulted in a tear in the friendship. Perhaps you have some ideas as to how it can be mended.

Already your child is learning that actions have consequences. You will know when to act empathetic and when to point that out.

If your child realizes that they look at the world differently, or that they are "different," and they wonder why, you can explain how BPD affects them without using the term itself (see chapter 5). Here's an example of a parent acting in a calm manner when her daughter had a meltdown.

Shonda, who exhibits BPD traits, was playing a soccer game when she had a minor spat with another child over whose fault it was that the ball went into the woods. They complained to the coach, who didn't want to hear who started it or who was right or wrong. Instead, he said he was ending the argument. His solution was for both children to run the perimeter of the soccer fields.

The other girl started off running, but Shonda began stomping off to the car. "It's not fair!" she told her mother Adelle, adding, "I want to go home! I hate soccer!" Adelle knew that Shonda had some issues, and she decided that this might be a teachable moment. Adelle decided to use SET-UP and said, "Wow, you really have loved soccer, so I am concerned something so bad would happen that it would make you want to quit (support). I can see you're angry. Maybe you're feeling frustrated too. I know if I were punished for something I didn't do, I would feel the same way (empathy)." At this point, Adelle doesn't know whose fault it is, so she gives Shonda the benefit of the doubt. *"The fact remains, though, that you have a choice. You can do what the coach says, or, like you say, you may have to give up soccer (truth)."* Notice that Adelle is not concerned about whose fault it is or assigning blame. She is concerned with helping Shonda manage her out-of-control feelings.

Adelle continues, *"I would really hate to see you quit soccer because you enjoy it so much. Remember when we all came to your match and you scored a goal? You were so happy and proud. Do you also remember how much you enjoy the friends you've made on the team?"* Here, Adelle is helping Shonda with splitting—black-and-white thinking—by pointing out that soccer is not all bad. *"I tell you what. Let's run it together if the coach lets us. I'll stay off the track and cheer you on. What do you say? Let's try it!"*

Shonda was not happy at first, but her mom acted silly and that made her laugh. Pretty soon she forgot how mad she was. "I'm faster than you, Mom!" she shouted, feeling proud of herself. Now, that is out-of-the-box thinking by the mother.

Walk Away

Sometimes, you just need to walk away from an argument with your child. Whatever you do, don't JADE (justify, argue, defend, or overexplain), especially with a young child. Tell your child what you want them to do in clear, simple language (they can easily get confused), and then walk away.

> When I refuse to argue, my daughter may mutter some vile comments about me, but often she does what I asked her to do.

And when the child *does* do what you ask, be sure to notice and to praise them. The first time your child does it, be effusive, even if it's not a great job. Then hold your praise back a bit until your child does a little better—give them an A for effort with each little improvement until they do a job you can honestly praise.

Use Distractions

Some parents set aside intriguing toys to serve as distractions on a freezing, wet, or snowy day, or when their child is feeling down, mildly ill, or bored. That's what Rebekah did.

> Jacob, age eleven, was home with a cold and couldn't go to school or go outside. He was sick of video games and said he was having "the worst day ever."
>
> He began kicking his bedroom door hard, shrieking repeatedly, "I'm bored! I'm bored! I'm

bored! I have nothing to do, and it's your fault, Mom!" After reminding Jacob of the limit on destroying property and giving him a time-out, Rebekah went into her closet and pulled out a kalimba, an African instrument she had purchased for just such a moment.

"Maybe you could play with this. I just found it," said Rebekah. Jacob asked her if it was supposed to be a birthday or Christmas present. "Maybe, and it never got to you for some reason," said Rebekah. Jacob was intrigued by the toy. He read the instructions and played with it for hours.

Sometimes all it takes to redirect your child with BPD traits is a little distraction. Here are some common situations you might encounter and how to handle them with distractions.

The situation: Your child Mary Ann, age eight, is playing dolls with Olivia. Suddenly, Mary Ann grabs Olivia's doll and Olivia starts to cry.

The wrong response: "Mary Ann, you give that doll back! I've told you a million times you need to share! And don't you give me that *look*."

A better response: "Maybe we could try something else. I know—how about if we go into my old trunk and find clothes to dress up in? There are all sorts of clothes in there. And hats and shoes too!"

The situation: Your child bonks another kid in the head with a rubber ball. The other child is fine but mad.

The wrong response: "You're not supposed to hit other kids in the head, ever! What if your friend got a traumatic brain injury or something? Or his parents sued us? Go to your room right now and think about what you've done!"

A better response: "I'm happy nobody was really hurt. But it wouldn't hurt if you played with balloons. Honey, why don't you apologize for hitting your friend and then we can play with some balloons.

The situation: Jimmy laughs at your child Eduardo when he gets whipped cream on his nose, and Eduardo takes offense.

The wrong response: "Don't worry, Jimmy. Eduardo gets way too upset too easily because he has issues. It's no big deal."

A better response: "Some things that make people laugh aren't funny if they happen to you. Jimmy thought it was funny when you got whipped cream on your nose. But you didn't think it was funny, did you, Eduardo? Wait a minute. [You spray some whipped cream on your own nose and a startled Eduardo laughs.] Oh, I guess it was a little funny!"

School Issues

School may feel like hell for children with BPD traits, often starting in the fifth or sixth grade when puberty hormones proliferate. This is also a time when children may feel more vulnerable and at odds with themselves and others. Remember, children with BPD have the same emotions as everyone else; they just have them more intensely, they swing to other emotions more quickly, and it takes more time for their emotions to return to baseline. These issues, plus splitting (black-and-white thinking), cause the dysregulated behaviors you see.

Children with BPD traits may be struggling so much with their internal issues that they don't or cannot pay attention enough to complete their schoolwork—or even start it. Parents need to contact teachers to ensure the work is getting done and to identify any problems that may crop up. The work may be too hard, or your child may be anxious, depressed, or have some other underlying problem, such as school bullying (a common problem today).

Some elementary and middle schools offer online information about when assignments are due and whether or not they've been turned in. If such an asset is available to you, then use it! Ask, and you may be surprised to find that such a resource is available at your kid's school. Let's look at some other school-related issues.

Trouble with Other Students

Many children who are diagnosed with BPD or exhibit its traits are victimized by school bullies. This is likely because kids with BPD seem odd or different from others, and being different is not a good thing for a school-aged child. Going with the herd is the norm, and anyone who violates this norm will be noticed.

Ask your child if they're being bullied in school (or on social media), and if they are, talk to them about how to handle this problem. Nearly all schools have antibullying policies, but if faculty don't know that bullying is occurring, nothing will happen.

Obtaining an Individualized Education Program (IEP)

Children with BPD or BPD traits often need an individualized education program (IEP). The school takes your child's special needs into consideration and puts together a written plan that specifies the extra help they will need, such as extra time to take examinations or more help with certain subjects, such as language arts or math. IEPs are most often used for learning disabilities but may sometimes be evoked for "behavioral issues."

However, because many mental health professionals won't diagnose BPD in children, you'll have to use a different diagnosis to obtain an IEP if you can't get one for your child's behavioral issues. Since children with BPD nearly always have co-occurring diagnoses (see chapter 3), such as depression or anxiety, one of these could be used. There is also an "other" category for children with emotional issues. Some parents hire IEP advocates to help them obtain or create an IEP, but there are many resources available to help parents navigate the process. Entire books have been written on the subject.

The Rehabilitation Act of 1973 (specifically Section 504), the Individuals with Disabilities Education Act (IDEA) of 2004, and the Americans with Disabilities Act Amendments Act (ADAAA) of 2008 are the primary federal laws that deal with IEPs. They dictate which children need an IEP, what must go into the IEP, when updates to an IEP are needed, and many other aspects of providing extra help for children. Section 504 may allow for an individual plan of action for children who don't meet the criteria for an IEP under IDEA.

States must follow federal laws or risk losing federal funding; however, this doesn't mean it's easy to obtain an IEP. It is not. If you need information about IEPs, visit https://www.wrightslaw.com, a free legal source.

Most schools are resistant to placing children in one of the available federal programs because so many other children already have IEPs. They create a great deal of extra work for staff, including an enormous amount of paperwork in a very specific format, as well as many reporting requirements. Educators, who are already overstretched, often view IEPs as an added burden. So, parents who believe their child needs an IEP must be proactive, even if it means rocking the boat or disagreeing with the school and teachers. You must be your child's advocate, because if not you, then who?

Check In with Teachers

It's *not* surprising that most teachers don't understand borderline personality disorder, because most people have never heard of any personality disorder (other than narcissistic personality disorder). Often people confuse BPD with bipolar disorder because they sound similar, and both have to do with moods. However, teachers do notice if a student acts odd or out of sorts and doesn't seem to fit in, and they also notice if a child acts out. Talk to your child's teacher to find out if your child is exhibiting problematic behavior in school. It might also be helpful to see if your child's teacher would be willing to validate negative emotions to decrease their power. Validation is an extremely helpful tool for all children, not just those with BPD.

Offering Too Much Help

It's my job to make my son's life as stress free as possible, but I can't always anticipate problems that come up that set him off. I just don't know what to do. Isn't he already handicapped enough by this mental disorder?

When children are little, it's difficult to remember that your job as a parent is not to make life easy for them, but to teach them to tolerate frustration, become independent, and accept accountability for their actions. If you have a preteen with BPD traits, you have an enormous advantage over parents whose children don't show signs until adolescence or adulthood: you can help them from the very beginning, before they have the chance to develop bad habits.

Trying to determine what to expect of children is a constant juggling act for parents. Though your preteen may look to you to solve problems for them, do something for them, or fix it for them, instead focus on loving and supporting them while letting them take a chance at finding a solution for themselves. You will be so very glad you did once they become an adolescent.

Team Sports and Activities

Learning that it's okay to fall down, how to get right back up, and how to accept losing are important lessons taught in team sports. Other team activities like the yearbook committee or chess club also give your child a chance to work with others toward a collective goal. Your child will learn invaluable life lessons, like how to work with others, complete tasks, handle conflict, and win and lose gracefully.

If you encourage participation in team activities, don't be surprised if your child wants to quit if they feel criticized or they know they made a mistake. Or maybe the teacher or another student gives some constructive criticism and your child has a meltdown. If this happens, use SET-UP to show your support, empathize, and then point out why it's important to continue playing. Remind your child that every member is important to the team. Help them to see the strength in continuing to play when things don't go their way.

Lucy didn't know if her son would stay on the soccer team because he frequently complained that he wasn't as good as the other players. He also thought that the coach was too critical, and that the rules of the game were hard to learn. Then a disabled child joined the team.

That child couldn't run fast, and he was much smaller and weighed significantly less than the other children his own age, but he clearly had a lot of heart. He always tried his best, and everybody liked him. During practice, the other team members went out of their way to include him in plays. During games, when the child had success, his teammates cheered wildly. The presence of the disabled child helped Lucy's son realize that it's good to do your best, whatever that is.

Other People's Advice

When you're a parent, other people, including total strangers in the supermarket and elsewhere, will offer you advice about how you should parent. Those other people don't know your child. Listen to their advice, if you want to, and then do what you think is best. For example, let's say your eight-year-old launches into a major tantrum in a store. Some people might tell you that you should spank your child, yell, threaten, and so forth. Sometimes your own parents and siblings give such advice, which is harder to ignore.

Before you take your child to the store again, use the limit-setting process and communicate the rewards and consequences—a good one in this case is that you won't buy their favorite food—to your child. If neither works to correct the behavior, leave your child at home and implement your consequence. Here are examples of unhelpful advice you may hear from others, as well as bad and good ways to respond.

Comments relatives and others may make: "Tommy does *not* respect his elders at all! Why don't you teach him respect for adults?"

Things you may *wish* to say (don't do it): "Oh yeah? So, I should use ways that never work for anyone, like berating a kid if he makes a mistake or hitting him like you do? I'm not doing that!"

Responses you might offer: "It's a process and Tommy is learning to respect others. It's hard for him because of some issues, but he's working on it."

Comments relatives and others may make: "Olivia is so bossy and nasty and always wants to be in charge. Someone should take her down a few pegs."

Things you may *wish* to say (don't do it): "Talk about being bossy and nasty! Consider the source of this comment, the bossiest and nastiest person in the universe!"

Responses you might offer: "Olivia sometimes has trouble separating her needs and wants from what other people need and want—but we're working on it."

Comments relatives and others may make: "I can't believe the hissy fits Jimmy pitches over nothing! You'd think he was two years old, not ten!"

Things you may *wish* to say (don't do it): "Oh yeah? What about the time someone made a tiny nick in your car door and you had a total psychotic meltdown! I thought you were going to give yourself a heart attack. Don't talk to me about self-control."

Responses you might offer: "Jimmy has trouble controlling his emotions sometimes, but he's learning how and we're helping him." (You don't need to answer follow-up questions about *what* you are doing. Just say you are working on it as many times as you need to.)

Role Modeling

We'd like to finish out this chapter with some role model advice to keep in mind for parenting a preteen who has BPD traits, or a BPD diagnosis.
- Don't lie to your child. If you don't want to share certain information, say it's private or you don't want to discuss it.
- Whenever possible, deliver on your promises. Avoid making promises you're likely to have trouble keeping.
- If you don't want to hear your child using the "F" word, then don't use it yourself.
- If you want your child to spend less time on the internet, then spend less time online yourself. Find activities you can do together, like disc golfing, bike riding, or going for a hike. We all have busy lives, so if you need

to schedule fun time in order to make it happen, then do so!

Top Takeaways from This Chapter

In this chapter we discussed the difficulties parents have getting a BPD diagnosis for their preteen who exhibits BPD traits. We talked about formal and informal traits, and ways to help your child even if you can't get a diagnosis. Here are some key takeaways from this chapter:

- Preteens exhibit traits not typically seen in adults with BPD, such as issues with sensory processing, making friends, sleeping, transitioning from one activity to the next, and changes to routines. However, this information is anecdotal, not research based. We offer it here because it will be a long time before children under age twelve will be formally studied with BPD in mind.
- No amount of validation is too much. Remember, you're validating their feelings, *not* their thoughts or actions. Combine validation with limits.
- If you believe your preteen has BPD traits, or if they've been diagnosed, fight for your child to get the right treatment and the right schooling. Do it *now* while the pathways in their brain are still developing. No one else will do it. If you act now, you'll save yourself

and your child a *lot* of trouble as they mature and become an adult.
- Remember that your preteen has no idea that they think, emote, and (to a certain extent) behave differently than people who don't have BPD. They can't differentiate between themselves and the disorder. They have never experienced any other life, and how they act and feel comes naturally to them because of their disorder.
- People with BPD have a difficult time empathizing with others because BPD is all they know, and it's all consuming. If your preteen doesn't understand how to get along with people, help them put themselves in the other person's shoes. Ask them how they would feel if something similar happened to them.
- At this age, humor and distraction are good tools for when things go wonky. Also, you are the primary role model for your preteen. Take it seriously, because they're always listening, watching, and learning.
- Consider encouraging your child to join a sports team. Group activities can offer many opportunities for preteens to learn how to interact with others, how to lose, and how to deal with frustration.

- Some people, even those close to you, will offer unsolicited advice. *If your child acts badly, it must be the parent's fault, right?* Wrong. If the advice giver is a stranger, forget about them. If they're someone you care about, show them this book.
- In short, simple terms, learn how to explain to others how BPD affects your child. You will need to explain it to teachers, doctors, and many others. You may choose to avoid using the words "borderline personality disorder." Perhaps, "My daughter is going through a difficult period right now in which her emotions overwhelm her ability to think logically. Those heightened feelings make her act in extreme ways. We are looking for treatment to help her."

CHAPTER 11

Parenting an Adolescent with BPD

Daniel: *I am pretty sure my sixteen-year-old son has BPD. He hates being alone, even for a minute. If I'm sitting on the couch with him and I get up to walk across the room to get something, he will whimper and ask, "Aw, you're leaving me?" He expresses feeling empty and not like a "real person." He says he feels like killing himself and has stayed in a mental hospital twice—two weeks each time. He has cut himself three times. He exhibits extreme, over-the-top emotional reactions to minor events and is very easily slighted or offended. He plays the victim constantly—my wife and I are always the bad guys and his birth mother is the savior. Even when things are going well, he finds something to be upset about.*

Coping with a teenager with borderline personality disorder can sometimes feel more like crawling through ground glass than walking on eggshells. Even teenagers considered "normal" can be tough to parent. Some parents say that on a scale of 1 to 10 of difficulty, raising an adolescent with BPD is about a 1,000. But there *are* actions you can take to help your teenager.

These may be the most important years for not "feeding the monster" that is your child's BPD. Your overall goal for your child's adolescence is to prepare them for living independently when they reach ages 18 to 21. Every time you feed the monster, think of it as adding more time to your child staying at home, unable to take care of themselves because you've made life too easy for them. Since they equate you doing things for them with love, it's going to be hard to get them to act independently. So, resolve to show your love in a million other ways.

Before we delve into those, let's talk for a minute about the teenage brain. Studies have shown that brains continue to mature and develop well into early adulthood. (To be specific, the neurons in the teen brain are still in the process of making connections between the emotional part of the brain and the decision-making center.) Much like a person is sexually mature *long* before they're ready to be a parent, your kid can legally drive (and do much more) before their gray matter is "fully cooked" (American Academy of Child and Adolescent Psychiatry 2016b).

That's why adolescents have problems thinking things through and act in irrational, risky, and impulsive ways (yes, impulsive on top of impulsive). The "uncooked" brain is why they don't always make good decisions and why they give in to peer pressure. If you have a teen, then you know that they're not always great at solving problems and making decisions. There is not much you can do about this biological fact except perhaps share it with your teenager in the hopes that they'll keep it in mind when faced with choices. When it comes to the underdeveloped brain, BPD adds a layer of complexity to already challenging behaviors.

This table compares how the behaviors of adolescents with BPD differ from those of typical teens. Essentially, teens with BPD often use these behaviors to cope with profound misery, intense emotions, fears of abandonment, and self-loathing, unlike nonborderline teens, who are just going through a stage.

Average Teen	Teen with BPD
Does not try to self-harm and probably does not think about self-harming.	Cutting makes them feel more "real" and alive, so the cutting behavior becomes a coping action when they feel overwhelmed or upset. The more a child self-injures, the more it becomes a hardwired coping skill.
May bust curfew, arriving home at midnight instead of 11 p.m. Is remorseful.	Stays out all night, comes in at 5 a.m. or later, and tells parents it's none of their business what they do.

Average Teen	Teen with BPD
Tries alcohol or marijuana a few times. It doesn't interfere with life in general.	Probably uses alcohol and marijuana—and is way more likely to use harder drugs like opioids. Mostly uses drugs to cope with the severe emotional pain of BPD—but the mental, emotional, financial, and career costs almost always make their mental health worse (Friedel, Cox, and Friedel 2018).
Goes back and forth between liking their parents; gets mad and shouts angry, nasty things at them.	The idealizing and demonizing of their parents is more intense and dramatic—to a power of 10. For example, in the morning, Carly told her mother she was terrible and should go to jail or maybe just die because she refused to replace the brand-new smartphone Carly had just lost. When Carly found her phone in the afternoon, she swept her mother into her arms and told her she was "the best-ever Mom" for having made her favorite snack.
Has an argument with boyfriend and is very upset. Cries and tells parents they can't possibly understand how it feels.	Has an argument with boyfriend and believes that he despises her and that she is worth nothing and is evil. She may also believe the boyfriend is evil. (Relationships are unstable, and the teen with BPD splits their boyfriend or girlfriend using black-and-white thinking [splitting].)

Average Teen	Teen with BPD
Is angry with parents for restrictions, like a limit on phone time until grades improve. Says parents don't understand and must hate them.	Is out-of-control angry at parents for phone restrictions and says if they don't immediately lift these restrictions, they will report them to child protective services (CPS) for abuse. The parents don't lift the restrictions and the child does call CPS. CPS investigates, upsetting the entire family.
Experiments with sex, usually with one or two partners, as part of growing up.	Has unprotected sex with multiple partners to feel better about themself, to feel desired, to feel connected, and to avoid feelings of abandonment.
Is upset with their mother after a disagreement and kicks a door hard, causing no real damage.	Is in a rage with their mother after a disagreement and throws several glasses at a door. Purposely (or not) steps on a piece of glass, and the mother must call 911 because of profuse bleeding.

As you can see from the table—and may already know firsthand—the behaviors of teens with BPD are more extreme than those of nondisordered teens. In this chapter we're going to discuss issues surrounding sexuality, social media, and your teen with BPD; and cover ways you can parent your teen more effectively in these arenas.

Sexuality

In our surveys, many parents responded that acting out sexually is a huge problem with their adolescents. This is not surprising. In our experience, people with BPD of all ages are more likely to be preoccupied with sex, have sex at a younger age, engage in casual sex, and have sex with a greater number of people than the unaffected person. They also have more high-risk sex, such as not using protection or having sex with a stranger. Here's some of what we heard from parents.

Lucia: *My daughter uses sex as a coping tool when she feels empty, numb, lonely, or bored. Sex generates a temporary positive emotional response and feelings of acceptance. I think that's true for lots of girls and women, but at a factor times 25 in teens with BPD. My husband and I allowed our daughter to get birth control implant put in when she was fifteen. We emphasized it would not prevent STIs. It may not stop everything, but she is not ready to be a mother.*

Kanesha: *My son has lots of weird, uncomfortable messages on social media, which he is not allowed to use. We had a crisis one day when we suspected he was sending out images of himself on social media and on his phone, and we saw that he was having sex with an adult woman he had met on online.*

Vicki: *My child wants a baby who will always love her. That's all she can talk about. It terrifies me. Thankfully, there are times when she changes her mind. But she usually goes back to "I want a baby." She has no conception of what that really means. She is* *not ready to be a mother, and I am not ready to be a grandmother because I am still raising her! We put her on a birth control implant. I pray she makes it to adulthood, at least, before she decides to go down that road.*

Katie: *When my daughter was thirteen and wanted to date and have sexual relationships with men in their twenties, she didn't understand our objections. She angrily told us we were controlling and abusive.*

Bettie: *My thirteen-year-old daughter was promiscuous and refused to use any protection during sex. She didn't need birth control, she told me, because she had "willed" herself to not get pregnant and to not contract any STIs.*

Before deciding on the best course of action for addressing your teen's sexual promiscuity, it's a good idea to investigate the causes of their behavior. Often there's more than one reason. Sex is a way that some people with BPD address feelings of emptiness, low self-worth, low self-esteem, and insecurity (in relationships); impulsive self-destructive behaviors; the need to belong; a lack of identity; depression; an inability to handle frustration; and the desire to be wanted. Sex is a way to fit in and be at least one kind of "popular." It can also be a marker of earlier sexual abuse.

The positive effects of sex are short term, like that from a hit of a drug, and the high doesn't last very long. So, the action has to be repeated, often with another partner because the teen "split" the old partner when they inevitably disappointed them. You can't control your teen's behavior, but you should know about the risks involved. This is why it's important to talk about the risks of teen sexual activity, such as pregnancy and sexually transmitted infections (STIs).

Risks of Compulsive Sex

- **Sexually transmitted infections:** For example, the human papilloma virus (HPV), the most common STI, is the primary cause of cervical cancer. It can be contracted by having sex with someone who is already infected with the virus—and who may not know it. However, a vaccine against HPV may be given to adolescents and young adults starting at about age twelve. Ask your child's doctor about this vaccine.
- **Pregnancy:** Do you and your child agree on what should be done if she becomes pregnant? Would she have the child and expect you to raise it? Or do you agree on the subject of abortion or adoption? This should be part of "the talk," which we will discuss shortly.
- **Getting hurt:** Does having sex mean the same thing to your child as it means to their partner? If not, someone is going to get hurt. If their partner just sees it as "hooking up"

with no commitment, and your child thinks they're now dating, your child could be in for a very long fall to the ground. If it's vice versa, they could really hurt someone else.

Talking About Sex

The last person a teenager wants to talk to about sex is their parent—but it's important, especially for teens with BPD. As we've already made clear, their behaviors are generally more extreme and riskier than those of nondisordered teens. Sometimes teens are crying for help and actually want their parents to step in and offer advice. We suggest that you try to view this conversation as an important bonding opportunity between you and your child, an opportunity to set your adolescent straight on what is okay or not okay in sexual relationships. For example, you may wish to say that sex is an intimate and caring act between people who care about each other, making each person vulnerable to the other. And, unless they've agreed on an exclusive relationship, their partner may also be having sex with other people, which puts them at risk physically and emotionally. Or, if they're having sex with someone eighteen and older, let them know that may be a felony crime, depending on state laws, and their partner could get into a lot of trouble. (Don't threaten to turn them in.

Instead, elaborate on what could happen if an authority figure found out.)

Bring up the risks of sex without shaming or judging your child—as much as you might want to, such behavior will just chase them away. If they can articulate the reasons why they're having sex, you can validate their *feelings* before speaking practically about the risks and (not many) rewards of this behavior. Talk about consent, birth control, sexually transmitted infections, pregnancy *(What if that happens?)*, and common myths, such as you can't get pregnant if you douche right after heterosexual sex or if the female didn't have an orgasm. Or that birth control pills are effective from day one. Or that, if the sex occurred with the female on top, pregnancy can't occur. You may wish to make an appointment with your child's pediatrician or family doctor to discuss contraception and protection against STIs. Tell the doctor in advance that you want them to cover these topics, so they allow for extra time.

If your child is already sexually active, hold them accountable. Set limits. For example, to prevent teens from sneaking out, parents can install cameras and locks on the front door that, when opened, send an alert to their phone. Ultimately, you cannot control your child's body. But talking with them about the risks of sex may help them avoid making impulsive choices.

> **A Reminder**
>
> If you decide not to tell your child their diagnosis, you can explain how BPD affects them without using the term. See chapter 5.

Change Can Be Hard

Any kind of change is difficult for children with BPD to handle. *Prepare for the worst but hope for the best* is a mantra common among parents of kids with BPD. If any of the following changes are going on with you or your family, you might want to prepare for the worst, as they might very well set off your child's BPD. But that doesn't mean you can't also hope for the best.

- Your teenager has a new romantic relationship.
- A romantic relationship has ended for your child.
- Someone is sick or has died, such as a grandparent or uncle.
- Your child has returned to school after a long summer off.
- Your child has a new friend or lost an old friend.
- Your child is in a new school.
- Your family has moved (this includes moving to a new house in the same city).

- Your child has been ill for an extended period, or has an injury, such as a broken leg.
- You child has started going through puberty and their body has started changing.
- You and your partner are not getting along, or you have a new partner.
- Your child is being bullied.

> ### Talking About Substance Abuse
> Drug abuse is a dangerous co-occurring condition to have with BPD. It happens because people with BPD are self-medicating to make their painful feelings go away. The combination of substance abuse and BPD can doubly harm relationships, goals, academic or career success, and physical and mental health. For more about substance abuse, see chapter 14.

Social Media

A 2020 study analyzed the effect of interpersonal functioning in 620 people with BPD traits, ages 18 to 77 years, who used social media. Researchers found that people with a higher number of BPD traits posted more frequently on social media. These individuals were also more likely to block and unfriend people than those who didn't have BPD. In addition, people with BPD said that social media was important in their daily life (Ooi et al. 2020).

Some adults don't realize how pervasive and important social media is in the average teen's life. Many kids constantly post updates about their daily life or try to attract a following on a popular online forum. Sometimes, adolescents with BPD (whom, as you know, behave impulsively and inappropriately), do so on social media. They may post mean, defamatory, or even threatening comments about someone they're angry with. They might even flat-out lie about others, as well as make wild speculations about people's personal or sexual behavior or physical appearance. They may post inappropriate pictures.

It's important to talk with your teen with BPD about the real-life consequences of posting on social media. Besides the real possibility of hurting themselves or others with posts, social media activity can affect their future prospects. Anyone, including employers, can review your teen's social media activity and develop an opinion about them without ever meeting them. Since their identity is constantly changing, help them avoid putting themselves in a social media box. This table highlights some key social media points to warn your child about.

What Your Teen Shouldn't Do on Social Media	The Reasoning Behind It
Send or post a picture of an intimate body part—theirs or someone else's. Don't send one via a messaging app either—not to a boyfriend, girlfriend, partner, or anyone.	If the picture is of a person under age eighteen, it's considered child pornography in some states. Warn them that if they share an intimate picture of themself with a boyfriend or girlfriend, that person might post it online if they break up—or even if they don't.
Say how much they hate or despise another person or point out how fat, thin, or [something else] a person is.	This is cyberbullying, something teens have killed themselves over. This behavior also pushes others away. They may not chide your teen in print, but they may shun them, fearful of what your child might say about them if they stay friends. Also, warn your teen to avoid being part of the crowd engaging in this behavior.
Make up stories about another person, such as a teacher.	This could harm the other person. And if harming the person is your teen's intent? Well, you may want to let them know that they (and you) can be held financially liable for negative consequences, such as a job loss.
Say they want to harm or kill anyone.	If that person is hurt or murdered, your teen becomes a suspect. Even if nothing happens to the person, such behavior is cruel and serves no purpose. Also, online threats can lead to restraining orders and lawsuits.

Adolescents can be brutal when it comes to social media; for example, they rate each other's personal appearance. They take selfies and spend hours making sure they look just right. Many teens want to be "influencers" who create a following on social media platforms. Teenage boys like to gross out other people, and they also

like to brag. They sometimes lie about their sexual conquests and other adventures. And teenage boys with BPD are more likely than other boys to maximally exaggerate the grossness, getting into the competitive spirit and not realizing they have totally crossed all lines. In short, teenagers with BPD, who are more emotionally volatile than other adolescents, are at greater risk for distress and upset over social media.

If you think your teen spends too much time on social media, and you want them to reduce their use, consider the behavior you're modeling. Be discreet about *your* use. Instead of posting endlessly on Facebook, spend more time talking to family members (especially your teen or their siblings) or taking care of yourself per the suggestions in chapter 5. If reading Facebook *is* your way of taking care of yourself, then, as we said, be discreet.

Should you decide that you need to cut your teen off from social media, which generally means taking away their phone, anticipate that they'll act as if you amputated their arm. Some reasons for shutting off social media or the internet include:
- Overusing it to the exclusion of real-life activities
- Cyberbullying others
- Accessing porn

- Accessing information about illegal activities (drugs)
- Sharing inappropriate photographs of themselves or others
- Using it to meet up with strangers
- Sexting
- Being exploited in some manner

If your child needs online access to receive and submit school assignments, you can allow them to access a shared computer until the penalty phase is up. Develop criteria for getting back internet access and maintaining it. You may want them to agree to allow you to view their history, to avoid certain types of material (for example, pornography), and to limited hours of usage. Your teen's phone, and access to social media, are likely things they really care about, meaning they can serve as useful leverage for you in the behavior-change department. When doling out consequences, however, keep in mind that a few phoneless days in their life will seem like an eternity.

Notice When Your Teen Does Something Right

When your adolescent exhibits "bad" behaviors, such as those related to sex and social media, it's easy to only notice the behaviors you don't like. But everyone does something right now and then, so start looking for good behavior, no matter how minor. For example, if you ask your teen to take the trash out, and they *do*, acknowledge it with a smile and a thank you. Leave out any sarcastic additions, such as "Finally!" or "I thought I'd never live to see this day." This is hard! But try it. You may also wish to give a gentle touch, such as a pat on the back or the shoulder. Many teens don't want their parents hugging and kissing them but appreciate a positive touch—even if they don't say so.

This table lists minor good behaviors you can keep an eye out for, and how you might acknowledge them. Though we're focused on small behaviors, don't forget to notice and praise major behaviors too.

Behavior	Don't Say This	Say This Instead
Your teen remembers to put the toilet seat down.	*OMG! Contact the local news station. Jimmy remembered to put the seat down on the toilet.*	*Thank you for remembering to put the seat down, Jimmy! I really appreciate it.*
You ask your teen to fold his clothes. He mutters to himself, but he does it.	*What are you saying under your breath? I bet it's something mean and terrible!*	*I appreciate you doing this for me. It's really helpful. (Smile—not a fake smile, but a real one. You can do it.)*

Behavior	Don't Say This	Say This Instead
Your teen hates math, but he's doing his math homework anyway.	*Hallelujah! You're finally doing your math. I can't believe it.*	*Good for you, working on your math! I'll leave you alone, but please let me know if I can help.*
Your child is angry with you, but doesn't use swear words.	*Oh, did you forget a few nasty words to go with your complaining?*	*I can see you're angry, and I appreciate you speaking to me with respect.*

Your Teen Still Needs You

As cool as your teen tries to be, as much as they avoid you or argue with you, they still need you. They need you to notice when they're happy or sad. They need you for the quiet moments, when you both notice the sun rise, just as much as they need you for the times you take them to an amusement park or on a fishing trip. They need you to make them feel special—in a good way.

Think about everything you like about your child, and once in a while, just mention it. You like that they are high energy and always ready for an adventure. Or you like that they stick up for their friends when others are mean to them. Or you just like them completely, the total package. Recall trips you've made together and ask them what they remember best about these vacations. And listen to your child tell you about moments they have enjoyed with you.

We asked parents of adolescents with BPD if they would do anything differently, knowing what they know now. Here's what some of them had to say:
- I probably wouldn't have lectured my son so long and so often, and I would have noticed the positive things and given him much more praise—which often seems hard to do.

- I would have gotten my daughter into therapy sooner and would have stuck with the one therapist who really understood BPD. We were convinced to try something different after a hospitalization, and then we couldn't get that therapist back to see her after that failed.
- I'd have started my son on DBT therapy at a much younger age. I would have advocated for him to have special support in school. He is smart, and the school always talked me out of it because of that. Bright kids can need extra help too.
- I would have told my daughter that she was beautiful, smart, and wonderful. Not when she was acting like a monster, but when everything was calm. This positive feedback is so important. Otherwise, all they get is negative attention, which makes everything worse.

Top Takeaways from This Chapter

In this chapter we discussed some of the unique challenges that come with parenting a teen with BPD, including those surrounding sexual promiscuity and social media usage. Here are some key things to keep in mind as you read on:

- Remember that the teenage body is willing and able, but the teenage brain still wants a nap and milk and cookies. Let this fact help quell your frustration when you think your child is out of their mind. Always remember that, for your child, feelings equal facts.
- Parenting a teen is hard. Parenting a teen with BPD takes a village. Fortunately, it only lasts for a maximum of seven years. That may seem like a long time. If you've been able to do the groundwork laid out in this book, you'll have an easier time. If your child is already a teen, it's never too late to engage the protocols described in this book.
- Teens with BPD have the same problems other teens do—but their problems are on steroids. Whatever you do, don't take their behavior personally. Remember when you were a teen?
- It's usually uncomfortable to have "the talk" about sex, but sex is a common way for teens to deal with pain, emptiness, feelings of worthlessness, and so on. And they can start having sex very early. Pain makes people do things they wouldn't ordinarily do.
- If you can, monitor your child's social media accounts. If they have abused them, make this a requirement. If their feed looks too mild, they may be using an alias and another

account with their friends. There are parental controls you can use, and you can also require them to keep their computer in a public place. Abuse of this policy, as always, should result in natural consequences, such as losing access to their accounts for a certain period of time or something similar.
- **Notice your kids being good and let them know that you noticed. Rewards can be as simple as a smile and a touch to show appreciation.**

CHAPTER 12

Parenting an Adult Child with BPD

George raised two daughters with BPD. Life with these girls, now women, was challenging, and George learned a lot, both during the girls' adolescence (they were two years apart in age) and their adulthood. George says one daughter has—with therapy and plenty of hard work—overcome nearly all of her BPD-related issues and is now a self-supporting adult any parent would be proud of. Sadly, the other daughter is a drifter who relies on drugs to get by, and he rarely hears from her.

The problems triggered by BPD don't end when your child attains adulthood. As you know, the motto of this book has been to teach your child independence and accountability. But what if your child is already an adult? My first recommendation is to read one of my other books: *Stop Walking on Eggshells, The Essential Family Guide to Borderline Personality Disorder,* or *The Stop Walking on Eggshells Workbook.*

The number-one problem most parents of adult children with BPD tell me is that they are frustrated that their adult child wants to stay at home and take advantage of free food, board, and maid service. If this sounds like your adult child, that is a sign that either they are simply low functioning, or that their disorder has been fed time and time again, and now they don't know how to cope on their own. Your child may not be appreciative of this privilege, and if you let them, they'll make messes, take the car, have unruly friends over, disobey rules, and otherwise make themselves hard to live with. Whether they live with you or not, parents tell us that their adult children with BPD behave aggressively, rely on drugs and alcohol to anesthetize their ups and downs, don't take adequate care of their children, quit job after job (or get fired), and pressure their parents to perform basic parenting jobs, such as cleaning up after grandchildren and supporting them financially. Their kids refuse to further their education, get a job, go to treatment, or grow up.

Holding Your Adult Child Accountable

It is never too late to stop feeding the monster, teach the lessons of accountability and independence, or overcome fear, obligation, and guilt (chapter 8). For the adult child, you can teach these lessons a little faster. One way is phasing out whatever support you no longer wish to provide over time, such as giving them six months to find a new place to live, reducing the amount of money you give them each month, or giving them three days to put

> their stuff away before you toss it into a box into the garage (or the trash). This needs to be communicated in a validating manner—first with SET-UP and then with BIFF if needed.

If you are ever to have peace, your own life, and freedom—*and yes, you deserve them*—you need to develop the skills and fortitude to radically accept what you can't change (chapter 5); overcome fear, obligation, and guilt (chapter 8); set limits and observe them (chapter 9); reset your expectations; cherish but disengage (later in this chapter); and, sometimes, have no contact with your child (the main topic of this chapter). The good news is it's never too late to teach these lessons of accountability and independence, and you can teach an adult child a little faster than you can a preteen or adolescent.

Reset Your Expectations

It sounds negative to say that you should lower your expectations of your adult child, but it's something that millions of parents need to do when they have a child with a severe mental or physical disability. At first doing so will be disappointing. But giving up the ghost of what could have been and living with your child in the here and now helps enormously. You'll just be celebrating new goals, and your adult child may make you just as proud.

We're not saying you should have *no* expectations, but rather to consider realistically what your child may be able to achieve. For example, perhaps you wanted your child to have a career, but instead you need to focus on the far more realistic goal of your child having a job, which is still a good goal. Maybe you assumed your child would go to college, whereas graduating from high school or getting a high school equivalency diploma is a positive goal that your child can actually achieve. When they do achieve these changed objectives, you will be just as happy. The following table provides some other examples of changed expectations.

Former Expectations	Changed Expectations
My child will hold a professional position or a good job.	My child will have a job.
My child will go to college.	My child will graduate from high school or get their GED.
My child will marry a wonderful person.	My child will have a successful relationship with someone.
My child will stay out of trouble.	My child will obey the probation department rules and eventually get off probation.
My child and I will have a good relationship with each other.	My child and I will be on speaking terms if we can.
My child will never take drugs.	My child may go to rehab and to meetings.
My child will help me when I'm old.	My child will manage their own life, with help from therapy.
My child will be a great parent, and I'll love being a grandparent someday.	My child can't cope with raising kids, so I am going to raise my grandchildren.

Once you've changed your expectations, help your adult child set some realistic goals, then help them problem solve (see chapter 9) the practical issues related to these goals, such as finding transportation to work, having enough money for rent, and so forth. For every step forward, they may take two steps back. Expect this. They may split themselves, seeing themselves as all bad or a complete failure. We've all had setbacks, but of course they feel worse for people with BPD. Encourage them by telling them that lots of people make mistakes and don't succeed the first time they try something. Remind them that people who succeed are not necessarily smarter or more talented. They may just be people who didn't give up, or people who learned from their mistakes and kept going.

Janet: *You can really see the positives when you step back and look at the whole picture. It's like not seeing a child for a long time and then seeing them again and gasping at how much they've grown—you don't see it when you're with them every day.*

First it's doubting your kid will finish the ninth grade, but by the middle of the tenth, you realize they did and that's worth celebrating. Then it's doubting they will get their driver's license. But a year later than most kids, they do. Next it was wondering if they'll ever finish high school, and three months out, it looks good.

So for us, the key is to find and celebrate the positives, to step back and remember the things that worried us that never came to pass, and to be pleasantly surprised and pleased at all of their baby steps forward.

Letting your child explore their own independence makes them feel competent and gives them a sense of accomplishment. They need to experience those feelings a few times so that the emotional thrill of being able to do things on their own outweighs the reassurance they feel when you do something for them. You will never know what your child can do unless you give them the space to do it. They will never know what they're capable of either. We've all been faced with scary situations we weren't sure we could handle (for example, going to a university with fifty thousand students in a strange city), and we had to take a leap of faith that we could manage. Your child may have to take a leap of faith too. They will face setbacks, but they may be surprised with the outcome if they stick to it.

Tell them you have faith that they can do whatever they put their mind to. Let them fail and pick themselves up again. Most of us fail at first, but the key is to try again. It's hard to watch your child fail, but imagine how you would have turned out if your parents rescued you from every mistake or did everything scary for you. You wouldn't have learned from your mistakes or experienced discomfort. Your child may or may not be ready for this kind of adulthood. But you won't be around forever, and your primary job as a parent is to foster as much independence as possible. To do this, you can't be there to provide a soft landing every time.

It's not easy giving up on your imagined child, because it may seem like everyone else's children are successful doctors or high-powered attorneys, whereas your child barely made it through high school and struggles to hold a job—if they have a job. When others brag about their children, what do you say? What can you do? For starters, keep in mind that you don't really know what's going on in all those "perfect" families. Your friend's kid, the successful doctor, could have a drug problem, and the attorney your daughter went to school with might be on her third husband. For this reason and many others, it's best to not compare your children to others.

Problem	What You Can Do	What You Can't Do
Your child threatens to kill themself.	Take your child to the emergency room. Call the police or an emergency mental health hotline.	Make your child suddenly feel much better.
Your child is abusing dangerous drugs, such as heroin or methamphetamine.	Tell the child they cannot use drugs in your home. Tell the child's doctor about the drug abuse. They can't talk to you about your child because of medical privacy, but *you* can report information to them.	Make them stop taking illegal drugs. Transform them into a healthy person. (They have to want to do this for themselves.)
Your child is abusive and/or neglectful to their children.	Tell them their behavior must change. If their behavior continues, report them to child protective services in your county or state.	Make them be a good parent. Make the abuse or neglect end.
Your child continually gets in trouble with law enforcement.	Tell them you won't pay for an attorney or bail them out the next time it happens. (And stick to this plan!) Tell your child they will probably go to prison if they don't change their behavior.	Make your child obey the law. (Telling your child about laws is probably useless. They know what they are; they just don't want to obey them.)

Problem	What You Can Do	What You Can't Do
Your child's behavior is terrible, and you want to evict them.	Tell your child if their behavior doesn't change immediately, they must find another place to live within a specific time period. If the behavior does not change, talk to a lawyer and evaluate your options. Alternatively, just tell your child to leave.	Make your child follow the rules you've set for your home—they must *choose* to comply with them. (However, you can provide consequences for noncompliance, such as that they must leave your home.)
You don't allow smoking in your house, but your child keeps lighting up inside.	Inform your child they can only smoke outside of the house. Offer the idea of nicotine-replacement medications to curb their desire to smoke.	Make your child stop smoking, even though you know it's unhealthy.
Your child brings people into your home whom you don't like.	Tell them that if they want to see friends you don't like, they can see them outside of the house or elsewhere.	Choose your child's friends. (Sometimes people with BPD befriend outcasts because they are the only type of people who will hang out with them.)

Your Adult Child Lives with You

If your child lives with you, don't make things too comfortable for them. You may let them live with you because you want them to have a stable home base, but you also want them to be motivated to be out on their own. The key is to remember that they're no longer a kid but a grown adult who still needs your help. Unless you want them at home forever, the idea in letting them remain in your home is to provide them with a bridge to living on their own. You want to see progress, no matter how slow. Here are some ideas for building that bridge.

Set a reasonable target move-out date. Help your child think through the steps they need to take before that can happen. Be supportive, but firm; these steps need to be accomplished by a mutually agreed-upon date.

Charge them something every month for room and board. This reinforces the reality that becoming an adult means adult responsibilities. If they don't pay some kind of rent, getting an apartment will be a very rude awakening. Even if it's only a symbolic amount, insist that it be paid on the same day every month.

Don't do their chores. Impress upon them that clothes don't magically appear in their dresser, their room doesn't get cleaned by house elves, and their trash doesn't disappear with the wave of a wand. They should be responsible for all of these chores. Remember, they are an adult renting a room in your house. Don't pick up after them, get them up in the morning, continually remind them of important things, or treat them as if they have a disability that completely prevents them from doing things for themselves. Things may be harder for them to do, but that's not an excuse. If they can do something for themselves, and yet you still do it for them, that's enabling; if they can't do something for themselves, and you do it, that's supporting. If they get fired because they don't get up in the morning, they have learned something important. You're teaching them accountability.

Expect them to participate in household tasks. Besides the minimum expectations of showering and dressing each day, expect them to pick up groceries, cook a meal, clean the living room, unload the dishwasher, and do other things adults do. Being productive and giving back to the family will make them feel good (eventually), and they will develop important skills.

Set limits. Naturally, you're going to wonder, *What if they refuse to do any of this?* This is where limit setting comes in (chapter 9). Come up with consequences that protect your values, needs, and wants, or ask them to find another place to live with a clear deadline. There's a difference between being unable to do something and refusing to do something, and by now you should have a pretty good idea of which is which. Limits might include no drug use, threats of violence, displays of rage, name calling, stealing, disobeying rules, picking on a sibling, having overnight guests—whatever you decide.

Establish household boundaries. If you don't want anyone in your bedroom besides your spouse or partner, say so. If necessary, put a lock on your bedroom, so a child addicted to drugs can't steal the jewelry you inherited from your grandmother or the sleeping pills you sometimes take. Put a lock on the inside *and* the outside of the door, so no one can go in when you leave home.

Write it down. Put rules and limits in a written lease, which you and your child should sign and date. Keep a copy for yourself and give one to your child. They can't protest that they didn't know the house rules if they're in writing. Demonstrate anything they might not grasp, such as how you like a room cleaned or what "making dinner" means (for example, it doesn't mean picking up a pizza with your money). If they tell you that you're being mean, you are on the right track to making them accountable for their decisions and actions, which is only a fraction of what they'll need to know to be out on their own.

Let's say your adult son lives at home and is apparently happy to live in squalor in his bedroom. You are not. You need to have a conversation with him before the bugs carry you all away. Here's an example of how that might go.

Mom: Tom, I'd like to talk to you about something important. Do you have a minute?

Tom: Sure. [He continues his activities.]

Mom: I would appreciate it if you could pay full attention to me, because, as I said, it's important. You see, I made a mistake. [Notice that she asks for what she wants in the positive rather than phrasing her desires in the negative by telling him what to do—turn off the TV, stop playing with your phone. This is an especially effective technique. Notice how she teases him with something he's dying to hear—his mother making a mistake. *What could it be?*]

Tom: [Interested, he puts down his phone.] What kind of mistake did you make?

Mom: Well, remember when your father and I laid out the conditions for you when you first moved in?

Tom: Sort of. That was a long time ago.

Mom: Well, one of them was that you clean up after yourself—like do your own dishes and laundry. We wrote it down. But I am so used to thinking of you as my little boy that I've been doing everything for you and not giving you a chance to be a man on your own. At the same time, this has doubled my workload.

Tom: Are you calling me messy? Because if you look over there, you'll see Dad's plumbing stuff, and over there you have a bunch of paperwork, and John has his basketball stuff in the hall. I am not the only person creating all the messes!

Mom: No, you're not. We could all use some improvement. I'm not going to clean up Dad's messes either. [She doesn't overexplain, offering reasons he could challenge.] I'm going to stop doing your laundry, cooking your meals, and cleaning up after you. [She's brief and firm, using the BIFF communication technique from chapter 7.]

Tom: I can't believe this! I am like your servant! It is so----ing unfair. I hate this.

Mom: That's the way it's going to be, starting now. I've made you one last meal, lasagna, and it's in the fridge. Your laundry is by the dryer. Everything you left around the house I put in your room. If you leave anything around the house, I'll put it in your room. I'll need you to clean up after cooking. If you don't, that will be a separate conversation [informative and firm].

Tom: You're being so mean to me. You're not acting like a mother!

Mom: No, I'm not. I'm an adult treating my adult son like the adult that he is. That adult is someone I really want to get to know.

Tom: Oh yeah, sure you----ing would.

Mom: Tom, you already agreed to keep the place clean—I take full responsibility for not following through. [Notice that she doesn't use a word such as "enforce," which would make her sound like the police.] So, I understand this is coming at you quickly. I care that this is hard for you, and you look surprised and angry [offering support and empathy using the SET-UP communication technique from chapter 7]. If there had been an easier way to tell you, I would have done so. But your father and I are very firm about this [firm].

Tom: What are you going to do if I'm not Mr. Clean? Throw me out on the streets?

Mom: I'm hoping you'll do as you promised, and we won't have to worry about any what-ifs. I love you [friendly, using BIFF]. I like lots of things about you being here. I think this is the way to go. Why don't you think about it, and we'll talk later if you have questions? [Notice that she does not JADE: justify, argue, defend, or overexplain.]

Parenting Your Grandchild

According to reporting by *PBS NewsHour*, about 2.7 million grandparents were raising their grandchildren in the United States in 2016, and that number will most likely increase when the full results of the 2020 Census are released (Cancino 2016). We suspect that many of the parents of these grandchildren have BPD. Adult children are unable to parent their children for many reasons, but these are the most common:
- Drug or alcohol (or both) abuse
- Mental illness (Including BPD)
- Incarceration
- Abusing or neglecting their children
- Death, such as from an overdose

If the state places a child in foster care, they usually seek out relatives to care for the child. But sometimes the state doesn't take custody, and an adult child may ask their parents to care for their grandchild. If you find yourself in this position, and you agree to care for a grandchild, be sure to consult with a lawyer experienced with custody law. Get permission to take your grandchild to the physician and to school, in writing, signed and notarized, from your adult child with BPD. You may also be able to obtain emergency custody through the local courts, but every state has different laws.

Unfortunately, if the grandparent doesn't obtain some form of legal custody, in many states the parent can snatch the child back anytime they feel like it. Unless your grandchild is adjudicated as a ward of the court by child protective services and/or a judge, the birth parent is in charge.

Some grandparents report their adult child's neglectful or abusive behavior to child protective services (CPS), and, as you can imagine, this infuriates their adult child. Sometimes these adult children retaliate by not letting their parents see their grandchildren again. Our best advice is to do the right thing for the minor child, even if that means taking custody from the neglectful parent. Don't factor in possible retaliations from your adult child. Act in a way that protects your grandchild.

CPS officials don't like to remove children from a family home, but they will if they believe children are in danger or are seriously neglected. Here are some examples of abuse and neglect that they will act upon:

- The child doesn't receive regular meals and has no access to food.
- The child is frequently beaten or punished for minor infractions.
- The child is extremely fearful of their parents.

- The child is being or may have been sexually abused.
- The child is frequently left alone and is expected to care for a younger sibling (say a four-year-old who's expected to watch a one-year-old).
- The child doesn't have warm clothes in the winter.
- The child is given marijuana and other drugs.

If you think you may soon be raising your grandchildren, or you already are, we recommend *The Grandfamily Guidebook: Wisdom and Support for Grandparents Raising Grandchildren* (Adesman and Adamec 2018). This comprehensive book will help you navigate the tricky situation you find yourself in. Besides reading this book, here are some key tips for custodial grandparents.

Now you're a parent. Undoubtedly you feel sorry for your grandchild, so much so that you want to go easy on them. However, you can't be the spoiling grandparent anymore. You need to act like a parent would, enforcing basic rules and teaching the child how to act responsibly toward themselves and others.

What they call you. Young children hear other children call their caregivers "Mommy" or "Daddy," so they naturally use the names themselves. If it really bothers you, just tell the child to call you "Grammy," "Grandad," or whatever name you've chosen for yourself.

Friendships. Try to talk with friends about things other than parenting issues and seek out parents who are facing the same issues you're now encountering. You can meet younger parents at soccer practice, PTA meetings, children's birthday parties, or any place parents gather. An ice breaker might be, "I'm raising my grandchild now and looking for a [good dentist, karate teacher, or some other expert]." Most people love to give advice. Also, be sure to avoid talking down to younger parents, even though they may be as old as—or even younger than—your adult child. In this case, you are equals, as parents.

Communication. Do expect some tough questions from your grandchild, often at difficult times, such as while you're driving down the highway at rush hour. If you need to concentrate, tell them that you'll talk about it when you get home. Then be sure to talk about the issue when you arrive home. For example, your grandchild may ask why you, not their parents, are raising them. You may not wish to get into drug abuse or other issues with a young child. Instead, one answer that covers all situations is that their parent was unable to be a good parent, so you (and your partner, if this applies) took on this important job because you love them. In addition, many children think that they did something wrong to not be parented by their parents, so remind them that their parent's issues were in no way their fault.

Going "No Contact"

Once a child with BPD becomes an adult, it is not unheard of for the child and parents to go "no contact" for a certain period of time. "No contact" means what it says: no visits, phone calls, messages, and so forth. Some parents very reluctantly initiate this because of substance abuse, parental abuse, or chaotic behavior that's making their lives so miserable that they don't see any other option.

Sometimes the adult child initiates no contact for reasons that are vitally important to them, leaving parents baffled because they don't really understand what they did "wrong." This can be extremely painful for them, especially for grandparents. Sometimes the cause is something as petty as an argument about what to buy in a grocery store, but even in such cases the argument must have triggered deeper issues. The no-contact decision can also be mutual. Here are some stories from parents who decided to go no contact.

> **Miriam:** *I had to go no contact with my son. I will never contact him, but he knows my number. It's better this way, until his medication helps him regulate. I love him, but I'm scared of him. Arm's length is best in my situation. He lives with his bipolar ex-girlfriend. Toxicity is strong.*

Gabriela: *My daughter went no contact with me. My therapist advised me to let my daughter make contact with me when she's ready. This is devastating. When I ask her why she doesn't want contact, she says, "You know why!" I'm at a loss. I am hopeful one day she will change her mind.*

Gina: *We've had no contact with our adult daughter. It was very difficult at the beginning, and I spent hours crying. I miss my grandchildren so much. I send them birthday cards. I don't know if they receive them. I still think and pray for my daughter every day, but I had to make a choice to focus on myself and move forward with my life.*

Cho: *I'm at the point where I'm not going to reach out to my daughter anymore. We went through twenty-plus years of extreme chaos. Last message from her was, "You are the worst blanking mother in the world and I hope you have another heart attack and die." The door has been open all these years. But now there will be no more contact or gifts from me anymore.*

Stephanie: *My son is twenty-three and I initiated the no contact. He suffers from drug addiction, and I won't be in his life when he is using. Even when there have been waves of normalcy, it is still toxic and abusive. I used to feel terrible about this, but I have done everything to fix it and nothing works. I hope my son seeks rehab/treatment, but I will not* have anything to do with him while he is addicted. He is homeless and that is his choice.

Paris: I decided to stop all communication between my daughter and myself because communication never ends well. It is difficult because she is still living in my house, but I am moving in two months, and she needs to find a place to go in the meantime. Every time I try to communicate with her and just say hi, she either ignores me or uses the opportunity to fight about something. I am hurt that this is what it has come to. I am sad because I love her so much, but she does not seem to care. I want to be there for her, but I am useful only when she wants something. So I am sad, angry, and relieved that I do not have to keep trying anymore.

Cherishing Your Child, But Disengaging

Another technique for dealing with an adult child with BPD is cherishing your child, but disengaging. It is similar to "detaching with love," a concept promoted by Al-Anon, a support group for people whose lives are affected by someone who abuses alcohol. When you cherish your child, but disengage, you've learned that your involvement, your worrying, and your anxiety don't change a thing except get you upset. You recognize that you are not responsible for your child's disorder or their recovery from it. You will no longer obsess about their behavior and situation, which you cannot control, so you can lead a happier and more manageable life. In short, you let your child claim their own life, and you live a life of your own.

When you cherish your child, but disengage, you make a promise to yourself that you will:

- No longer suffer because of the way your child chooses to live.
- No longer allow yourself to be used or abused by your child.
- No longer do anything for your child that they can do for themselves.
- No longer create a crisis.
- No longer prevent a crisis if it will occur in the natural course of events.

Cherishing your child, but disengaging doesn't mean you stop loving them. Don't forget the "cherishing" part. You may still support them in a way that they cannot support themselves—or not. You can still be in contact. Disengagement is more of a mental state than anything else. It is like hearing news that makes you upset, but you can go on with the rest of the day without obsessing over it. You care, but you're not governed by it. You're living in the state of *you* instead of the state of *them*, trusting your child to learn from their own mistakes. If they can't, it is not your fault. You tried your best. You may give them advice, but you don't take it personally or get too upset when they don't take it. You have radically accepted that their life is theirs, and they have the right to live it as they want—and so do you.

You don't have to answer those 2a.m. phone calls in which they berate you. Their crisis is not necessarily your crisis. You have space in your life for you, and space in your mind for you too. Your emotional life no longer revolves around the ups and downs or their life. You've gotten off the roller coaster ride. You have finally realized you can't fix them. You no longer have catfish hope. All that time you spend obsessing over them can now be filled with friends, hobbies, travel—whatever you want. Yes, you will still be sad sometimes. Your heart will still ache. But once you have had a glimpse of having a real life after a lifetime of subsuming yourself in someone else's, if you are like the parents I interviewed, you won't want to go back.

Parents Cherishing Their Child, But Disengaging

> **Mary:** *About six months ago, I realized that I wouldn't like me as a person if I were looking from the outside in: Angry. Tired. Having arguments with my brother over my son's behavior, which I can't change. The only thing I have control over is me. I've had to learn to recognize and shut off the mental rehashing of*

arguments to get some sleep. Enjoy my cup of tea. My conversations with friends and family are now about something fun, or at least something outside of my own worries. I change the topic when my brother asks about my son. The only control I have over the situation is my own reaction and my own mental counseling. When I can succeed at achieving either of those, I feel good about myself.

Louise: When we first received advice from a professional, I was shocked that he encouraged us to step back and take care of ourselves. In my case, I realized that I was continually focused on how I could help my daughter, and I did manage to get her to try some types of help. But when it came to the point that I was still encouraging her to get help and she just flatly refused, I finally realized that there was nothing I could do. It does keep popping into my mind, how to find ways to help her, but I know now that unless she is willing, there is no point in my energy being used up that way. I keep up the mantra "I have done all that I can."

Disengaging is not cruel and nor is it nice. It is simply a means that allows you to separate yourself from the adverse effects that another person's disorder has upon your life. Disengaging helps you look at your situation realistically and objectively, thereby making intelligent decisions possible.

> **Memorize the Three Cs and the Three Gs**
>
> I didn't cause it. I can't control it. I can't cure it. I need to get off my child's back, get out of their way, and get on with my own life.

Top Takeaways from This Chapter

Parenting an adult child with BPD presents many unique challenges, such as navigating having a child still living at home or being responsible for raising grandchildren. Here are some key points from this chapter to keep in mind as you figure out the best way to manage your relationship with your adult child:

- Once your child with BPD is an adult, you are no longer legally responsible for their actions. They are now accountable for their own actions.
- It's never too late to instill a sense of independence and accountability in your child. Just do so gradually, with validation, reassurance, and encouragement, while also setting limits. Tell your child that you have faith that they will be rewarded with persistence. Share a time when you had to do something difficult and eventually

succeeded. Let them know that one step forward and two steps back is normal.

- Lower your expectations and accept that you didn't get the child you thought you wanted. Accept the child you have, and with them set new goals that they can achieve. Point out obstacles that might get in their way and help them problem solve. As hard as it is, let your child struggle without stepping in. You can support them, encourage them, and give them unconditional love, but don't solve their problems for them. Let them feel that pride and sense of accomplishment that comes from doing things for yourself and not being dependent on someone else. Reward independent actions. For example, go out to dinner to celebrate a work milestone, such as keeping a job for six months.
- Don't compare your child to other children, or your life to that of other parents. You don't know what goes on behind closed doors. How many people know everything you struggle with?

CHAPTER 13

Parenting a Child Who Self-Harms or Is Suicidal

> *For some people with BPD, the need to escape is so overwhelming and the pain is so intolerable that no thinking or planning happens.... Attempts aren't necessarily planned. And a lot of times, they're instantly regretted. I have a less stereotypical relationship with suicide. I don't attempt it often, and usually only after enduring a long string of incremental sufferings. Suicide is like a little cyanide capsule in my pocket, just in case the enemy [pain] comes too close—always there, but only to be used when facing seemingly insurmountable odds.*
>
> —Kiera Van Gelder, *The Buddha and the Borderline*

On the day your child was born, you vowed to keep them safe. You made sure they saw the doctor, wore a bike helmet, and flossed. You cautioned them to stay away from strangers. So, it's shocking when you find out that they may be one of the greatest threats to their own well-being.

If your child self-harms or is suicidal, you're probably frightened, distressed, and worried. These threats are so severe that they change the way you parent. For example, you're more tempted to give your child whatever they want, even when it's not in their best interest, just to keep them safe. You may walk on eggshells to make sure you don't do anything to trigger them.

Although self-harm and suicide are scary, you don't have to deal with them all by yourself. In fact, you shouldn't. If your child refuses to see a therapist or go to a hospital, you can seek out advice from therapists and doctors on your own. You may not be a therapist or doctor yourself, but you can take steps to improve the situation for your child, and yourself.

Julie: *I cope with my suicide fears by reading and learning as much as possible about BPD and dialectical behavior therapy. I spend more time with my daughter watching shows, doing puzzles, and shopping, her favorite pastime. I am thankful for every morning that I hear my daughter up at 6a.m., as I know I have her for one more day.*

Suzy: *I deal with my suicide fears by educating myself as much as possible. I asked her caseworker to teach me how to make and successfully implement a safety plan for our home. I learned how to get the services I need and be an advocate for my daughter.*

In this chapter we're going to discuss self-harm and suicide, and what you can do to mitigate their impact on you and your child.

Self-Harm

Self-harm is any emotionally driven, deliberate behavior that results in some kind of physical damage to the body, such as scratching deeply, cutting, or burning one's skin; banging one's head against the wall; and punching or hitting oneself. Other forms of self-harm include excessive tattooing, drinking toxic substances, eating disorders, drug abuse, and excessive exercise.

The most important thing to know about self-harm and suicide is that, in general, kids with BPD hurt themselves to feel *better*, not because they want to die. Self-harm may release endorphins, chemicals that make one feel better. However, self-harm can be dangerous enough to require emergency room visits. And despite what people often think, self-harm is a "bid for attention" only in about 10 percent of cases—it's rarely the main reason (Aguirre 2014). In fact, many kids do it in secret, often to a part of the body that's not usually exposed, such as the belly, inner thighs, and between the toes. Because of the feel-good chemicals, self-harm can become an addictive habit that's hard to kick.

Responding to Self-Harm

> When it comes to self-harm, one of the biggest challenges parents face is responding in a way that doesn't reinforce the child's behavior. Reacting too negatively can increase the child's shame and subsequently their risk of self-injury (Aguirre 2014).

People with BPD say that self-harm helps them:
- Feel alive, less numb and empty
- Distract themselves from emotional pain with physical pain
- Feel numb (the absence of pain)
- Express anger at others
- Punish themselves or express self-loathing
- Relieve stress or anxiety
- Feel "real"
- Communicate their emotional pain to others

If your child self-harms, they need to see a mental professional right away for four reasons:
1. They are at higher risk of suicide, even if they don't consciously want to die.
2. They could accidentally injure themselves very badly.
3. They need to learn better ways to cope with painful emotions.
4. Self-harm can cause scarring, which your child may come to regret when they get older.

The parents we've interviewed have handled their child's self-harming behaviors in a myriad of ways. Here's a sampling.

Using natural consequences and not reinforcing the behavior. Shelly: We had always parented from a "natural consequences" viewpoint, so we handled the self-harm in a similar way. The natural consequence of cutting was a loss of privacy. I would literally put my son on twenty-four-hour watch, sleeping on his floor, following him from room to room, until the episode had passed. If he refused to have me monitor him or if it was a more serious attempt, the consequence was a hospital stay. It took a big-time commitment, including lots of sick time from work, but it kept him safe. The added negative consequence was having me at his side constantly—although it helped to dispel his fear of abandonment! Also, we handled each incident in a very matter-of-fact way; no drama, no emotion. Just clean up the wound and start the watch. This way we didn't reinforce the behavior by equating cutting with attention.

Using visual aids. Carmine: We printed up visual aids of "negative thought processes." When my daughter is in a rage, talking and reasoning are out, but seeing the pictures seems to help. There are several similar aids out there, but I got mine online at https://iqdoodle.com.

Not making it a power struggle. Janice: My daughter wanted to stop but had a difficult time. She successfully hid the self-harm for a long time. Once I found out, I explained the consequences of infection, and I got her bandages, antibiotic cream, and hydrogen peroxide. I showed her how to clean and take care of her cuts. In front of her, I stayed calm and didn't make an issue out of it so it wouldn't become a power struggle. Behind the scenes, though, whenever she wasn't home, I searched her room and bathroom for anything she could use to cut. I would confiscate the contraband and never say anything. Working with her therapist, she found better coping skills and eventually stopped.

Installing a telephone app. Nia: My teenage daughter has an app on her phone that tells her how many days she hasn't cut. I think it helps her to see her successes.

Validating messages and frank conversations. Jazmin: Our child is in a secure hospital unit but still manages to self-harm by using ligatures from ripped clothing, headbanging, and even carpet and paper burns. I tend to make validating statements like:

- I am taking care of myself so that you don't have to worry about your pain hurting me.
- I'm sorry you're in so much pain right now. I am committed to being here to help support you.
- I have confidence that you can get help to reduce your suffering.

All of these statements have helped us. It's crucial not to get drawn into the drama, but to just acknowledge and validate.

Creating an emergency kit with loving messages. Antonne: I made my son an emergency kit for when he felt like self-harming. I told him to open it only in an emergency. I wrote a letter with some loving messages and positive inspirations. I added a list of things he could do instead of self-harming, such as snapping rubber bands on his wrists or putting his hand in a bucket of ice water. I added some treats, like snacks and a $5 gift certificate for video games to download. He used it once, and as far as I know, he hasn't self-harmed since. His therapist also had him write a list of calming activities. He made himself a Spotify list of happy songs, and I reminded him in the emergency box note to listen to his happy playlist.

Employing limits, coping strategies, and natural consequences. Rhonda: We locked up all her meds and sharps and used natural consequences. If she self-harms, she loses privacy privileges. We take her to the ER every time for an evaluation. She hates it. During one bad two-month period, she was there every weekend; and once, twice in one week. We came up with coping strategies: red marker on her skin, lavender to smell, bracelets with beads to count and fiddle with, journals, and countless other things. She will go months without self-harming now. She occasionally relapses. With no emotion,

I validate the struggle, then praise her for all the months she was harm free. She cleans it up, we talk about what led her to self-harm, and then we move forward.

As you can see, parents have found all sorts of interesting ways to deal with self-harm behaviors. One other piece of advice we'd like to offer is to reward your child when they come to you because they feel unsafe. If your child tells you that they're worried they're going to hurt themself, take them seriously. Spend time with them, perhaps doing something the two of you enjoy, or even working on therapeutic skills they've been taught by a therapist. Cancel your plans if you need to and be sure to thank your child for trusting you enough to come to you with their fears.

CLINICIAN'S CORNER WITH DANIEL LOBEL

A professional should always assess thoughts of self-harm, and parents should allow a trusted professional to guide you as to how you should respond to your particular child.

Because you can't prevent your child from having thoughts about self-harm, it can be helpful to suggest alternative activities they can do to occupy their mind. You may participate with them, depending on what your child prefers. Of course, if you think your child is suicidal, it is

imperative to obtain help from a mental health professional as soon as possible. Here are some suggestions:
- Drawing up a list of the pros and cons of stopping self-harming behavior. In other words, what potential gains could they get from quitting?
- Distracting themselves with pleasurable activities. When they're engaged in something interesting, they won't be self-harming. After a break they can revisit what's causing their distress with a fresh perspective.
- Volunteering. They can volunteer at the Humane Society, teach a younger sibling a skill, or become active with a particular cause, any of which can offer them a break from their worries and emotions.
- Taking a mental vacation. They can put their problems on hold for a half hour or an hour. Anything that helps avoid impulsive activities is good.
- Spending time in nature, which has tremendous healing powers. Each season, even winter, can be a delight.
- Engaging the senses: taste, hearing, sight, smell, touch. They can bake something delicious, stroke the soft fur of the family pet, or listen to their favorite music.

- Doing something spiritual, whether it's prayer or going to church, temple, or synagogue.
- Learning a new skill—perhaps one you can teach them.
- Being a tourist in their own hometown. They can do what tourists do when they visit your community.
- Exercising. They can set goals (within reason) to become fitter and keep track of how they're doing. (You can combine this with muscle relaxation; instructions are available online.)
- Writing a story, song, or poem about how they feel. Writing is healing. Keeping a journal has been shown to reduce distress.
- Researching "DBT distress tolerance techniques" online. There are loads of suggestions. (Of course, attending a DBT program in person is even better.)

Your child can do these activities at any time, not just when they're feeling mildly depressed, and you can do them with them anytime as well—if they want you to. However, if they associate self-harming behaviors with special attention from you, they will be positively reinforced for self-harming.

Suicide

Suicide is a problem in the United States, and according to the Centers for Disease Control and Prevention (CDC), suicide is the second leading cause of death for all people ages 10–34 (2021). Studies report that suicide rates for patients with BPD *within the mental health system* (which they may have entered due to a suicide attempt or self-harming) are 8 to 10 percent—approximately 50 times greater than that of the general population (Aguirre 2014). According to psychiatrist Joel Paris, up to 10 percent of people with BPD will die from suicide (2019). However, these studies were conducted only on people with BPD who entered treatment. In our experience, it is not as common among people with BPD who don't believe they need help.

In chapters 1 and 2 we discussed the immense amount of pain that people with BPD experience, which helps explain suicidal thinking. However, there are many reasons why people consider suicide:

- To end the pain
- Feelings of hopelessness about the future
- To punish themselves for feelings of shame and worthlessness
- The belief that their family would be better off without them

- To communicate the intensity of their pain because they don't believe others truly understand
- To cope with real or perceived loss, rejection, or abandonment

As noted, BPD increases the chances that your child will consider or attempt suicide, as will co-occurring psychiatric issues (see chapter 3) and upsetting life events:

- Major depression (If your child is seriously thinking about suicide, it's likely they're suffering from unaddressed or under-addressed depression. Make sure your child is being treated for clinical depression.)
- Substance abuse (Abusing alcohol or other drugs often lowers a person's ability to think and act rationally—something that requires great effort when someone with BPD has been triggered.)
- Especially poor impulse control (People with BPD have poor impulse control. Keep tabs on your child when they experience a major loss, such as a breakup with a boyfriend or girlfriend.)
- The death of a loved one (The death of a parent or other loved one is traumatic to everyone, but it's extremely traumatic for someone with BPD. It is the ultimate abandonment that can lead to depression and

sometimes suicidal thoughts and feelings. Talk with your child about their grief, which is probably more intense than you think it is, and validate them.)
- Failing in school or work (If your child believes that success is everything, then failing in school, college, or work is a really big deal. Talk to them about struggles you had in school, college, or work.)
- Trouble with law enforcement (Some adolescents with BPD routinely get in trouble, be it for shoplifting, vandalism, drug possession, or something else. They may worry that they'll be going to prison for life. Or they may believe that they've shamed their family forever. We talk about criminal behavior and what you can do in the next chapter.)
- Past suicide attempts or a family history of suicide
- A highly publicized suicide in the news or the suicide of a peer
- Relationship problems
- Medical problems
- Bullying
- Anxiety
- Rigidity in thinking
- A gun in the home

Suicidal Behaviors

Here are three behavioral mind-sets that may lead to suicide. However, keep in mind that some people move quickly from thinking about suicide to making a plan and carrying it out, while others never take it from the "thinking about" stage. It's impossible to know what's going on in your child's head, so if they are thinking about suicide, that alone means they need help.

1. **Thoughts about suicide, or "suicidal ideation":** For example, your child might have thoughts like *If I were dead, I wouldn't have to experience this pain.* Thinking that death is an option makes some people feel better. (Try to have a good relationship with your child—or stay in touch with someone who does—so you can keep an eye on this.)
2. **Suicide plan:** Your child thinks through how they might take their own life, writes letters to important people to be opened after their death, and gives away cherished possessions. Some people don't go through this step. Instead, they impulsively make an attempt when one more unendurable thing is piled on their large mountain of unendurable things. (If your child is extremely impulsive, keep a keen eye out for these "one last straw" kinds of triggers.

Remember, what might seem small or fixable to you could feel like the end of the world to your child. Again, talk with your child about the issue of suicide. You may wish to chat with their siblings, parents of friends, teachers, or anyone else who might know your child and be willing to talk with you. You are going to have to determine what crosses an ethical boundary: their privacy is important to them, but so is their life.)

3. **An actual suicide attempt:** It doesn't matter if your child only took five baby aspirins. It's the *intention to die* that makes it a true suicide attempt. If your child tries to take their own life in any fashion, help should be sought. Either take the child to an emergency room or call 911.

Your child may not share with you that they're feeling suicidal—or that they have a suicide plan in place. Because of this, it's important to watch for signs such as these:
- Talking about wanting to die, feeling hopeless (or like life has no purpose), or feeling that they're a burden to others
- Not making future plans
- Increasing substance abuse
- Acting reckless or anxious
- Sleeping too little or too much

- Withdrawing from people and becoming isolated
- Not taking care of their hygiene
- Even worse mood swings and anxiety
- Writing a will or giving away possessions

What should you do if you see any of these signs? It's all right to ask your child directly if they are planning to take their own life. It shows that you care, and the question reduces the risk of a completed suicide because it gives the suicidal person the opportunity to open up.

Once you've asked, listen to your child without offering immediate solutions, which they might see as invalidating. Don't dismiss their emotions or experience, which is also invalidating. You may have gone through the same thing, but you don't have BPD. Remember, your child's feelings are much more intense, and they think in black and white. When something bad happens it's a tragedy for them, and it feels like things will *never* be good again. If you try to tell them logically that this isn't so, you will invalidate them and make them feel worse. All you need to do is to try to get them to hold on until their emotions and/or their circumstances change. And they will.

Here's how the conversation with your child might go.

Mom: You've been wearing the same shorts and shirt for four days, and I don't think you've taken one shower. That's not like you. What's up?

Child: Nothing, Mom. Leave me alone. Go away.

Mom: I love you and I'm worried about you. I want to support you in whatever you're going though [support].

Child: You can't help me. Nobody can help me. Everything is hopeless.

Mom: I'm hearing that you are feeling hopeless. I wonder if you're feeling depressed too. Can you tell me more about how you're feeling? Whatever the problem is, people usually feel better when they talk about it. Whether or not you do, I'm here for you [support and empathy].

Child: You can't possibly understand!

Mom: Maybe I can't. Then again, there is a chance that talking about it will help you feel less hopeless and depressed.

Child: [Very sarcastic] Fine. Carrie broke up with me.

Mom: Oh, dear. Breaking up with someone you love can be heartbreaking [validation].

Child: Well, that's obvious.

Mom: If that's what happened to you, I am so sorry. That hurts a lot, I know [support, validation].

Child: [Quietly] There's no other girl like Carrie. If she dumped me, who else would want to date me? I will never be happy again, that's for sure.

Mom: I'm concerned that if you feel you'll never be happy again, that you might do something to hurt yourself again. Can you tell me if you have any plans to do that? [Truth]

Child: [Sighing heavily] I don't know.

Mom: Please tell me if you get to that point, because I need to keep you safe. If you don't want to talk right now, why don't we go out and do something? Getting moving can distract you from feeling bad. I know it's not a solution, but I'm asking you to give it a try. Let me help [support].

Child: [Opening up] What am I going to do when I see her at school?

Mom: Let's think that through together [support]. [She helps her child problem solve; see chapter 9.]

If you think your child is suicidal and they're seeing a therapist, call the therapist—now. If your child is a minor, talk with the therapist about the possibility of admitting your child to a hospital. You can take your child to the hospital even if the therapist disagrees. You probably know best. Trust your gut. The same is true when it comes to the discharge date. If your child has been admitted to a hospital and you don't think they're ready to leave, fight for them to stay. Find out what happens if you refuse to take them home. Call your insurance company. You can also consider another hospital.

If your child is an adult, only they can decide if they want or need to go to a hospital—unless they are a danger to themselves or others. State laws provide for very limited hospitalizations against a person's will. However, you can always offer to drive your child to the hospital, or to see a physician, therapist, or psychiatrist. You could also call an emergency number for assistance (see appendix C). If your child is already in danger (for example, has already taken pills), call an ambulance.

Hospitalization

Psychiatric hospitals (or regular hospitals with a psychiatric floor) are stigmatized in our society. People only imagine them as places where patients are strapped to a bed and given electroshocks. In reality, these are settings in which people participate in different groups, talking about what brought them to the hospital, and learn better ways to manage their emotions and cope with life. The hospital has one overriding purpose: to keep your child alive. In these settings there are people with different types of disorders, thus hospitalization is not the same as a treatment program. Clinicians will work with your child to develop a discharge plan that addresses aftercare measures, such as seeing a therapist, so they can avoid another hospital visit.

When your child enters the hospital they're assigned a psychiatrist unless they already have a psychiatrist who's able to handle the role. That psychiatrist is the decision maker when it comes to your child's case—what medication they take, or whether they can leave the floor (for example, to go to the cafeteria). The psychiatrist will see your child regularly to monitor their progress. Oftentimes psychiatrists change the medication a patient is taking, the reason being that if the patient is suicidal, the current meds may not be working. Ask to be informed of all such changes in the same way you would if you were seeing the doctor as an outpatient.

> ## CLINICIAN'S CORNER WITH DANIEL LOBEL
>
> Hospital personnel should never make changes in psychiatric meds without knowing what the patient is already taking. The only exception is if the person is so agitated that their safety or the safety of others is at immediate risk. Under this circumstance they may administer a sedative on an emergent basis.

If your child is a danger to themselves or others but isn't willing to go to the hospital, you may have to consider involuntary commitment. Involuntary commitment can only happen under very specific conditions, and state laws dictate that people receive treatment in the least-restrictive setting possible. Laws vary from state to state, but they all include two basic criteria (Hairston 2019):

1. The person must have or be suspected of having a mental illness.
2. The person must be at risk of harming themselves or others. (The definition of this risk varies from state to state.)

If your child is involuntarily committed, call their therapist, who may wish to visit the child in the hospital. So call ASAP. If they don't have a therapist, and you think the involuntary commitment is a problem, call an attorney.

> ### CLINICIAN'S CORNER WITH DANIEL LOBEL
> It is a good idea to have a mental health lawyer to advocate for your child in involuntary custody. The attorney will protect the child's civil rights while at the same time be available in case there are legal charges against the child associated with the involuntary hospitalization.

Top Takeaways from This Chapter

The risk of self-harm and suicide are very real for kids with BPD, but, as we discussed in this chapter, there are many ways to head off or deal with both:
- Like everything else, self-harm should have its own natural consequences.
- Priority number one is to keep your child alive and safe.
- Get support for yourself if your child self-harms or is suicidal. You need someone to talk to, even if it's a therapist—in fact, as you know, we recommend that you see your own therapist anyway.

- Be alert to signs of suicidal ideation or plans. Seek dialectical behavioral therapy (DBT) for your child, and do your best to convince your child that therapy will help them feel better. If you can't find DBT, look for a therapist who knows how to deal with suicidal people, specifically those in the borderline population.
- Talk to your child about how they feel. You will not put the idea of suicide in their mind just by talking about it. Don't sound judgmental, which will just make them lie to you. Just show love and concern.
- Know what you can and can't do when it comes to suicide. You can talk to your child, love them unconditionally, tell them how devastated you would be by their death, help them find therapy, stay with them (for a time) when they're feeling suicidal, remove sharp objects, call an ambulance, visit them in the hospital, and so on. *But only your child is responsible for their own life. You cannot live it for them.* You can't watch them 24/7 for the rest of your life, because eventually you will die—or at least need to use the restroom. And if you could control every aspect of your child's life—take away their agency—would it be the ethical thing to do?
- If your child is suicidal but won't go to treatment, you may be able to have them

committed to a hospital. In the event that your child is involuntarily committed, try to retain the help of a mental health lawyer advocate.

CHAPTER 14

Parenting a Child with Extreme Behaviors

LaVerne: At first, the abuse my husband and I endured from our daughter with BPD was verbal, such as shouting, screaming obscenities, and general disrespect. But then she graduated to grabbing my wrists, pinching my arms, restraining me, holding my arms behind my back, using her body to block the exit, pressing her face and body against mine, and grabbing the steering wheel and hitting me while I was driving.

Most kids with BPD don't steal, abuse drugs, or throw terrifying rages that drive you out of the house seeking safety. But some of them do, and it's extremely frightening, depressing, and disturbing. It's easy to feel compassion for your child when they're acting vulnerable and depressed, but not so much when they're throwing vases, doing drugs, and getting arrested. But children who exhibit the aggressive behaviors described in this chapter are just as hurt and feel just as much pain. Rather than turn their pain inward via self-harm and suicide, they direct it outwardly—the name calling, the objects they break or damage, the substances they abuse, and the laws they break. If your child with BPD is one of the ones who does exhibit extreme behaviors, take heart, because we're going to discuss techniques for dealing with these issues.

Physical Violence

BPD children commit two kinds of violence: violence against a person (slapping, hitting), and symbolic violence (throwing things, destroying property, putting a fist through the wall). Both are frightening, and both are unacceptable. If your child threatens you or family members with physical violence, don't assume it's an idle threat any more than you would consider talk of suicide as just talk. Just like verbal violence, your first priority is keeping you and your family safe, whatever it takes. You don't want your child with BPD to live with the fact that they hurt you or another family member, nor should you accept abuse from your child. Would you accept it from a stranger? Now is not the time to worry about the fallout from taking action to protect yourself and others.

If your child is threatening violence:
- Don't argue with or confront your child. Either you need to get to safety, or your child needs to be taken to a place where they can't hurt you.

- Try validation, speaking in a soft voice, telling your child you love them, and anything else that might calm things down.
- If all else fails, call the police.

Calling the police should always be considered a last resort. However, the most important thing to do is to keep the whole family safe, and hard as it may be, that may mean calling the police if all other options fail. It's not easy for a parent to call the police on their child, but sometimes it's necessary. And when you have a child with BPD, often doing what the siruation demands is harder than taking the easy way out.

My twenty-five-year-old daughter is especially impulsive and aggressive. All she does is criticize me and say I am the worst mother ever (my son disagrees). She was staying at home the summer between college years, and she went completely ballistic. She provoked her stepmother into a screaming fight; then things escalated, and my daughter said she was going to bash in the entire house and steal our documents and passports.

Then she falsely accused her stepmother of slapping her and pushing her down the stairs. We told her to leave immediately. I am devastated, but we need to protect our two younger children, and I won't let my wife be put in the middle like this. Although I feel destroyed, I am going to find out what our legal rights are regarding the false accusations and getting a restraining order.

Although it's hard to imagine your own child ever physically attacking you, it happens, usually in the heat of the moment when the child is completely out of control. If your child is threatening physical violence, do not assume it's an idle threat, and *do not argue or confront your child of any age.*

This is not a time for self-help or to worry about what the fallout might be. *Your number-one job is to keep yourself and the rest of the family safe.* Here are some actions to take:

- Don't let your child get between you and the door, but don't make it obvious by gazing desperately at it. Move slowly and calmly toward an exit. If you must climb out of a ground-floor window, do it.
- Don't look directly into your child's eyes. Instead, look and speak past them. If possible, stand next to them, as if it is you and them against the world.
- After one warning—"If you don't sit down, I am calling 911"—follow through immediately if they do not heed it. Worry about whether this was the right action later. If you feel unsafe now, it *is* the right action.

Here are some signs that your child may become physically violent with you or other

family members (McVicker 2015; American Psychological Association 2013):
- Punching walls and throwing things
- Verbal threats of violence
- Expressions of violence in social media, to friends, and elsewhere
- Being a victim of violence or witnessing violence
- History of vandalism
- History of discipline problems or problems with authority

If violence is a continuing problem in your home, contact a family violence organization, an elder or parental abuse hotline, or a general domestic abuse hotline. If your child is an adult and you need to protect your other children or grandchildren, call child protective services. Document the behavior and keep copies of any police reports—especially if you're a grandparent. You may need this documentation to prove to a caseworker or family court judge that your adult child has acted in a dangerous manner toward you or others in your home. Here are some coping strategies for dealing with anger and aggression, as well as behavior to avoid when confronted with them.

The problem: Your child threatens you verbally and you are a little scared.

Try this: Limit setting: "That is not okay. I will not allow you to treat me that way." (Impose consequences that allow you to take care of yourself according to your values, wants, and needs.)

Instead of this: "Don't you dare threaten me! I'm the parent and you're the child, and you should just do what I say."

The problem: Your child shoves you, mildly or hard.

Try this: Walk away, cool down, and let your child calm down, then try limit setting. Later on, say, "That was not okay. I will not allow you to treat me that way." (Impose consequences that allow you to take care of yourself according to your values, wants, and needs.)

Instead of this: You shove them back harder and say something mean and angry to them.

The problem: Your child is so angry that they damage their bedroom door.

Try this: Take away the bedroom door and deprive them of privacy for two weeks. They can change in the bathroom. This is a great example of linking the consequence to the behavior. Some parents remove the door of children who self-harm in private.

Instead of this: Yelling at them to "Cut it out!"

The problem: Your child calls you a bunch of vile names.

Try this: Limit setting: "I have told you that it's not all right to call me those names. You have no right to speak to me that way." (Be specific and impose consequences.)

Instead of this: "Oh yeah! Well, you're a...!"

The problem: Your child wants to know *right now* if she can stay at her friend's house all night. You don't approve of her friend, who you suspect is using serious illegal drugs.

Try this: Delaying: "Let me think about that. I must discuss it with your mother because we're on the same team. I also must check our family schedule for this weekend. But if you need to know this minute, my answer is no."

Instead of this: "You want to know right now? Okay, then the answer is a big *no!*"

Substance Abuse

People with BPD may abuse substances (sometimes several at the same time) to numb their pain, feel better about themselves, and mask their BPD symptoms (especially their nearly constant self-loathing and fear of abandonment). The substances provide a feeling of calm and momentarily fill the dark hole of emptiness. In our experience, the use of drugs and alcohol aggravates some of the most dangerous BPD traits, especially mood swings, impulsivity, interpersonal issues, rage, and depression.

Teens who use alcohol and other drugs are more likely to exhibit poor judgment, drive impaired, have risky sexual encounters, get more sexually transmitted infections, perform poorly at school, and make more serious suicide attempts (Child Mind Institute n.d.). The effects on the adolescent's developing brain—with or without BPD—are even more worrisome. As you learned in chapter 11, the brain doesn't stop developing until adulthood. Vaping, drinking, or using substances can damage the brain's wiring, increasing the likelihood of cognitive difficulties. Substance use also changes the brain circuits involved in rewards, stress, and self-control (National Institute on Drug Abuse 2020).

No single factor determines whether a person becomes addicted to a substance, but, as the following table indicates, the more risk factors (and fewer protective factors) your child has, the more likely they are to become addicted to a substance. In addition, the younger your child starts the use of substances, the more likely they will become addicted. (National Institute on Drug Abuse 2020).

Risks	Protective Factors
Aggressive behavior in childhood	Belief in self-control
Lack of parental supervision	Parental monitoring and support
Low peer-refusal skills	Positive relationships
Drug experimentation	Avoiding experimenting with substances
Availability of drugs at school	School antidrug policies
Community poverty	Neighborhood resources
Genetic or biological factors	Genetic or biological factors
Borderline personality disorder	No mental disorders

Treatment for an individual with a dual diagnosis (BPD and substance abuse) is difficult because of the likelihood that they are abusing more than one substance, including prescription drugs. Your child may need a dual-diagnosis program. It's vital that both disorders, substance abuse and BPD, be treated at the same time—or substance abuse first, because it interferes with BPD treatment (Aguirre 2014). Talk to your mental health professional. Ideally, treatment should begin as soon as possible. Treatment for dual diagnosis is most effective when therapists with consistently positive attitudes, high expertise with both conditions, and the ability to offer skills training as well as psychotherapy treat both disorders simultaneously.

Letting your substance-abusing child stand on their own two feet is terrifying because you're scared they will die without you. However, if you continue to enable them, they're likely to continue to buy drugs with the money you give them, do drugs on the furniture you provide, and do nothing but take drugs, since you offer a free place to stay (with all the food they can eat), removing any incentive for them to get a job.

By all means, try to get your substance-abusing child into treatment. *But you cannot want them to get well more than they do.* Not enabling or being codependent with a substance-abusing family member—especially a substance-abusing child—is beyond the scope of this volume. However, we can say that when it comes to substance abuse and BPD, all the advice boils down to this: *There is only hope for change when you stop taking responsibility for your child's drug problem, including all the fallout that comes with it, and give the responsibility to them.* Anything else feeds the monster of addiction. Here are some examples of enabling behavior and not-enabling behavior.

> **Situation:** Your daughter won't take her psychiatric medication for depression, anxiety, or another problem.
>
> **Enabling behavior:** You sneak it into her food. This will undermine your child's trust in you and the medical profession when she finds out what you did.
>
> **Not-enabling behavior:** You advise her of the consequences of not taking the medication (such as experiencing depression, anxiety, and so forth).

Situation: Your daughter got very drunk last night and feels terrible today.

Enabling behavior: You give her some acetaminophen and comfort her. You clean up the vomit from the floor next to her bed.

Not-enabling behavior: You advise her on what to do about a hangover and encourage her to take care of herself. Let her clean up her own mess.

Situation: Your son wrecks his car, but he's okay.

Enabling behavior: You buy him another car.

Not-enabling behavior: You let him go without transportation. He can take the bus or walk. And no, he can't use your car. You need it.

Situation: Your child dumps her girlfriend and then feels terrible about it.

Enabling behavior: You agree to explain to the girlfriend that your daughter was in a funk and didn't really mean her behavior.

Not-enabling behavior: You problem solve with your child on how to handle the problem. She can try to get back together with the other person or not. This is not your problem to resolve.

For space reasons, we cannot go through everything you should know when your child is

a substance abuser, but we recommend these suggestions and cautions:
- Become familiar with your child's friends' parents and learn their stance on supervision and substance use.
- Encourage your child to socialize with friends at your house and keep an eye or ear on them.
- Have a policy that your child can ask you to come pick them up, no questions asked, as long as they don't abuse the privilege. You don't want them to drive a car drunk or ride with a friend who is drunk.
- Talk to your child about their non-BPD reasons for using drugs, such as peer pressure and how substances let one's guard down, making it easier to connect with others.
- Don't allow others to bring alcohol or illegal drugs into your home.
- Check to see if alcohol will be served at parties your child wants to go to, and check to see if the parties are supervised. Call parents to make sure they will be there.
- Communicate your expectations to your child and schedule check-in talks.
- Model healthy behaviors (for example, don't drink too much yourself).

- Be aware that alcohol and many drugs lower inhibitions, which can lead to violence in people with intense anger and mood swings.
- Offer empathy and compassion for the struggles and the factors that compel your child to abuse substances. Validate how tough it is *before* emphasizing how important it is to make the right choices. As always, offer treatment options and other ways of dealing with their stress (see chapter 5).
- Set aside time for you and your child to have fun. (Remember to schedule time for their siblings too.)

Legal Trouble

BPD symptoms can cause your child to get in trouble with the law. Here are some potential problem areas for kids with BPD:

- **Arrests:** As you know, people with BPD may suffer from impulsivity, instability, and aggression. The combination of intense emotions and impulsivity might lead your child to drive recklessly, shoplift, and get into fights, resulting in arrests (Salters-Pedneault 2020b).
- **Truancy:** Teens with BPD who are struggling in high school tend to skip classes, leading to run-ins with truancy laws. You may be legally responsible for their attendance at school, so call your child's school to inquire about their

attendance. If they've been skipping, figure out limits and consequences or contingencies and ask an attorney about your legal responsibility.
- **Childhood neglect or abuse:** Your adult child may not be taking adequate care of your grandchildren (see chapter 12). This can lead to encounters with child protective services and other government and private agencies involved with things like foster care, adoption, and termination of parental rights.

If your child steals your possessions to sell for drugs, consider making a deal with them: either they willingly go into treatment or you will press charges. If they don't work hard in therapy or they drop out, press charges. If you let their behavior slide, they're likely to steal from you again. Some people with drug-addiction issues will do almost anything to get money for drugs so that they can avoid withdrawal (which can range from exceedingly uncomfortable to fatal). If they commit a crime against their sibling, it's important that you stick up for the sibling, who has already been affected enough by having a sibling with BPD.

Your Child Is Arrested

Holding your child accountable for their actions becomes very tricky when they're arrested. One moment, you have the final say in what happens to your minor child—the next, the government does. It's just as scary when your adult child is arrested. If your child is arrested, you need to strike a balance between holding them accountable for their actions and ensuring that they're not being railroaded by the criminal justice system, which may decide to punish your child too lightly or too severely (in your opinion).

If your child is a minor and they're being arrested for the first or second time, you may want to be more involved, whereas if you're dealing with an adult who's been arrested many times, you may wish to be less involved. You have to ask yourself, *Is my child acting recklessly while knowing, in the back of their mind, that I will get them out of trouble?* If the answer is yes, then have minimal involvement. If the answer is no, and your child can learn a lesson, you may wish to become more involved. This is something you need to get a feel for on your own. If you decide it's in the best interest of your minor child to post bail for them, make sure your child has a plan for paying you back. Hold them to it.

If your child (especially an adult child) gets arrested for a serious or violent crime and goes to jail, we advise against rushing to bail them out. Jail is scary for most people and may be terrifying for your child—at least the first time. One visit may convince them that they never want to go there again, leading to behavior change. If you bail them out, they may learn nothing, except that you will get them out of trouble if they get caught again—which they assume won't happen. When your child learns that their parents will clean up their messes, they have no reason to change.

Once your child is arrested, there are limits to what you can do for them. Attorneys typically offer the following helpful information and advice in the case your child is arrested:

- Each state has its own laws about juveniles who commit crimes. You'll have to research the laws in your state. Some states let the parents be present for questioning, some do not. Your child *does* have a right to have an attorney present.
- Your child should remain calm and polite without aggravating or arguing with the police. They should avoid saying anything incriminating. If the police think drugs may be involved, they may screen your child medically. They will book them, taking their photograph and fingerprints.
- If you are there, remain calm and don't rush to judgment. Calmly try to find out as much as you can about the circumstances of the arrest. You may or may not be able to speak to your child face-to-face (again, laws vary by state).
- Your child should say nothing until an attorney is involved. Your child should state, "I want a lawyer," and any questioning

underway should cease. The police may act like they have more information than they do. Remember, they are not on the side of the suspect (your child).
- If you're there, don't try to act like a lawyer; engage one instead. Don't waive your rights or agree to a search of your home without a lawyer present. If you do hire a lawyer, it should be one who specializes in juvenile cases if your child is a minor. Any witnesses should be referred to this person. You may wish to explain BPD to your child's attorney.
- Your child may be required to go through a community program, such as counseling or community service. If your child is a minor, help them get to those appointments for the first few times. Emphasize how critical it is that they go. Otherwise, they may have to go back to court and perhaps face more charges.
- The outcome of the case will depend on the judge, police jurisdiction, the state you live in, the severity of the offense, biases in our criminal justice system, and luck. The court uses the following additional kinds of information when making its decision: the child's age, past record, social history, and school records; the evidence; and the family's history and structure.

- Depending on how involved you choose to be, you might want to say to a minor child, "This is a serious situation, and I need you to explain in detail exactly how we got here." And, "We still love you, but your actions are hurting us." It's important for your child to understand that their actions have consequences for their future. A record could seriously mess up their life. If they don't want to talk to you, they may wish to speak with a counselor or someone else in the family.

Seek Mental Health Treatment for Your Child

Parents should insist that their arrested child of any age receive mental health treatment. If your child has not yet been diagnosed with BPD or any other psychiatric problems, seek a diagnosis from a mental health professional *before* your child's trial date. The attorney may be able to use this information to plead them out to a lesser sentence, or to persuade the court to send them to a treatment facility instead of giving them a jail or prison sentence.

For example, if your child has BPD and an alcohol abuse disorder, your child's case could be sent to a special drug court that many states have. These courts might order treatment and random drug screenings, which are far preferable to a prison sentence. If you do only one thing when your child is arrested, get them mental health treatment. It is not enabling behavior. It is being a good parent.

Top Takeaways from This Chapter

Parenting a child who exhibits extreme behaviors presents challenges, but as with all the other challenges we explored in this book, there are proven methods for caring for yourself, your child with BPD, and other family members. Here are the key takeaways from this chapter:

- Yelling, calling people names, and illegal behaviors are acting-*out* behaviors. They are parallels to the acting-*in* behaviors related to suicide, self-harm, and depression, in that they all spring from the same pain and emptiness caused by BPD. This does not excuse the behavior, nor your child for hurting themselves, you, and others.
- Soothe your own emotions (see chapters 5 and 8) before tackling the problem at hand. You don't want to add your own anxiety, stress, and so forth to the mix. Give your child a chance to calm down and become less impulsive. Using validation is one good way.
- When the family is unsafe, your duty is to get them to safety, even if that means calling the police. As needed, call on advocates, such

as child protective services, family violence centers, lawyers, and so forth, to aid your child.
- Do not enable your child or "love them to death." Strike a balance between holding them accountable on one hand while offering support and help on the other hand.

Epilogue

When we began this book, the parents we interviewed asked us to include stories of hope. We thought such tales were going to be hard to find, but we had plenty—way more than we can use. The key to the positive mind-set of these parents is that they celebrated all the little pieces of progress that their kids—and they themselves—experienced along the path to recovery. With the help of this book and others like it, we hope that you too will become a BPD-savvy parent. We'll let these parents have the last words.

Darlene: *I'm proud of myself for not running to the hospital or calling there every hour or so. It's hard, but I'm trying.*

Laurie Ann: *I'm proud that I required my daughter to turn in missing school assignments before going out with her boyfriend, even though I knew it would mean tantrums.*

Jenny: *I am proud of my son. It's been an uncertain year with his health, but he never gave up and he kept up with track at school. Today they called to inform him that he has almost $30,000 for a scholarship.*

Brittany: *I am proud of myself for taking on a meditation practice so that I can stand in the storm with some level of equanimity. I am proud of my teen for recognizing that DBT skills will enable her to* find coping strategies that are not harmful and will heal past traumas and limit future traumas.

Xandria: I'm proud that I'm not caretaking my granddaughter over her love life. She is communicating with an ex (who I really like), but I'm staying as neutral as I can. It's their lives. Believe me, this is a huge one for this grandma!

Cindy: We started our hard journey last year. It was extremely difficult to first find a diagnosis, and then the answers about treatment. Fortunately, we tried so hard and found a residential treatment center with DBT for our daughter. One year later, we can finally can take a deep breath.

Charlotte: I am proud that I have learned to depersonalize my daughter's verbal attacks. It's not about me!

Ted: I'm proud that I'm standing my ground ... most of the time! It's one step forward and two steps back sometimes, but I'm learning to live with that.

Avery: I am so happy that my youngest is finally starting to take some initiative. He's taking a physics class (and is doing the work!), just got a job (which I don't think he's going to like), and has given himself the goal of getting his pilot's license. Where this goes, I have no idea, but it's been three weeks of positive movement forward. I'll take it!

Acknowledgments

First, I would like to acknowledge my wife, Diane, and my sons, Zachary and John, for their support in this endeavor and everything else I take on in my life.

Next, I would like to thank my mentors: Drs. Miklos Losonczy, Alan Gray, and Arnold Wilson. Without your teaching and guidance, I would not have the skills and insight to achieve this point in my career.

I would like to thank all of my readers and all of my patients who have taught me about pain, healing, and growth through their own journeys and suffering.

Finally, I would like to thank Randi Kreger and the editorial staff at New Harbinger for giving me the opportunity to collaborate on this project.

—Daniel S. Lobel, PhD

I would like to acknowledge the emotional support from my husband, John Adamec, and also from my other family members, including my daughter, Jane Adamec, and my grandson, Tyler Adamec, for their patience and understanding during the process of researching and writing this book with my excellent coauthors. Also, many thanks to the editors at New Harbinger for their valuable suggestions on improving the book even more.

—Christine Adamec

A big hug and thank you to all the members of my online support group Moving Forward—a warm, caring, and compassionate group that helps educate and support people with a borderline or narcissistic family member. You're a great group, and you've been especially kind to me. Special thanks to Thana, Karen, and Kim Haverly for making our twice-weekly Zoom meetings possible. The three of you have tremendous initiative and follow-through. I couldn't even begin to quantify how meaningful these meetings have been for people, and it's all due to you.

Donna Toone, the moderator of the Facebook group for Parents of Children with BPD, gave me free and full access to her members, allowing me to interview them and ask them questions. Most of the quotes in this book came from her group. I will always remember Donna's kindness in helping me help her members. Thanks to everyone in that Facebook group who contributed.

Fran Porter, the author of a memoir about her daughter with BPD, *When the Ship Has No Stabilizers: Our Daughter's Tempestuous Voyage Through Borderline Personality Disorder*, did more than write the foreword, for which I thank her. She gave me feedback on some sections of the book, for which I also thank her. Fran, I wish we knew as much about BPD when your daughter was born as we know now. That's a sentiment shared by almost every parent: *if only we had known.*

Special thanks to Meghan O'Neil for her insight and contributions for the sibling section in chapter 6. She was invaluable and raised that section far above what I, a nonsibling, could have done by myself. Siblings are such an overlooked group, and one of the most affected by their brother's or sister's disorder. I hope that section will help siblings all over the world. If it does, it will be due to Meghan.

Dan Slapczynski, a brilliant writer who is not even a professional writer, wrote appendix A, "Top Ten Tips for Dads," based on his own experiences. I asked him to do this because about 90 percent of the people I interviewed were mothers who told me they wanted more involvement from their husbands. On the other hand, if you are a father whose partner won't get involved, you may wish to show them that appendix. If you are a father who has stepped up, thank you!

Thanks too to the gang at New Harbinger, especially Catharine Meyers, for trusting me so much. As a writer, I have freedom that most authors would give their right arm for. I trust everyone at New Harbinger to always have my books' best interests at heart, from conception to promotion (again, the right arm).

Most of all, I would like to thank my coauthors, Daniel S. Lobel and Christine Adamec, who made this book possible. I never could—or would—have done it without them. Christine leapt into the project with both feet, and on her own initiative learned everything she could about BPD—even ordering clinical textbooks. Dan, who was with patients night and day, was very accessible and answered my questions in a timely manner. Thanks to both of you.

—Randi Kreger

APPENDIX A

Top Ten Tips for Dads

Over the course of my research, I learned that the mothers would almost always like more involvement from their husbands when it comes to parenting their child with BPD. This heartfelt letter was written by a father of a daughter with BPD. He boiled down this entire book into the most important things he believes all fathers need to know.

—Randi Kreger

Dear Fellow BPD Dad:

I wish I could say, "Welcome to the club," but I know we both wish our children were healthy, and that we'd never heard of BPD.

Let me introduce myself: I'm one of the lucky dads. My daughter's life has been impacted by BPD every day. It has cost her a night in jail, a week in a psychiatric facility, two wrecked cars, a string of countless broken friendships, and her peace of mind. We were forced to have her move out and live with her grandmother at seventeen. She suffers emotional pain every day, and sometimes talks of ending her life.

But like I said, I'm one of the lucky ones. For all her problems, my daughter has graduated high school and attends college, has had steady boyfriends, holds a job, and now lives on her own. She's trying hard to be an adult, and, most of the time, is succeeding. Part of that, I hope/think/believe, is because of how we—meaning my wife and I—learned to handle her BPD.

If you're like me (and I have to assume you are, since you're taking the time to read this), you want to help your kid more than anything else in the world. But sometimes, even when reaching out to other BPD parents for help, you feel alone. As a dad, you're outnumbered, and often stereotyped. You're told you just want to "fix things" and "don't understand BPD," and, more often than not, you're dismissed right off the bat as some odd trespasser in a land owned by moms.

That's bunk. You've been there through thick and thin. Your opinions and your feelings count.

So, to help you out, I'm going to offer you some advice. Not because I'm an expert, or even because I always practice what I preach (I don't—I screw up like everyone else). I'm just passing on the advice I wish someone had told *me* years ago, because it might have made things just a little bit easier.

Anyway, without further ado, and not necessarily in order of importance, here are what I consider the "Top Ten Tips for Dads."

1. Read Chapter 7 on Communication Techniques

I know, I know—it's kind of cheating to imply I'm going to offer you precious pearls of wisdom and then start off by saying, "Go read a chapter of a book," but in fairness, at least it's *this* book and you've already paid for it. You're welcome.

You, your wife, your BPD child, and their siblings—you're all living under the same roof, and the math of that suggests that you're going to *have* to communicate with each other. That gets harder with a child with BPD because they don't always experience the world and their feelings in the same way we do. Chapter 7 will give you some well-researched tools that have been tested for years, tools that will help bridge that gap between you and your child. Ideally, those tools can minimize arguments and improve your relationship with your child by avoiding common mistakes. Is it easy? Not always. But if your child lost their hearing, you wouldn't hesitate to learn sign language to communicate with them. Think of this as the BPD equivalent of that effort.

The chapter even teaches a technique that (finally!) addresses the infuriating lack of respect your kid often shows to you and their mom. "Form before content" teaches you how the child must comply with basic rules of respect and courtesy before *any* conversation can take place. That's worth the cost of the book right there.

2. Respect Your Wife's Knowledge

No, your wife didn't force me to write that. I know you've been there in the trenches every day, and that's invaluable, but I'm assuming your wife has been the one to take the lead on studying BPD and the ways it impacts your child. She's the one who probably picked out this book and handed it to you, right? If that's the case, don't ignore what she's learned.

If she makes a decision regarding how to handle your BPD child, roll with it. That doesn't mean you can't question the decision—the last time I checked, no healthy marriage is a dictatorship—but don't do it openly, in front of the child; always present a united front. My real-life tip: use your technology and conduct the conversation silently via text.

3. Work as a Team with Your Wife

Think of this more like tip number 2.5, because it's a natural outgrowth of what I suggested above. Parenting is exhausting in the best of times; throw BPD into the mix and all bets are off. The easiest way to get through it—and brother, I said "easiest," not "easy"—is to do it together.

Your child should see a united parenting team at all times, even if behind the scenes that "solid" wall needs some tuck-pointing. Doing that will not only minimize arguments within the marriage, but it'll also minimize any attempts at manipulation by your kid.

Compromise and work together, and even when you stumble on that, never fail to have each other's back.

4. Be Consistent

This point, to me, is "Parenting 101," BPD or not. Whatever course of action you decide, stay with it and don't go wobbly.

Let's take a simple example. Your BPD child wants something, and for good and legitimate reasons, you say no. BPD children being persistent, you say no four hundred more times before giving up and saying, "Whatever. Do what you like."

I guarantee you, you just bought yourself a heap of trouble. Intermittent reinforcement will encourage future disobedience, feed into your child's disorder, and drive you crazy. Give in once, and you'll be taking on a hundred battles that didn't need to happen.

Please, for your own sake, as well as your child's, *stay the course.*

PS: You know, I'm reluctant to once again point to another chapter of the book and say, "Read this," as I like to think that my brief advice is enough for anyone and everyone, *but* chapters 8 and 9 (really one chapter divided into two) really delve deep into specific parenting skills that will help you with your BPD child (and their non-BPD siblings too). Plus, the information teaches you ways to *actually* improve life with your child—not only helping them, but also scratching that itch to finally "fix" something.

Between the two you'll learn:

Why you shouldn't cave: When you say yes to avoid a fight, even though you know you should say no, you're "feeding the monster" (BPD) because it only makes the disorder worse. It rewards negative actions and encourages them to be repeated. These chapters explain what you should do instead.

Why it's important to not give in to emotional blackmail: We all act with a degree of fear, obligation, and guilt when it comes to our kids, and saying no stirs all of that up in our gut. Stop listening to it, and learn to do what's necessary, not what's easiest in the short term.

How to set realistic limits: And in the process, how to discard the harmful myths that screw up our plans.

How to help your child with their problems: A wide-ranging skill that will show you everything from how to handle a BPD crisis to how to respond when your child comes to you for relationship advice.

How to encourage your child's independence: That's the end goal for every healthy parent, right? Learn how to get to that point with your child.

If you don't want to read the chapters, ask your spouse to do it, then quiz them endlessly about the content; because, one way or another, you'll need the information. But please note: if you think *that* advice is good for your marriage, then you need all the self-help books you can find.

Read the chapters!

5. Validate, Don't Invalidate

Note: If you aren't sure what this concept fully means, don't be discouraged. Turn to chapter 7 again for a brief overview. (Again, you bought the book. Might as well get your money's worth.)

Children with BPD often seem to have a history that only they experience. Their perception of conversations, actions, and even large-scale events, often differs from what you or your wife may remember or know to be true.

But whatever your BPD child is feeling, *it is what they are feeling and how they perceive the world* at that point in time. Invalidating that—saying, "It's not that bad" or "That's not what happened"—not only reminds them of how differently they see the world; it also reinforces the child's belief that they have no one to turn to when they're in distress.

Validate your child's emotions. It is *the* most powerful tool at your disposal to help manage your child's moods, and it has a direct impact on minimizing their suffering. Don't let that opportunity go to waste.

6. Be a Role Model

Since we're more than halfway through the list, let's get to one that I admit I failed at too often.

I grew up in a very loving family, but one in which shouting was as commonplace as "please" and "thank you" in other homes. I curbed the vast majority of that as a parent—honestly, it was night and day in my childhood home—but I admit that that wasn't good enough.

The actions you model for your kids are more powerful than a dictionary's worth of words. If you show them that screaming is okay, then screamers they will become. If you show them that tantrums are okay, then (Spoiler alert!) your kid is going to throw tantrums. Guaranteed.

You *must* manage your emotions and exhibit the very same behaviors you hope to see in your child, because *your child is watching*.

7. Don't Keep It a Total Secret

As a rule, a family is as sick as the secrets they keep. The stress of parenting can be backbreaking; the stress of parenting a BPD child, heartbreaking. Combined, that's too much for a person to shoulder alone.

Find someone to confide in, someone with no axe to grind and no agenda, someone who is there just for you. For my wife, close friends fit the bill. I like to keep my cards close to my vest in my personal life, and so I found a professional counselor to be a much better option for me.

Whatever option you choose, I hope you find some much-needed solace.

8. Keep Fun in Your Marriage

I know, I know—quite the jarring segue there, but number 7 was kind of a bummer, and I thought the room needed some livening up.

As I mentioned earlier, a solid marriage is an invaluable tool when raising a child with BPD. Keeping that relationship healthy is vital to your success as a parent. And, if that mercenary outlook isn't enough, I suppose you could fall back on the whole "I love my spouse" trope.

Seriously, though, before BPD, before your child, there was just you and your wife. Ideally, long after your child moves out, there will still be "just" you and your wife. There is no longer or more important relationship in your adult life. Nurture it.

No matter what, no matter how tough things seem at home, make time for (kids-free) time with your spouse.

9. Help Around the House

I admit, your wife *did* ask me to include this one.

Your wife takes a big amount of parenting your BPD child on her shoulders. Maybe she works outside the home too. That's a whole lot of responsibility, a whole lot of stress, and a whole lot of time devoted to everyone not named Mom. If that woman cracks, no one wins, least of all your wife (or you).

So, show your wife you care. Step up and help around the house. Cook. Clean. Help get the kids to their soccer practice.

It's not only smart; it's also fair.

10. Pay Attention to Your Non-BPD Children

I'm going to end on what may be the most important tip of all, because it involves the health and success of your other children.

Your non-BPD children are tremendously affected by the drama surrounding their sibling. It is not unusual for a non-BPD sibling to require therapy of their own to deal with the trauma of events. In addition, given that the BPD child is inadvertently consuming more time, focus, and effort on the part of you and your wife, your other children run the risk of getting the short end of the parenting stick.

For the sake of their own mental and emotional health, make a conscious effort to recognize them. Validate their feelings, spend time with them alone, and make an effort to participate fully in their lives.

They are worth every bit as much as your BPD child, and they deserve the best you have to offer them.

·

I'd like to finish by asking you to think of the day your BPD child was born, of that fresh newborn in your arms, and of all that you wished for their future. Those were dreams, and this is reality. You have to play a balancing game. You have to realize that your child suffers from an illness; and just like a physical malady might stop them from playing for the Yankees, BPD may derail some of those grand plans you had for them. You may not become the father of a president or watch your child cure cancer, but when things seem dark and hopeless, you can't let go of *all* of that hope and expectation you once held dear.

BPD is not a death sentence, nor an automatic end to success. Your child can still forge an adult life on their own, and can still accomplish things that make them happy and successful—and I hope for you both that they do—it just takes a lot more work and a *lot* more support from loved ones.

Good thing they've got you then, eh?
Good luck, Dad. You've got this!

APPENDIX B

Clinician to Clinician: The Underdiagnosis of BPD in Children

Many clinicians are reluctant to diagnose borderline personality disorder (BPD) in children and adolescents, and some never do so. In this very brief appendix, I will explain why, under certain circumstances, children and adolescents who have a number of BPD characteristics should be considered for a diagnoses of BPD or BPD tendencies.

Reasons for Not Diagnosing Children and Adolescents

First, let's review the most common reasons for not diagnosing children with a personality disorder:

- The belief that children and adolescents don't have fully formed personalities and therefore cannot be diagnosed as disordered
- The belief that having a personality disorder diagnosis is stigmatizing
- The fact that many insurance companies don't cover treatment for personality disorders

Rather than diagnosing personality disorders, child and adolescent clinicians often focus on comorbid disorders, such as anxiety, depression, and ADHD, which are less socially stigmatizing. These disorders are generally treated, and the personality disorder symptoms go unaddressed until early adulthood, once they've crystallized as part of an individual's personality.

Unfortunately, waiting for personality disorder symptoms to crystallize before treating them compromises the effectiveness of treatment, as well as the individual's prognosis.

Reasons for Diagnosing BPD Earlier

In the *DSM-5* definition of BPD, the American Psychiatric Association states that BPD begins by early adulthood (2013). This suggests that characteristics of this disorder appear in childhood and adolescence, and become chronic in early adulthood if left unaddressed.

Other sources suggest that clinicians should diagnose BPD earlier than previously thought:

> Two things are absolutely clear. First, adults with BPD almost always recognize that their symptoms and suffering started in childhood or adolescence. Second, some adolescents have symptoms that are so consistent with BPD that it would be

unethical not to make this diagnosis and treat them accordingly. (Aguirre 2014, 26)

Recent data indicate that an estimated 18 million Americans will develop borderline personality disorder in their lifetimes, with symptoms commonly emerging during early adolescence and adulthood.

BPD has been a controversial diagnosis in adolescents, but this is no longer justified. Recent evidence demonstrates that a diagnosis of BPD is as valid among adolescents as it is in adults, and that adolescents with BPD can benefit from early intervention ... BPD diagnosis and treatment should be considered part of routine practice in adolescent mental health to improve these individuals' well-being and long-term prognosis.

All available data indicate that adolescence is a critical point for early identification and therapeutic treatment of BPD. (Fossati 2014)

The failure to identify and treat premorbid characteristics of BPD in childhood and adolescence is inconsistent with modern health care directives, which focus on preventing diseases rather than initiating treatment once symptomology has maximized.

Children and adolescents who meet the full criteria for a personality disorder should be diagnosed with one. In this book we described interventions targeted at children and adolescents at risk for developing BPD by early adulthood. The interventions are designed to mitigate the development of the full personality disorder.

Children and adolescents who have characteristics of BPD but don't meet the full criteria should be diagnosed with "BPD tendencies," and these characteristics should be treated with the techniques described in this book. Doing so can help avert the development of more serious forms of BPD later in life.

—Daniel S. Lobel, PhD

APPENDIX C

Resources

Books About BPD in Minors

Borderline Personality Disorder in Adolescents: What to Do When Your Teen Has BPD, 2nd ed., B.A. Aguirre, 2014, Fair Winds Press, Beverly, MA.

Blaise Aguirre is the medical director of an inpatient unit for teens with borderline personality disorder. He gives lectures around the world on the topic. If you are the parent of a teen with BPD, this is a must-have.

When Your Daughter Has BPD: Essential Skills to Help Families Manage Borderline Personality Disorder, D.S. Lobel, 2018, New Harbinger Publications, Oakland, CA.

This practical book will further explain some of the concepts in *Stop Walking on Eggshells for Parents* and serve as a guide as you weather the storm of BPD and restore balance in your home. You'll discover ways to help your child while maintaining appropriate limits for yourself and other family members. Lobel is also the author of *When Your Mother Has Borderline Personality Disorder: A Guide for Adult Children* (Rockridge Press, 2019). Lobel can be reached at

914-232-8434, Katonahshrink@gmail.com, and https://www.mysideofthecouch.com.

Parenting a Teen Who Has Intense Emotions: DBT Skills to Help Your Teen Navigate Emotional and Behavioral Challenges, P. Harvey and B.H. Rathbone, 2015, New Harbinger Publications, Oakland, CA.

Dialectical behavior therapy, or DBT, is an evidence-based treatment for BPD and other diagnoses. This book is about young adults as well. It includes a step-by-step guide for handling disruptive, risky, and substance-abusing behaviors.

Parenting a Child Who Has Intense Emotions: Dialectical Behavior Therapy Skills to Help Your Child Regulate Emotional Outbursts and Aggressive Behaviors, P. Harvey and J.A. Penzo, 2009, New Harbinger Publications, Oakland, CA.

A guide to de-escalating your child's emotions and helping them express feelings in productive ways. It contains strategies for when your child's emotions spin out of control.

Books for Family Members of Someone with BPD

The Essential Family Guide to Borderline Personality Disorder: New Tools and Techniques to Stop Walking on Eggshells, R. Kreger, 2008, Hazelden, Center City, MN.

This is a great reference book from a psychiatric/medical point of view, covering everything related to BPD, such as the exact BPD mechanisms in the brain. It covers the five basic tools: taking care of yourself, uncovering what's keeping you stuck, communicating to be heard, setting limits, and reinforcing the right behavior. It also has chapters that cover treatment, finding a therapist, and the risk factors of BPD.

Raising Resilient Children with a Borderline or Narcissistic Parent, M. Fjelstad and J. McBride, 2020, Rowman and Littlefield, Lanham, MD.

This book can help grandparents concerned about their grandchildren, but it's mostly directed at parents.

Loving Someone with Borderline Personality Disorder: How to Keep Out-of-Control Emotions from Destroying Your Relationship, S.Y. Manning, 2011, Guilford Press, New York.

Stop Caretaking the Borderline or Narcissist: How to End the Drama and Get on with Life, M. Fjelstad, 2013, Rowman and Littlefield, Lanham, MD.

This book shows caretakers of adults with BPD and narcissistic personality disorder (NPD) how to get out of destructive interactions and take new, more effective actions to focus on themselves and the rest of the family—all while allowing the adult with BPD or NPD to take care of themselves and take responsibility for their own behavior. It stresses how to not be abused.

The Stop Walking on Eggshells Workbook, R. Kreger and J.P. Shirley, 2002, New Harbinger Publications, Oakland, CA.

General Psychiatric Book About BPD

Borderline Personality Disorder Demystified: An Essential Guide for Understanding and Living with BPD, rev. ed., R.O. Friedel, L.F. Cox, and K. Friedel, 2018, Da Capo Lifelong Books, New York.

A great psychiatric book about BPD that covers a wide range of topics, including BPD in children, the history of BPD, the brain as it relates to BPD, treatments, medications, and so forth.

Skills-Building Books

Better Boundaries: Owning and Treasuring Your Life, J. Black and G. Enns, 1997, New Harbinger Publications, Oakland, CA.

A book on limit setting based on your values, needs, and wants.

BIFF: Quick Responses to High-Conflict People, Their Personal Attacks, Hostile Emails, and Social Media Meltdowns, B. Eddy, 2011, HCI Press, Scottsdale, AZ.

This book discusses the BIFF communication technique in depth.

Emotional Blackmail: When the People in Your Life Use Fear, Obligation, and Guilt to Manipulate You, S. Forward, 1997, HarperCollins, New York.

The Gaslight Effect: How to Spot and Survive the Hidden Manipulation Others Use to Control Your Life, R. Stern, 2018, Harmony Books, New York.

The Power of Validation: Arming Your Child Against Bullying, Peer Pressure, Addiction, Self-Harm, and Out-of-Control Emotions, K.D. Hall and M.H. Cook, 2012, New Harbinger Publications, Oakland, CA.

This book is directed at parents of young children, but it has good information for any parent.

Radical Acceptance: Embracing Your Life with the Heart of a Buddha, T. Brach, 2003, Bantam Books, New York.

Talking to a Loved One with Borderline Personality Disorder: Communication Skills to Manage Intense Emotions, Set Boundaries, and Reduce Conflict, J.J. Kreisman, 2018, New Harbinger Publications, Oakland, CA.

This book goes over the SET-UP communication technique we discussed in chapter 7.

What Shamu Taught Me About Life, Love, and Marriage: Lessons for People from Animals and Their Trainers, A. Sutherland, 2008, Random House, New York.

This book shows you how to use behavioral reinforcement and similar methods.

Books That Help Parents' Mental State

Conquering Shame and Codependency: 8 Steps to Freeing the True You, D. Lancer, 2014, Hazelden, Center City, MN.

Don't Let Your Kids Kill You: A Guide for Parents of Drug and Alcohol Addicted Children, C. Rubin, 2010, NewCentury Publishers, Petaluma, CA.

The Gift of Loving-Kindness: 100 Mindful Practices for Compassion, Generosity, and Forgiveness, M. Brantly and T. Hanauer, 2008, New Harbinger Publications, Oakland, CA.

Pocket Therapy for Emotional Balance: Quick DBT Skills to Manage Intense Emotions, M. McKay, J.C. Wood, and J. Brantley, 2020, New Harbinger Publications, Oakland, CA.

The Relaxation and Stress Reduction Workbook, 6th ed., M. Davis, E.R. Eshelman, and M. McKay, 2008, New Harbinger Publications, Oakland, CA.

Self-Compassion: The Proven Power of Being Kind to Yourself, K. Neff, 2011, William Morrow, New York.

When Things Fall Apart: Heart Advice for Difficult Times, P. Chödrön, 2016, Shambhala Publications, Boulder, CO.

When Your Adult Child Breaks Your Heart: Coping with Mental Illness, Substance Abuse, and the Problems That Tear Families Apart, J.L. Young and C. Adamec, 2013, Lyons Press, Guilford, CT.

BPD Memoirs by Women with BPD

Get Me Out of Here: My Recovery from Borderline Personality Disorder, R. Reiland, 2004, Hazelden, Center City, MN.

The author of this book, a mother of two young boys, discusses eating disorders, BPD, and suicide. This is okay to give to your teen, although they would probably relate more to the next book. Both books will give you remarkable insight into what it's like to be inside the head of someone with BPD.

The Buddha and the Borderline: My Recovery from Borderline Personality Disorder Through Dialectical Behavior Therapy, Buddhism, and Online Dating, K. Van Gelder, 2010, New Harbinger Publications, Oakland, CA.

The author discusses having BPD from her late teens to her thirties, as well as sexual content, self-harm, and suicide.

Memoirs by Parents of Children with BPD

And I Don't Want to Live This Life: A Mother's Story of Her Daughter's Murder, D. Spungen, 1983, Ballantine Books, New York.

When the Ship Has No Stabilizers: Our Daughter's Tempestuous Voyage Through Borderline

Personality Disorder, F.L. Porter, 2014, Crossfield Publishing, St. Marys, Ontario.

Books for Children and Teens with BPD

The Anger Workbook for Teens: Activities to Help You Deal with Anger and Frustration, 2nd ed., R.C. Lohmann, 2019, New Harbinger Publications, Oakland, CA.

Don't Let Your Emotions Run Your Life for Kids: A DBT-Based Skills Workbook to Help Children Manage Mood Swings, Control Angry Outbursts, and Get Along with Others, J.J. Solin and C.L. Kress, 2017, Instant Help Books, Oakland, CA.

Written to give children ages seven to twelve a toolbox for emotions as they arise.

Don't Let Your Emotions Run Your Life for Teens: Dialectical Behavior Therapy Skills for Helping You Manage Mood Swings, Control Angry Outbursts, and Get Along with Others, S. Van Dijk, 2011, Instant Help Books, Oakland, CA.

The Grit Workbook for Kids: CBT Skills to Help Kids Cultivate a Growth Mindset and Build Resilience, E. Nebolsine, 2020, Instant Help Books, Oakland, CA.

This book offers exercises grounded in mindfulness and self-compassion to help teens overcome crippling self-criticism and respond to feelings of self-doubt with greater kindness and self-care.

The Grit Guide for Teens: A Workbook to Help You Build Perseverance, Self-Control, and a Growth Mindset, C. Baruch-Feldman, 2017, Instant Help Books, Oakland, CA.

The Relaxation and Stress Reduction Workbook for Teens: CBT Skills to Help You Deal with Worry and Anxiety, M.A. Tompkins and J.R. Barkin, 2018, Instant Help Books, Oakland, CA.

Books for Adults with BPD

The Big Book on Borderline Personality Disorder, S. Rooney, 2018, Unhooked Books, Scottsdale, AZ.

Borderline Personality Disorder: A Guide for the Newly Diagnosed, A.L. Chapman and K.L. Gratz, 2013, New Harbinger Publications, Oakland, CA.

Borderline Personality Disorder Toolbox: A Practical Evidence-Based Guide to Regulating Intense Emotions, J. Riggenbach, 2016, PESI Publishing and Media, Eau Claire, WI.

The Borderline Personality Disorder Workbook: An Integrative Program to Understand and Manage Your BPD, D.J. Fox, 2019, New Harbinger Publications, Oakland, CA.

The Dialectical Behavior Therapy Skills Workbook: Practical DBT Exercises for Learning Mindfulness, Interpersonal Effectiveness, Emotional Regulation, and Distress Tolerance, 2nd ed., M. McKay, J.C. Wood, and J. Brantley, 2019, New Harbinger Publications, Oakland, CA.

This book is the next best thing to attending an actual DBT group. Each item in the subtitle is one of the skills sections of DBT.

Hard to Love: Understanding and Overcoming Male Borderline Personality Disorder, J. Nowinski, 2014, Central Recovery Press, Las Vegas, NV.

Mindfulness for Borderline Personality Disorder: Relieve Your Suffering Using the Core Skill of Dialectical Behavior Therapy, B.A. Aguirre and G. Galen, 2013, New Harbinger Publications, Oakland, CA.

What's Right with Me: Positive Ways to Celebrate Your Strengths, Build Self-Esteem, and Reach Your Potential, C. DeRoo and C. DeRoo, 2006, New Harbinger Publications, Oakland, CA.

BPD Websites, Support Groups, and Organizations

National Education Alliance for Borderline Personality Disorder (NEABPD). https://www.borderlinepersonalitydisorder.org

NEABPD runs the Family Connections classes for parents and other family members of loved ones with BPD. Family Connections™ is a free, evidence-based, twelve-class course that meets in person for two hours and requires one to two hours of homework/practice weekly. It provides education, skills training, and support for people who are supporting a sufferer of borderline personality disorder.

NEABPD also offers a virtual option for families living far from Family Connections™ meeting locations, or for those who prefer to take the course online.

Family Connections™ is based on research funded by the National Institute of Mental Health (NIMH). Surveys show that after completing the course, family members experience decreased feelings of depression, burden, and grief, and more feelings of empowerment.

References

Adesman, A., and C. Adamec. 2018. *The Grandfamily Guidebook: Wisdom and Support for Grandparents Raising Grandchildren*. Center City, MN: Hazelden.

Aguirre, B.A. 2014. *Borderline Personality Disorder in Adolescents: What to Do When Your Teen Has BPD*. 2nd ed. Beverly, MA: Fair Winds Press.

American Academy of Child and Adolescent Psychiatry. 2016a. "Residential Treatment Programs." September. https://www.aacap.org/AACAP/Families_and_Youth/Facts_for_Families/FFF-Guide/Residential-Treatment-Programs-097.aspx.

American Academy of Child and Adolescent Psychiatry. 2016b. "Teen Brain: Behavior, Problem Solving, and Decision Making." September. https://www.aacap.org/AACAP/Families_and_Youth/Facts_for_Families/FFF-Guide/The-Teen-Brain-Behavior-Problem-Solving-and-Decision-Making-095.aspx.

American Institute of Stress. 2019. "7 Signs You May Be Too Stressed." *Daily Life* (blog).

November 6. https://www.stress.org/7-signs-you-might-be-too-stressed.

American Psychiatric Association. 2013. *Diagnostic and Statistical Manual of Mental Disorders*. 5th ed. Arlington, VA: American Psychiatric Association.

American Psychological Association. 2013. "Warning Signs of Youth Violence." https://www.apa.org/topics/physical-abuse-violence/youth-warning-signs.

Bansal, V. 2020. "How to Opt Out of the Drama Triangle and Take Responsibility." *Tech Tello* (blog). April 23. https://www.techtello.com/how-to-opt-out-of-the-drama-triangle.

Bergland, C. 2017. "Diaphragmatic Breathing Exercises and Your Vagus Nerve." *The Athlete's Way* (blog). May 16. https://www.psychologytoday.com/us/blog/the-athletes-way/201705/diaphragmatic-breathing-exercises-and-your-vagus-nerve.

Brown, B. 2012. "Listening to Shame." Filmed March 2012 at TED2012, Long Beach, CA. Video, 20:38. https://www.ted.com/talks/brene_brown_listening_to_shame/details?language=en.

Cancino, A. 2016. "More Grandparents Raising Their Grandchildren." February 16. *PBS News Hour.* https://www.pbs.org/newshour/nation/more-grandparents-raising-their-grandchildren.

Cardasis, W., J.A. Hochman, and K.R. Silk. 1997. "Transitional Objects and Borderline Personality Disorder." *American Journal of Psychiatry* 154: 250–55.

Center for Substance Abuse Treatment. 2014. "Understanding the Impact of Trauma." *Trauma-Informed Care in Behavioral Health Services.* Rockville, MD: Substance Abuse and Mental Health Services Administration.

Centers for Disease Control and Prevention. 2021. "Suicide Prevention." US Department of Health and Human Services. March. https://www.cdc.gov/suicide/index.html.

Child Mind Institute. n.d. "Borderline Personality Disorder and Substance Use." Accessed May 8, 2021. https://childmind.org/guide/parents-guide-to-co-occurring-substance-use-and-mental-health-disorders/borderline-personality-disorder-and-substance-use.

Chödrön, P. 2016. *When Things Fall Apart: Heart Advice for Difficult Times*. Boulder, CO: Shambhala Publications.

Cloitre, M., D.W. Garvert, B. Weiss, E.B. Carlson, and R.A. Bryant. 2014. "Distinguishing PTSD, Complex PTSD, and Borderline Personality Disorder: A Latent Class Analysis." *European Journal of Psychotraumatology* 5: n.p.

Davis, D.M., and J.A. Hayes. 2012. "What Are the Benefits of Mindfulness?" (1997). American Psychological Association, July/August. https://www.apa.org/monitor/2012/07-08/ce-corner.

Denworth, L. 2019. "How Much Time in Nature Is Needed to See Benefits?" *Brain Waves* (blog). June 13. https://www.psychologytoday.com/us/blog/brain-waves/201906/how-much-time-in-nature-is-needed-see-benefits.

Dierberger, A., and N. Lewis-Schroeder. 2017. "Borderline Personality Disorder and Complex Posttraumatic Stress Disorder." McLean Hospital. December 7. https://www.mcleanhospital.org/sites/default/files/shared/BPDWebinar-BPD-and-Complex-PTSD.pdf.

Dingfelder, S.F. 2004. "Treatment for the 'Untreatable.'" *Monitor on Psychology*, March, 46. https://www.apa.org/monitor/mar04/treatment.

Eddy, B., and R. Kreger. 2011. *Splitting: Protecting Yourself While Divorcing Someone with Borderline or Narcissistic Personality Disorder.* Oakland, CA: New Harbinger Publications.

Fast, J.A., and J. Preston. 2006. *Take Charge of Bipolar Disorder: A 4-Step Plan for You and Your Loved Ones to Manage the Illness and Create Lasting Stability.* New York: Warner Wellness.

Fjelstad, M. 2013. *Stop Caretaking the Borderline or Narcissist: How to End the Drama and Get on with Life.* New York: Rowman and Littlefield.

Forward, S. 1997. *Emotional Blackmail: When the People in Your Life Use Fear, Obligation, and Guilt to Manipulate You.* New York: HarperCollins.

Fossati, A. 2014. "Borderline Personality Disorder in Adolescence: Phenomenology and Construct Validity." In *Handbook of Borderline Personality Disorder in Children and Adolescents*, edited by C. Sharp and J.L. Tackett, 19–34. New York: Springer.

Friedel, R.O. 2004. "Dopamine Dysfunction in Borderline Personality Disorder: A Hypothesis." *Neuropsychopharmacology* 29: 1029–39.

Friedel, R.O., L.F. Cox, and K. Friedel. 2018. *Borderline Personality Disorder Demystified: An Essential Guide for Understanding and Living with BPD.* New York: Da Capo Lifelong Books.

Grant, B.F., S.P. Chou, R.B. Goldstein, B. Huang, F.S. Stinson, and T.D. Saha, et al. 2008. "Prevalence, Correlates, Disability, and Comorbidity of DSM-IV Borderline Personality Disorder: Results from the Wave 2 National Epidemiologic Survey on Alcohol and Related Conditions." *Journal of Clinical Psychiatry* 69 (4): 533–45.

Hairston, S. 2019. "Involuntary Commitment: When and How to Do It." *Open Counseling* (blog). August 19. https://www.opencounseling.com/blog/involuntary-commitment-when-and-how-to-do-it.

Hall, K.D., and M.H. Cook. 2012. *The Power of Validation: Arming Your Child Against Bullying, Peer Pressure, Addiction, Self-Harm, and Out-of-Control Emotions.* Oakland, CA: New Harbinger Publications.

Kaess, M., R. Brunner, and A. Chanen. 2014. "Borderline Personality Disorder in Adolescence." *Pediatrics* 134 (4): 782–93.

Kay, M.L., M. Poggenpoel, C.P. Myburgh, and C. Downing. 2018. "Experiences of Family Members Who Have a Relative Diagnosed with Borderline Personality Disorder." *Curationis* 41 (1): e1–e9.

Kornfield, Jack. 2008. *The Art of Forgiveness, Lovingkindness, and Peace.* New York: Bantam Dell.

Kreger, R. 2008. *The Essential Family Guide to Borderline Personality Disorder: New Tools and Techniques to Stop Walking on Eggshells.* Center City, MN: Hazelden.

Kreishman, J.J. 2018. *Talking to a Loved One with Borderline Personality Disorder: Communication Skills to Manage Intense Emotions, Set Boundaries, and Reduce Conflict.* Oakland, CA: New Harbinger Publications.

Lerner, H. 2014. *The Dance of Anger: A Woman's Guide to Changing the Patterns of Intimate Relationships.* New York: William Morrow.

Linehan, M.M. 1993. *Cognitive-Behavioral Treatment of Borderline Personality Disorder.* New York: Guilford Press.

Linehan, M.M. 2015. *DBT Skills Training Handouts and Worksheets.* 2nd ed. New York: Guildford Press.

Lobel, D.S. 2018. *When Your Daughter Has BPD: Essential Skills to Help Families Manage Borderline Personality Disorder.* Oakland, CA: New Harbinger Publications.

Matusiewicz, A.K., C.J. Hopwood, A.N. Banducci, and C.W. Lejuez. 2010. "The Effectiveness of Cognitive Behavioral Therapy for Personality Disorders." *The Psychiatric Clinics of North America* 33 (3): 657–85.

Manning, S.Y. 2011. *Loving Someone with Borderline Personality Disorder: How to Keep Out-of-Control Emotions from Destroying Your Relationship.* New York: Guilford Press.

Mayo Clinic. 2017. "Narcissistic Personality Disorder." November 18. https://www.mayoclinic.org/diseases-conditions/narcissistic-personality-disorder/symptoms-causes/syc-20366662.

Mayo Clinic. 2019. "Exercise: 7 Benefits of Regular Physical Activity." May 11. https://www.mayoclinic.org/healthy-lifestyle/fitness/in-depth/exercise/art-20048389.

McVicker, N. 2015. "Warning Signs of Teen Violence." *Hero911*. April 30. https://www.hero911.org/warning-signs-of-teen-violence.

National Institute of Mental Health. 2016a. "Generalized Anxiety Disorder: When Worry Gets Out of Control." https://www.nimh.nih.gov/health/publications/generalized-anxiety-disorder-gad.

National Institute of Mental Health. 2016b. "Panic Disorder: When Fear Overwhelms." https://www.nimh.nih.gov/health/publications/panic-disorder-when-fear-overwhelms.

National Institute of Mental Health. 2018. "Bipolar Disorder." October. https://www.nimh.nih.gov/health/publications/bipolar-disorder.

National Institute of Mental Health. 2019a. "Post-Traumatic Stress Disorder." May. https://www.nimh.nih.gov/health/topics/post-traumatic-stress-disorder-ptsd.

National Institute of Mental Health. 2019b. "Attention-Deficit/Hyperactivity Disorder." September. https://www.nimh.nih.gov/health/topics/attention-deficit-hyperactivity-disorder-adhd.

National Institute of Mental Health. n.d. "Borderline Personality Disorder." https://www.nimh.nih.gov/health/publications/borderline-personality-disorder.

National Institute on Drug Abuse. 2020. "Drug Misuse and Addiction." National Institutes of Health. July. https://www.drugabuse.gov/publications/drugs-brains-behavior-science-addiction/drug-misuse-addiction.

Neff, K. 2011. *Self-Compassion: The Proven Power of Being Kind to Yourself*. New York: HarperCollins.

Norcross, J.C., and B.E. Wampold. 2011. "Evidence-Based Therapy Relationships: Research Conclusions and Clinical Practices." *Psychotherapy* 48 (1): 98–102.

Ooi, J., J. Michael, S. Lemola, S. Butterfill, C.S.Q. Siew, and L. Walasek. 2020. "Interpersonal Functioning in Borderline Personality Disorder Traits: A Social Media Perspective." *Scientific*

Reports 10: 1068. https://www.ncbi.nlm.nih.gov/pmc/articles/PMC6978508.

Paris, J. 2019. "Suicidality in Borderline Personality Disorder." *Medicina:* 55 (6): 223.

Phutela, D. 2015. "The Importance of Non-Verbal Communication." *IUP Journal of Soft Skills* 9 (4): 43–49.

Porter, F.L. 2014. *When the Ship Has No Stabilizers: Our Daughter's Tempestuous Voyage through Borderline Personality Disorder.* St. Marys Ontario: Crossfield Publishing.

Ripoll, L.H. 2013. "Psychopharmacologic Treatment of Borderline Personality Disorder." *Dialogues in Clinical Neuroscience* 15 (2): 213–24.

Salters-Pedneault, K. 2020a. "Borderline Personality Disorder and Your Family." *Verywell Mind.* November 27. https://www.verywellmind.com/the-bpd-family-425215.

Salters-Pedneault, K. 2020b. "Legal Issues and Borderline Personality Disorder." *Verywell Mind.* December 7. https://www.verywellmind.com/bpd-and-the-law-legal-issues-and-bpd-425356.

Sander, L. 2019. "Time for a Kondo Clean-Out? Here's What Clutter Does to Your Brain and Body." The Conversation. January 20. https://theconversation.com/time-for-a-kondo-clean-out-heres-what-clutter-does-to-your-brain-and-body-109947.

Sansone, R.A., and L.A. Sansone. 2011. "Gender Patterns in Borderline Personality Disorder." *Innovations in Clinical Neuroscience* 8 (5): 16–20.

Schwartz, G.L., and J.L. Jahn. 2020. "Mapping Fatal Police Violence Across U.S. Metropolitan Areas: Overall Rates and Racial/Ethnic Inequities, 2013–2017." PLOS ONE. https://doi.org/10.1371/journal.pone.0229686.

Scott, E. 2020. "How to Relieve Stress with Art Therapy." *Verywell Mind.* January 24. https://www.verywellmind.com/art-therapy-relieve-stress-by-being-creative-3144581.

Smith, A. 2020. "37 Validating Statements (A Quick Guide for When You Are Stuck)." January 1. https://www.hopeforbpd.com/borderline-personality-disorder-treatment/validating-statements.

Substance Use and Mental Health Services Association. *Report to Congress on Borderline*

Personality Disorder. 2011. US Department of Health and Human Services. http://www.ncdsv.org/images/SAMHSA_Report-to-Congress-on-Borderline-Personality-Disorder_5-2011.pdf.

Treatment Advocacy Center. 2015. "The Role of Mental Illness in Fatal Law Enforcement Encounters." https://www.treatmentadvocacycenter.org/overlooked-in-the-undercounted.

Van Gelder, K. 2010. *The Buddha and the Borderline: My Recovery from Borderline Personality Disorder Through Dialectical Behavior Therapy, Buddhism, and Online Dating*. Oakland, CA: New Harbinger Publications.

Wasylyshen, A., and A.M. Williams. 2016. "Second-Generation Antipsychotic Use in Borderline Personality Disorder: What Are We Targeting?" *The Mental Health Clinician* 6 (2): 82–88.

Weiner, L., N. Perroud, and S. Weibel. 2019. "Attention Deficit Hyperactivity Disorder and Borderline Personality Disorder in Adults: A Review of Their Links and Risks." *Neuropsychiatric Disease and Treatment* 15: 3115–29.

World Health Organization. 2018. International Classification of Diseases (11th Revision). Retrieved from https://icd.who.int/browse11/l-m/en.

Zanarini, M.C., C.A. Reichman, F.R. Frankenburg, D.B. Reich, and G. Fitzmaurice. 2010. "The Course of Eating Disorders in Patients with Borderline Personality Disorder: A 10-Year Follow-Up Study." *International Journal of Eating Disorders* 43 (3): 226–32.

Randi Kreger is author of *The Stop Walking on Eggshells Workbook* and *The Essential Family Guide to Borderline Personality Disorder.* Her website, www.stopwalkingoneggshells.com, offers material related to borderline personality disorder (BPD). She also provides a free online family support group, Moving Forward, at www.groups.io/g/movingforward. She gives workshops throughout the US and Japan.

Christine Adamec, MBA, is a self-help author whose books include *When Your Adult Child Breaks Your Heart* and *The Grandfamily Guidebook.* She has authored and coauthored forty books, and is a member of the American Society of Journalists and Authors.

Daniel S. Lobel, PhD, practices clinical psychology in Katonah, NY. He is author of two books: *When Your Daughter Has BPD* and *When Your Mother Has Borderline Personality Disorder,* and numerous blogs on *Psychology Today.* He has taught at Mount Sinai School of Medicine, State University of New York, Hofstra School of Law, and lectures with the National Alliance of the Mentally Ill (NAMI).

Foreword writer **Fran L. Porter, BEd, MA,** is author of *When the Ship Has No Stabilizers,* a memoir about her daughter, who has BPD.

Real change is possible

For more than forty-five years, New Harbinger has published proven-effective self-help books and pioneering workbooks to help readers of all ages and backgrounds improve mental health and well-being, and achieve lasting personal growth. In addition, our spirituality books offer profound guidance for deepening awareness and cultivating healing, self-discovery, and fulfillment.

Founded by psychologist Matthew McKay and Patrick Fanning, New Harbinger is proud to be an independent, employee-owned company. Our books reflect our core values of integrity, innovation, commitment, sustainability, compassion, and trust. Written by leaders in the field and recommended by therapists worldwide, New Harbinger books are practical, accessible, and provide real tools for real change.

 newharbingerpublications

more books to help you stop walking on eggshells

Stop Walking on Eggshells, Third Edition
Taking Your Life Back When Someone You Care About Has Borderline Personality Disorder

The Stop Walking on Eggshells Workbook
Practical Strategies for Living with Someone Who Has Borderline Personality Disorder

newharbingerpublications
1-800-748-6273 / newharbinger.com

Back Cover Material

The skills & strategies you need when your child has BPD

If you have a child with borderline personality disorder (BPD), you are all-too-aware of the behavioral and emotional issues that come with this condition—including rages, self-harm, sexual acting out, substance abuse, suicidal behaviors, physical and emotional attacks, and more. Traditional parenting techniques that work on other kids just don't work with your child. But there are strategies and tools that can help.

Based on the self-help classic, *Stop Walking on Eggshells,* this essential guide offers powerful skills for navigating your child's disorder—without compromising your family or yourself. You'll discover a proven-effective approach to help you understand your child's world, and become a BPD-savvy parent. Included are real-life stories and advice from other parents who have a child with BPD. Most importantly, you'll find solid skills to help you handle crises, improve communication, and set limits that work. Whether your child is 10 or 35, this book offers tools to help you and your family thrive.

You'll learn:

- How BPD symptoms manifest in children, adolescents, and adults

- How coexisting conditions can complicate BPD
- What to do if your child self-harms or is suicidal
- How to help siblings
- How to find professional treatment

"A much-needed and welcome guide for families who have a child with borderline behaviors.... It fills a great need for practical, understanding support."

—Margalis Fjelstad, PhD, coauthor of *Raising Resilient Children with a Borderline or Narcissist Parent*

www.ingramcontent.com/pod-product-compliance
Lightning Source LLC
Chambersburg PA
CBHW010719300426
44115CB00019B/2955